VA VA FROOME

David Sharp is a freelance writer and a former deputy editor of
Procycling magazine. He spent seven years as a journalist with the
BBC and has written on travel and the arts for *The Herald* and
cycling for *Rouleur*. He lives in Berlin.

For Lesley

Va Va Froome:
The Remarkable Rise of Chris Froome

DAVID SHARP

This revised edition fiirst published in Great Britain in 2013 by Arena Sport,
an imprint of Birlinn Ltd.

Birlinn Ltd
West Newington House
10 Newington Road
Edinburgh
EH9 1QS

www.arenasportbooks.co.uk

ISBN 978 1 909715 13 4

British Library Cataloguing-in-Publication Data
A catalogue record for this book is available on request from the
British Library.

Typeset by FMG using Atomik ePublisher from Easypress
Printed and bound by Clays Ltd, St Ives plc

Contents

We shall not cease from exploration
And the end of all our exploring
Will be to arrive where we started
And know the place for the first time.

– T.S. Eliot, *Little Gidding* (the last of his *Four Quartets*)

'Send a boy where he wants to go and you'll see his best pace.'

– Nigerian proverb

2012 Tour de France

12 July 2012
Stage 11: Albertville–La Toussuire–Les Sybelles, 148km

Team Sky's plan was to control the race all day. Ride the opposition into the ground over the first three huge mountain passes, set a blistering pace up and over the summits and then start the peel-offs. Put the opposition on the back foot and keep them there. Hit the gas on the final climb to the ski station at La Toussuire. Then watch them scatter across the mountain in bits. Replicate the strategy that had worked so well at La Planche des Belles Filles on Stage 7. They'd stomped all over the opposition in the Vosges mountains, and Bradley Wiggins had taken the *maillot jaune*. The British rider was now the leader of the Tour de France. There was even the bonus that his loyal *domestique*, Chris Froome, had sprinted past Cadel Evans in the last 100m for a thrilling stage win. They had been in complete control. *Control the controllables* – one of the team's favourite mantras. Turn the screw, keep turning the screw, and then one by one they will pop.

On this glorious, sun-drenched Thursday, it was time to do it again. Stage 11. The first proper mountaintop finish of the race, in the heart of the French Alps. Definitely a day for specialist climbers. From Albertville the peloton headed due south through the spectacular Savoie, on a 148km trek that featured two *hors catégorie* (meaning 'beyond categorisation' or so ridiculously tough it defies a rating) climbs, Cols de la Madeleine and Croix de Fer, and one Category 2, the Col du Mollard, before they arrived at the foot of the final peak, a long drag up the Category 1 ascent to La Toussuire, on a stretch of mountain road that would be transformed for the afternoon into a giant open-air sporting amphitheatre.

This is what the Sky squad had been training for. Long, arduous weeks spent at training camps. In January, in Mallorca, tackling over and over again the 26 hairpins of the fearsome Sa Calobra climb. Then, in May, at a secluded retreat in Tenerife, in the nether regions of the back of beyond. Six-hour training rides at high altitude in suffocating desert heat in the shadow of a vast extinct volcano. They were in superlative physical and mental condition. At the top of their game. Ready to rumble.

It was a day of attack and defence. Defending champion Evans, the gritty Australian, threw down the gauntlet on the slopes of the Col du Glandon, on the steepest section, 8km from the top, just before the road turns onto the Croix de Fer. Between the twin peaks, the snarling, two-headed beasts of the great Alpine passes, Evans leapt away in a pre-planned, long-range kamikaze escape bid. It was 66km from the finish, but, lying third, 1:53 adrift of the yellow jersey, he was desperate to claw back time on Wiggins. Surely he'd gone too soon? He had. Sky picked up the gauntlet and threw it back in his face. But slowly, stealthily, to heighten his suffering. No need to panic. Ride at a high, steady tempo and eventually they'd reel him in. Sky's Michael Rogers turns up the power a notch or two and tows Wiggins, Froome, Richie Porte and anyone else who can stay on their coat-tails up the mountain. A few kilometres from the summit of the Croix de Fer, Evans is caught. He's toiling. Finished as a threat. Job done. Soon they are cresting the top of the next mountain, the Mollard. Up and over. They hurtle down the dizzying descent, snaking at high speed down a series of tightly packed hairpins, to the village of Saint-Jean-de-Maurienne.

The view south to the Aiguilles d'Arves is breathtaking. The northern needle of its three giant peaks, the Aiguille Septentrionale, with its bizarre cat's head, is clearly visible in the distance. As the sun burns away traces of morning fog in the Maurienne valley and scorches the top layers off the glaciers that permanently crown the French Alps, the crowd wait in their tens of thousands on the slopes of the climb to La Toussuire. The waiting is over. Here they come.

Team Sky hit the foot of the mountain – an unremittingly steep 18km climb to the out-of-season ski station. Tasmanian climber Porte begins his stint at the front, leading Wiggins and Froome up the horribly steep opening stretch. The cruel 9% gradient splinters the peloton. Sky's relentless pace repels any attacks. Further up the road from the head of the main field are the four breakaways. Frenchman Pierre Rolland – nursing a bloodied elbow after he took a tumble on the Mollard toboggan run – Croatian Robert Kišerlovski, Belarusian Vasili Kiryienka and the Dane, Chris Anker Sørensen. None is a threat to Wiggins. Rolland is the closest, in twentieth place, over nine minutes back.

Twelve kilometres to the finish. Suddenly Vincenzo Nibali swings off the back of the thirteen-strong yellow jersey group and catapults himself, as if launched from a pair of invisible pinball flippers, up the road past Wiggins. The Italian sits fourth overall, 2:23 behind the Londoner. He is a threat. Fluidly shifting through the gears, Nibali is five, ten, fifteen, twenty metres past before they even notice he's gone. As he dances up the climb on their blind side and appears again magically in their line of vision, Froome and Porte simultaneously turn to give Wiggins a comic-book double-take, as if to say, 'OK, boss, what do we do now?'

Nibali's devastating burst of acceleration has eliminated all but Wiggins, Froome, Evans, the young American Tejay van Garderen and Luxembourger Frank Schleck. The suddenly diminished group contains the first, second and third placed riders in the Tour de France: Wiggins, Evans and Froome.

No reaction to Nibali's attack. Froome and Wiggins just keep pedalling, expressions sphinx-like. Slowly, steadily, they know they will reel Nibali in. But Porte's goose is cooked. He peels off the front and quickly starts going backwards, like he's pushed the reverse button on an escalator. He'd buried himself to pace Wiggins over the mountains today, mark any dangerous breaks and keep him out of trouble at the front of the peloton.

Now it's Chris Froome's turn to take up the baton. It's down to him to bridge the gap to Nibali, drag Wiggins back into the race. The Italian was also racing to steal Froome's third place overall. Only sixteen seconds separated them at the stage start in Albertville.

Froome steps up the pace. Wiggins, Evans and Schleck follow. Van Garderen has become unhitched from the back, like unwanted ballast dropped from a hot-air balloon. Froome's head bobs and lists slightly to the right. Back hunched, long arms looped over the handlebars, shoulders swaying from side to side, elbows flailing, he's ungainly, but highly effective. He's steaming up the hill. Soon Nibali is nixed.

Wiggins puffs his cheeks, grimaces with the effort of holding Froome's wheel. Nibali pauses, hovers, and then tucks back in beside the Sky pair like a knife being pulled against a magnetic strip. Froome stands up from his saddle and forces the pedals round. With his bug-eyed Oakley sunglasses and long, gangly limbs he looks like a spider. Wiggins is clamped to his back wheel; their bikes almost merge tandem-like.

Ten kilometres to the finish. Wiggins is momentarily distracted, looking the other way, and Nibali goes again. 'The Shark' takes flight up the road and out of sight, gone in a fluorescent flash of Liquigas green. Evans's teammate, Van Garderen, wearing the white jersey of best young rider, rejoins the back of the elite group.

Now Froome looks like he's toiling, drained by his exertions in pegging back Nibali's first attack. Wiggins takes up the chase. It's the first time all day that the man in yellow has been without another Sky rider alongside. Nibali has fifteen seconds on Wiggins. He only needs one more second to leapfrog Froome into third. But Froome isn't here to worry about his own position. His only concern is to protect the yellow jersey of Wiggins. Keep the pace high. Ward off attacks. Keep him safe.

Froome rallies, glides to the front of the six-man train. Full gas. He dips his head and digs deep into the hurt locker. He appeared down and out. But he was just taking a breather. Now he's back, ready to do or die for his leader.

Evans suddenly crumples over his bike. Froome is going too fast. The defending champion's crown is slipping from his sweat-drenched brow. Van Garderen drifts back to help him. Evans looks haunted. He's dripping with sweat. Each rotation of the pedals is agony, his legs screaming *stop*. Behind the yellow reflective mirror shades his eyes stare into a deep, dark abyss.

Now it's only Wiggins, Froome and Schleck. Six excruciating uphill kilometres left to the finish. If they can just catch Nibali then their day's work is done. Wiggins will secure his position at the top. Evans is head-butting a brick wall into oblivion. Froome could steal second place. A Sky 1-2 at the end of the day? Dreamland.

Further up the road, Pierre Rolland has shaken off his break-away partners. Gasping for air, he ploughs a lonely furrow to the finish line. Stage victory is within his grasp. A yellow Mavic service motorbike sidles up next to him. The girl riding pillion, her name is Claire Pedrono from Brittany, holds up a chalkboard showing the Frenchman the time gaps with 5km to go. Thirty-six seconds on Sørensen and Kiryienka, 1:51 to the Nibali group with Jurgen Van Den Broeck and Thibaut Pinot and two minutes to the yellow jersey with Wiggins, Froome, Schleck.

The distinctive red car of Tour race director Christian Prudhomme tracks Wiggins and Froome. He stands tall out of the sunroof as if on safari, keeping pace with a herd of gazelles.

Nibali, the prey, is now within range. Froome's electrifying pace up the mountain has dragged the Italian back. It's time to cast the line, hook on to his back wheel and reel him in. Catch of the day.

Froome leads Wiggins up the climb. Then, *zap*, Schleck is gone, off the back, as if plucked from the mountain by Godzilla.

Now it's 5km to go for the yellow jersey group. And Froome has dragged Wiggins back to Nibali, Van Den Broeck and Pinot. Gotcha. Once more there are five riders snaking up the climb. Nibali is back in the fold. Sky's work is almost done. Wiggins can sit tight on Froome's wheel, enjoy a ski-lift ride to the summit.

The five settle into a steady rhythm as they approach the hamlet of Le Corbier at 1,508m above sea level. A lull in the action. Four clicks to go. A wall of shale to the left of the chain of riders casts a giant shadow on the road. Wiggins, Froome, Nibali, Pinot, Van Den Broeck.

Whoa! Suddenly number 105, Chris Froome, makes a sharp movement left and darts round Nibali, leaving Wiggins behind. The TV commentators explode into life. 'He's attacking him! He's attacking him!' commentator Phil Liggett shrieks. 'He's breaking them up, but look at this, Thibaut Pinot is straight on his wheel.'

What's going on? Has Froome gone rogue? Evans has long since cracked. He's out of the game. Nibali is in lock-up. So why is Froome attacking his own teammate?

Froome stretches his neck forward, craning into the climb like an emu on the run, as the road rises again, sweeping up and round a left-hand bend into the blinding sunshine. He accelerates through a colourful gauntlet of fans, cheering, clapping, screaming. A man in a leopardskin caveman outfit and curly blond wig parps wildly on a green vuvuzela. Another, shirtless, barefoot, arms flapping like a demented pigeon, fist pumping, shouting, sprints alongside Froome. The Sky rider motors on, unperturbed. The road straightens, ramps up. Now.

What's going on? What the hell is Froome playing at?

Co-commentator Paul Sherwen's voice rises to the strangulated pitch of an incredulous choirboy. 'I think he may well have been given the nod by Wiggins . . . but Bradley Wiggins has been left behind by Nibali!'

The TV images switch to an aerial shot of Wiggins, his yellow jersey flashing through gaps in the trees. He flickers in and out of view amid the foliage. Close your eyes and a yellow splodge appears, burned into the retina, like blinking at the sun. A lone fan chases Wiggins up the vicious incline filming his backside with a mobile phone. Capturing his strange humiliation. Alone, abandoned by his *domestique*. The leader of the Tour de France, dropped by his own teammate.

Liggett kicks in. 'Well this is . . . now . . . does Froome know what he's doing with that acceleration because he's got Bradley Wiggins on the defensive!'

Froome is speaking into the radio pinned to the left breast of his black jersey. Has he just received a massive telling off from the men in the Sky car? What was that acceleration all about? An attack, surely? A brazen, deliberate, anti-protocol attack. The time-honoured code is: defend the yellow jersey at all costs. Control the controllables. But what happens when your own teammate slips the leash?

Froome comes back into shot. With his right hand he reaches across his chest and fiddles with his radio, steering with his left hand. He pedals comfortably ahead of Pinot, but he's dropped his pace. He speaks into the mic. Two seconds . . . no more. One beat, two, then he swivels and looks over his shoulder back down the road. Where's Wiggins? Shiiiiit!

Sherwen explains: 'He's just got the word from team manage-ment – You've put your team leader in to a spot of bother here! Just sit up and wait for him.'

Froome looks down, breathes out, sits up slightly and drifts to the middle of the road. He twists his head round again to look for Wiggins. Pinot remains behind, mouth agape, at his limit. It is no sweat for Froome, relaxed, to stay ahead of the Frenchman.

A helicopter shot catches Wiggins, still alone on the road.

Froome, seemingly with all the time in the world, as if he might back-pedal, stop, go for a quick nap and then grab an ice cream, waits for Wiggins. Finally Pinot struggles past him. At last Wiggins comes back up to Froome. Van Den Broeck and Nibali are there too. The elite strongmen of the Tour de France. Pinot heads off alone.

The Wiggins yellow jersey group now has a minute on the incumbent champion Evans. The Australian will plummet down the standings. It *will* be a Wiggins–Froome, Sky 1-2. And Nibali will go above Evans into third.

Further up the climb Pierre Rolland, battered and bloodied, is clearly still in pain, the suffering etched on his face, but he doesn't wilt. He knows he's homing in on the stage win. He passes under the *flamme rouge*: 1km from the finish line, from victory.

Not too far behind him, just over a minute, Froome ups the pace again, out of the saddle. Wiggins follows, Nibali and Van

Den Broeck on his wheel close behind. They sweep up Pinot, Sørensen, Kiryienka.

One and a half kilometres to go. Froome, a one-man broom wagon, is sweeping up everyone ahead of him on the road bar Rolland. He speaks into the radio mic again. Cups his ear to hear the reply above the delirious racket of the crowd. Is he asking to go on the attack? He listens then replies, glances back at Wiggins.

The roadside gallery thickens. A United Nations of flags. The asphalt is covered in graffiti. The names of riders. Local hero Pinot's name is prominent. Excitable fans step out onto the road to take snaps of their heroes passing. Race motorbikes glide past on either side. It's a miracle no one gets hit. A man in a shark outfit stumbles backwards and almost disappears over the edge of the mountain. A fan of Nibali, perhaps?

Rolland turns into the final bend to the finish line. An ecstatic gallery of fans line the road, rattling the barriers, cheering and clapping. After nearly five hours in the saddle the 25-year-old from the Loiret takes a richly deserved stage win.

And then the yellow jersey group arrives. Round the corner and into the final 50m. Head down, Froome sprints full pelt for the line ahead of Pinot. But Pinot sneaks past for a French 1-2. Froome takes third, Van Den Broeck fourth. Across the line Froome immediately looks back, with a whip of the head, to make sure that Wiggins is with them. It's like a nervous twitch. The man in the yellow jersey crosses the line fifth, alongside Nibali.

Sherwen: 'Pinot looks to be a great star for the future but so too is Chris Froome – are we looking at a future Tour de France winner with this young man as well?'

Two British teammates now occupy first and second place at the Tour de France. Bradley Wiggins has taken a giant step towards becoming the first British rider to win the famous race. On the podium he is instantly recognisable. Clad in bright yellow, the famous *maillot jaune*, he's the leader of the Tour de France. Wiggo. The Mod. Whip-thin, with a beaky nose, and large sideburns framing his face like a pair of burnt ochre doormats. Everyone knows who he is.

But who is Chris Froome?

CHAPTER I
Kijana in Kenya

'Most of the time we looked on Chris Froome as a joker,' David Kinjah says. Static crackles down the telephone line from Kenya. The sound of rain beating a steady rhythm on a metal roof merges with a muffled hubbub of children's voices. 'At the beginning we didn't even think he'd be a serious cyclist, this footloose young boy who just wanted to come and enjoy some village life.'

A sudden thunderstorm has forced Kinjah to cut short a training ride with his Safari Simbaz cycling club and seek shelter within the cluster of corrugated-iron-clad buildings that is the club's headquarters in Mai-a-Ihii, a tiny village within the Kikuyu township, 20km north-west of Nairobi.

Inside the warren of rooms is an Aladdin's cave of cycling paraphernalia, bikes and spare parts. Myriad trophies and medals take pride of place in the workshops and living quarters, testimony to Kinjah's status as Kenya's most decorated cyclist. He captained his country at two Commonwealth Games and a host of international competitions. He even rode a season in Italy with the Index Alexia team, the former home of 2002 Giro d'Italia champion Paolo Savoldelli, earning the nickname 'Leone Nero', Black Lion.

The affable, dreadlocked 41-year-old is a legendary figure in the Kenyan cycling world. Now in semi-retirement, he is a one-man NGO, founder of the charitable cycling club, the Safari Simbaz Trust, dedicated to finding and developing cycling talent among underprivileged children in the communities in and around Nairobi. He is a coach and mentor to a motley crew of disadvantaged young riders, school dropouts and unemployed teenagers. All come from impoverished backgrounds, broken homes; some are orphans.

'These guys come from very poor families,' Kinjah says. 'Like any young child they love bicycles, so when you buy them their own you send them to heaven. When I go riding with them around the villages you really get to know how poor they are and how difficult life is for them. You just want to help them and let them have fun.'

In return for bed and board at Kinjah's base and opportunities to go for training rides with the great man they help to repair and clean the bikes. It nurtures an interest in cycling, Kinjah says, gives them useful skills and hopefully keeps them away from crime. In the red-dirt space outside the club grounds, Kinjah patiently teaches an eager, ragtag bunch of new recruits of all ages and sizes how to stay upright on two wheels and leads them on laps of the quadrant. Those with the raw ability to progress in the sport are singled out and coached more seriously by Kinjah. His ultimate dream is to start a cycling academy to nurture young Kenyan talent.

'I want to develop young boys and girls through cycling to enable them to have a sustainable future for themselves, either by being professional cyclists, mechanics or professional sport events managers,' says Kinjah. 'One of our dreams is to have the first professional cycling team in Kenya.'

For over a decade he has used his wages earned as a bike mechanic, winnings from races and any sponsorship deals he can attract for the Simbaz cause. When it's not raining – which is most days in February, in the dry, hot high season – Kinjah takes his young charges on training rides on their mountain bikes along the dusty roads of the Great Rift Valley.

★

Fifteen years ago a chance meeting at a cycling fundraiser saw him take on the role of mentor to another budding young cyclist, but one from a distinctly different background to those usually involved with the club.

'He was the fastest junior we ever had,' Kinjah tells me emphatically. 'But because he was *mzungu* nobody talked about him very much. It is a black country.' *Mzungu* means 'aimless wanderer' in Swahili, in essence a catch-all term for someone of foreign, usually western, therefore white descent. This particular *mzungu* was a thirteen-year-old boy called Christopher Froome.

'Cycling is traditionally for whites, not something for Kenyans. It would be easier to talk about running rather than cycling,' Kinjah says. The first image that springs to mind when thinking of Kenyan athletes is ebony-skinned, gazelle-like runners loping to another effortless gold medal at the Olympics or victory at a major marathon. Kenyans are indisputably the greatest long-distance runners on the planet. Of the top twenty fastest marathons ever run anywhere in the world, seventeen have been run by Kenyans. But cycling has no such pedigree in the country.

'I first met Chris in late 1998,' Kinjah recalls. Back then, the 26-year-old David Kinjah was Kenya's top professional cyclist. He was fresh off a plane from Kuala Lumpur and the 1998 Commonwealth Games where he'd finished a creditable 21st in the individual time trial (ITT), when a woman from Nairobi showed up in the Kikuyu township at one of the charity fun rides he regularly organised. Jane Froome introduced Kinjah to Chris, her reserved, button-nosed teenage son. She had heard that Kinjah coached local youths. Chris had boundless energy and was fond of tearing about on his black BMX bike, a present from one of his older brothers. 'She said to me, "My son loves bicycles, the school is closed for the holidays, and I don't know what to do with him! Do you think you could take him out riding?"'

Chris regularly cycled to school from their home in the leafy environs of Karen, an affluent suburb of Nairobi inhabited mainly by the descendants of white settlers and expats and named after the celebrated author Karen Blixen. It was a 20km round trip to the Banda School, situated on the north-western hemline of Nairobi National Park, a vast nature reserve teeming with a rich variety of wildlife. Known as 'Kifaru Park', it is a famous rhinoceros sanctuary (*kifaru* is Swahili for rhinoceros) and home to an abundance of wild animals such as lions and elephants, antelope and zebra, buffaloes and wildebeest who roam free, unperturbed by their close proximity to the city's bustling centre.

It was the Banda's very own wildlife playground, and science-class field trips had an added frisson. 'There are no fences in the national parks,' Froome recalled years later. 'Yes, you're riding with animals. It's common to cycle past elephants and lions. It's just normal there.'

His mother worked as a freelance physiotherapist and drove around the Nairobi area treating clients in their homes. It was inconvenient to drag her fidgety son along with her to house calls, so she asked Kinjah if he could keep Chris occupied on the weekends and long summer days, and teach him bike maintenance so he could fix the flat tyres he picked up riding on the potholed roads to and from school.

Kinjah says she was separated from her husband Clive, who had since moved to South Africa, and finding it difficult to juggle work commitments with looking after her hyperactive teenager.

Froome's maternal grandparents were latter-day colonialists, leaving England for the coffee plantations of Nairobi in the early decades of the twentieth century. The completion of the Uganda Railway Line in 1901 – running from Mombasa on the east coast of Kenya to the port city of Kisumu, on the shores of Lake Victoria – had enabled the British colonial administration to relocate from Kenya's coastal areas to the previously inaccessible interior – home to warrior tribes such as the Maasai – and the more temperate climate around Nairobi. By 1912 settlers had established themselves in the highlands and set up mixed agricultural farms, turning a profit in the colony for the first time. These first outposts, Naivasha and the Ngong Hills, including the suburb of nearby Karen, remain predominantly white-settled areas today.

The beginning of the end of Britain's colonial reign came in 1952 when a secret Kikuyu-dominated guerilla group, known as Mau Mau, began a violent four-year campaign against white settlers to drive them from their farms and reclaim the land the British had appropriated from Kikuyu communities during the building of the Uganda Railway. Rebel leader Dedan Kimathi was captured in October 1956 and hanged in Kamiti prison in February 1957, signalling defeat for the Mau Mau. In 1960 the state of emergency declared by the British in 1952 finally ended. The conflict had left tens of thousands of casualties, and the British government announced its plan to prepare Kenya for majority African rule. Kenya at last became independent on 12 December 1963. It had been a long time coming.

Froome's mother, Jane, was born in Kenya in 1956, the year the Mau Mau uprising was quelled, while his father, Clive, was born and grew up in England before moving to the eastern Africa country and subsequently working in the travel industry, running safaris. Froome's paternal grandparents still live in the small town of Tetbury, near Cirencester in Gloucestershire.

Christopher Clive Froome was born in Nairobi on 20 May 1985. His two older brothers – London-based Jonathan and Jeremy, who lives in Kenya – are both accountants. 'The right way to describe me,' Froome told *Cycle Sport* in 2008, 'is as a Kenyan-born Brit.'

More recently he has said, 'I'm not sure if you can call me African any more. Even though I've never lived in Britain, I feel British. I'm not Kenyan – I can't be, I'm white. My parents are British and I have British ancestry.'

In the morning Jane would drop her eager son off at Kinjah's place in Mai-a-Ihii and pick him up as dusk fell over the Ngong Hills on the distant horizon. Young Froome soon graduated from his BMX to a mountain bike, and quickly integrated with the small group of riders who would divide the day between tinkering with their bikes and heading off into the wilds of the Great Rift Valley. In the beginning his mother was a little nervous about leaving him alone, the only white face in the village, and this back in the days when there were no mobile phones to keep in touch.

But she relaxed, Kinjah says, when she returned at the end of the day to find Chris smiling and saying, 'I'm very happy. I like it here.'

'Cycling was my freedom from a young age,' said Froome. 'It was my way to see friends or go exploring.' Or even to use as a portable market stall. Froome confessed that as an eight-year-old budding entrepreneur he used to sell avocados off the back of his bike for pocket money.

His skin colour inevitably set him apart. 'We're all Africans here,' Kinjah explains, 'but having a *mzungu* in the village *was* slightly crazy.' But once Jane got to know and trust Kinjah she soon felt reassured that the village was a safe place for Chris. 'She understood that any place could be dangerous or safe, and it wasn't really a criminal village. She felt confident to leave him there not just overnight, but for days.'

Froome picked up a smattering of Swahili and made friends with other children in the village, something that helped put his mum even more at ease. Kinjah would collect sweet potatoes and vegetables from the *shamba* (small farm plots) dotted around the village, and Chris quickly embraced the local cuisine.

He even earned himself a few Swahili nicknames. One name in particular stuck – *murungaru* – a word from the mother tongue of Kinjah's tribe, the Kikuyu, used to tease the increasingly gangly teenager about his height. 'He was aware we had nicknames for him but never quite knew their exact translation,' says Kinjah with a chuckle. As he grew taller Froome would hunch down over his too-small bike and ride off, elbows flailing about (an ungainly riding style he has retained to this day), and Kinjah and his friends would laugh: 'Look, *murungaru* is starting to fly!' 'What is it?!' the teenager would turn and say, then laugh along in blissful ignorance.

However, Jane was inevitably concerned about her callow son pedalling blithely through hostile areas, certain townships and villages that were unaccustomed to white faces. Tensions were high in Nairobi in late 1998 when the Froomes first went to Kikuyu to meet David Kinjah. On 7 August Islamist extremists bombed the US embassies in the Kenyan capital and Dar es Salaam in Tanzania, killing 223 people and injuring thousands. The attacks, by al-Qaeda operatives, brought Osama bin Laden to international attention for the first time and only served to exacerbate an already edgy atmosphere in the country at large, but particularly Nairobi. The effect on the Kenyan economy was devastating, and it would take years to rebuild the shattered tourism industry.

On occasion, naturally mindful of Chris's safety, his mother would follow Kinjah's cyclists in her car, dishing out food and water along the way, like an ad hoc support car in a bike race. Kinjah recalls one time they were going camping in Kajiado, a predominantly Maasai town, 80km south of Nairobi. Africa's highest peak, Mount Kilimanjaro, provided a stunning backdrop for their journey south, its vast bulk brooding in the distance; three dormant volcanic cones shrouded in white cloud.

'Sometimes the mother would say to me, "Kinjah, remember he's only *kijana* (a young boy), don't push him too hard. I think it's getting to be too much for him." And I'd say to her, "Your son doesn't want to stop. This *kijana* is very determined."'

It was a long way to Kajiado, and the A104 highway, which led into neighbouring Tanzania, was dangerous. The road was rutted, and local drivers were prone to unpredictable manoeuvres. But young Chris showed little fear, even when riding among the older riders, and his stubborn determination not to buckle, to match the others, was soon apparent to Kinjah.

Even at such a tender age it was clear Froome had an ability to suffer on the bike. And he was confident, fearless. He wanted to do everything the others did, including tough hill climbs and kamikaze runs down the other side. In fact, he was often the first to hurtle down the most hair-raising descents.

'He was cautious, yes, but he wasn't afraid of what we were doing. He learned to be one of us,' Kinjah says. 'At first he didn't know that we were so serious about cycling. He really struggled to keep up with us, but then when he saw how hard we trained, he adapted to that.'

On the road to Kajiado, after about 60km riding in searing heat, Kinjah told Chris to stop cycling and ride in his mother's car. But he stubbornly refused and rode really slowly until the group were dots on the horizon. At a snail's pace he followed them all the way to Kajiado. 'He did this lots of times,' Kinjah laughs down the phone.

Despite his doggedness, the *mzungu* was still a bit of a joke to Kinjah and his crew. This Chris guy was fun to hang out with, Kinjah says. They were happy to take him under their wing and help out his mother, but he was just a kid. No one took him seriously, and initial impressions didn't suggest they had stumbled across a prodigious cycling talent.

★

Froome turned fourteen on 20 May 1999 and reached the end of his senior year at the Banda School. It was time to move on to secondary school. His Kenyan idyll was about to be rudely interrupted as he was whisked away to boarding school in South Africa. But it wasn't the end of his friendship with Kinjah. Their adventures together were only just beginning.

CHAPTER 2

Eton of the Highveld

Arriving as a boarder from Kenya, Chris Froome spent eighteen months at St Andrew's Junior School in Bloemfontein, capital of the Free State Province and known as the 'city of roses'. It was a culture shock for the boy from the Kenyan bush. Bloemfontein was at the heart of a staunchly Afrikaans province, and Froome barely knew a word of the native language.

From Bloemfontein he went north to the Highveld, the vast, inland high-altitude South African plateau, and to the city of Johannesburg. His father lived in the city, in the gentrified suburb of Parkhurst. Clive Froome's work demanded that he travel widely, so Chris was sent to a local boarding school in the autumn of 2000. But not just any old boarding school. St John's College is one of South Africa's most exclusive independent schools. Founded in 1898 by Reverend John Darragh, rector of the city's St Mary's Anglican Church, it has one of the best academic records of any school in the country with hefty annual fees for boarders.

Froome was required to sit an entrance test, which proved little trouble for the academically bright youngster, before being thrust into the ultra-privileged world inhabited by the children of Johannesburg's moneyed elite. The buildings and grounds of St John's resemble a five-star country club more than a school. There is a traditional College system, with five boarding houses: Nash, Hill, Hodgson, Runge and Clayton. From the tin huts of Kinjah's Kikuyu township to the lush green gardens and rarefied cloisters of St John's . . . it was light years away from his unconfined upbringing in Kenya.

'When the school started, it was very much modelled on

traditional English public schools like Eton,' says Allan Laing, who was the housemaster of Nash, Froome's College house during his time at St John's. Since 1907 the school has occupied the site of what was once a country school, in the up-market suburb of Houghton Estate – whose most famous resident is Nelson Mandela. Houghton, on the north-eastern outskirts of Johannesburg, has long since been absorbed into South Africa's largest city. Old traditions still linger at St John's, including an elaborate war cry performed at the weekly rugby matches.[1]

Although Froome possesses the clipped accent and polished manners of a typical public schoolboy, the experience hardened him. 'A boarding school like that makes you grow up earlier and learn how to do things on your own a bit more,' Froome has said. St John's tightly organised routine and strict discipline further instilled in him an independent spirit, already apparent as a boy growing up in Kenya and born of being left alone, a *mzungu*, in an all-black village; a child who needed to blend in, to become one of Kinjah's family.

★

Only five years prior to Froome's arrival in South Africa, the country was still ruled by a white minority, the Afrikaner National Party, which came to power in 1948 and enforced a policy of apartheid (from Afrikaans, literally 'separateness'), a system of segregation (and discrimination) on grounds of race. Black and white communities were forced to live in separate areas. Laws were passed forbidding marriage and sex between the races. Further legislation introduced racial segregation on buses and in schools and hospitals. The apartheid government forced the resettlement of three million people to black 'homelands' during the 1970s. The draconian pass laws, whereby Africans

---

1   St John's has become known for its war cry, accompanied by intricate drum lines, chants and movements, in which the letters SJC or the words of the school motto (Lux Vita Caritas/ Light, Life, Love) are spelled out in a sort of semaphore by the raising and lowering of school blazers to reveal the white shirt underneath.

were forbidden to live or work in towns without the correct documents, condemned much of the black population to exist in impoverished rural townships.

Despite rioting and terrorism at home and repudiation by the rest of the world, from the 1960s onwards the white regime maintained the apartheid system with only minor concessions until February 1991. South Africa finally emerged from international isolation in 1994 at the end of the apartheid era. But the cost of division and years of conflict would reverberate for years to come, not least in terms of lawlessness, social disruption and lost education for nearly two generations of young blacks. The wounds of apartheid were still raw in 2000 when Froome took up a place at St John's College, an institution of the former ruling white elite.

Plunged into the unfamiliar environs of St John's he found himself an outsider once again. This time, strangely, he was a white interloper in a predominantly white environment. His foreign status, as Kenyan, and his predilection for cycling, deemed an alternative sport (cricket and rugby were the traditional mainstays at St John's) set him apart.

'In Kenya I was in a mixed-race school all the way,' Froome said. 'It's not like South Africa. It's a lot more relaxed.' Laing tells me: 'You could definitely see that Chris was a Kenyan boy. He was an outdoorsy type of lad – he enjoyed being out in the fresh air. Cycling allowed him to escape the confines of being in a boarding school.'

Froome's passion for cycling would neither endear him to the school's traditional sporting fraternity nor gain him a prestigious scroll, or half-colours, which were woven into the blazer to signify sporting achievement. Indeed, at that time cycling was not even recognised as an official school sport. It was just something Froome pursued for his own enjoyment, in his spare time, and was tolerated by the school. 'He was clearly serious about it, so we made a few allowances and let him get on with it,' Laing says.

St John's most famous sporting old boy was Clive Rice, the former South African cricketer, whose career coincided with

South Africa's sporting isolation. Cricket was not for Froome, so he was never likely to follow in Rice's footsteps, but despite his slight build he participated in the school's second main sport, rugby, playing flanker for one of the school's lower teams until Grade 11. 'I was getting crunched,' Froome recalls. 'But I enjoyed it, loved it actually.'

His pleasure, Laing says, was tempered by the fact that 'he didn't show any real talent in the traditional sports like rugby and cricket that the school prides itself on. He was as he is now – thin and wiry but very athletic.'

★

The younger sibling of two older brothers, Froome had learned from an early age to fend for himself, make his own fun, and latterly was driven by a desire not to follow in their accountancy footsteps. ('I think a fear of falling into that world made me pedal faster!' Froome joked.) Then running wild in the great Kenyan outdoors, finding a kindred spirit in David Kinjah, he had been the only white face in a small Nairobi township. From there he became an English-speaking Kenyan at an Afrikaans school, then a bike-mad Kenyan, consumed by the great outdoors, holed up at a posh boarding school where a love of cricket and rugger was nigh on compulsory. He was a boarder, forced to sleep away from home and obey a strict code of conduct. It is little wonder Froome developed such a strong sense of independence, which runs through him still like the copper core of an electric cable.

These rich, diverse experiences would, whether he was conscious of it or not, leave an indelible mark on the young Froome and stand him in good stead for the challenges that lay ahead in his life, on and off the bike. Years later he said, 'I like to fight alone,' referring to his fondness for the solitary effort of time trialling and for the pleasure of riding in the mountains – the two disciplines in which he would go on to excel.

But, Froome, the free-spirited maverick, was also, as Laing asserts, a happy boy at school. He made friends easily and enjoyed the social side of mixing with the other boys in Nash. Popular with a number of close friends at the school, in sixth form he was made House Prefect.

★

A growing appetite for cycling could only be properly sated when term-time at St John's came to an end and he travelled back to Kenya to stay with his mother in Nairobi, a school-holiday habit he'd established during his time at Bloemfontein.

As David Kinjah recalls: 'Sometimes Chris would be gone for five months in South Africa, and then the schools would close, and all of a sudden he would appear and say, "Kinjah, I'm back." And then he would say, "Can I come tomorrow? Do you have a place for me to stay? Can I bring some food?"'

'I used to go up and stay at Kinjah's house in the village in Kikuyu for weeks every time I came back for the holidays,' Froome said. 'It was basic living, but I had the time of my life just training with them, heading up into the forests on our mountain bikes. That's where I got the love for cycling. Four or five of us would go down to the Great Rift Valley. I loved it but I suffered on those rides.'

As Kinjah's *protégé* grew stronger, at fifteen, then sixteen years old, the group would venture further, beyond the villages and open roads around Kikuyu, and up into the verdant Ngong Hills, made famous by Karen Blixen. The Danish baroness had arrived in Kenya in 1914 to manage a coffee plantation and wrote about the intense colours and ravishing landscapes – 'dry and burnt, like the colours in pottery' – in her 1937 memoir *Out of Africa*.

The word *Ngong* is a Maasai word meaning 'knuckles', a succinct description of the four noble peaks crowning the long ridge that rises from the plain around Nairobi and stretches from north to south, the hills falling vertically to the west, deep into the burning desert of the Great Rift Valley. The friends would ride up into these hills, through expat enclaves. In the early colonial days, many white settlers, like Blixen, established perfect reproductions of English farmhouses in the green and fertile hills, where the grass was spiced with the scent of thyme and bog myrtle.

According to Blixen, the 'chief feature of the landscape' in the Ngong Hills is the immense vastness of the canopy of the big sky overhead. 'Looking back on a sojourn in the African highlands you are struck by your feeling of having lived for a time up in the air. In the highlands you woke up in the morning and thought: Here I am, where I ought to be.'

The steep climbs and stunning vista of the Ngong Hills – rising to a peak of over 2,460m above sea level – suited Froome's early penchant for going uphill on his bike. The fresh-faced teenager lapped it up, breathing easily in the thin mountain air. 'I was born at altitude near Nairobi and have always enjoyed riding at altitude,' Froome said. Here he was, where he ought to be, at home.

'When we went out to do the hill climbs he wanted to do it all, to keep up with us,' Kinjah says. 'He wasn't scared. He was a very carefree, upbeat and fearless guy.' The teenage Froome's intrepid nature had clearly impressed him.

Local residents in the Ngong Hills area still reported seeing lions there during the 1990s, and confrontations with wild animals were a common theme of Froome and Kinjah's training jaunts into the untamed bush. An oft-repeated anecdote from Froome's childhood revolves around a fishing expedition to the Maasai Mara National Reserve. 'Every kid who has grown up in Kenya has had mock-charges from elephants or rhinos,' he said. 'The closest I ever came was being chased by a hippo. I was fishing on the Mara river, so I was probably asking for trouble, but a hippo did come out and chase me.

'Hippos really do move, but I dropped everything and ran up an embankment and held on to roots. I had to wait for a couple of hours. To me it's just a funny story; to most people in Europe, it's something completely foreign.

'Growing up in Kenya was just ... freedom. You learn so much about life so early – above all, you learn about independence. It is changing, but back then you could do what you wanted and discover life for yourself.'

By now Jane Froome had established herself as a physiotherapist at Karen Surgery on the Ngong Road and, in her son's absence, she had become one of Safari Simbaz's biggest supporters and a friend of Kinjah's. During time off from her duties at the surgery, Jane would make impromptu visits to Mai-a-Ihii laden down with baskets of food. 'She would talk to her friends and say, "You should come and visit Kinjah and see what he's done for my son and these other boys from the village,"' Kinjah says. 'She would collect donations for us and ask people to give food. She was very generous.'

Home on holiday from St John's, Chris and his mum would show up in Mai-a-Ihii with a picnic, and Froome, Kinjah and the others would head off on a camping trip on their mountain bikes, Jane sometimes following behind in the car. 'We rode on the highway a lot of times, which was a bit scary for his mum,' Kinjah says, referring to the fact that Kenya has one of the worst road safety records in the world – the country's motorists have a proclivity for improper overtaking manoeuvres, speeding and drunken driving. 'But Chris was one very confident young man.'

Kinjah has fond memories of their long bike rides south on the C58 highway through the Great Rift Valley's dramatic landscape to Lake Magadi, past ribbons of steaming and bubbling soda lakes. En route they would ride past giraffes striding elegantly across lacustrine plains and black rhinos snuffling by the lakeshore, lions lolling under trees, and zebras and ostriches roaming freely by the roadside.

The frisky Froome, says Kinjah with a laugh, 'really tried to drop me on every hill, but he couldn't'. And then their final destination, Lake Magadi, the most southerly of the valley's soda lakes, would appear shimmering in the distance. In the dry season it is almost entirely covered with a thick encrustation of soda, and the shoreline is fringed with massed pink colonies of flamingos, lending it a bizarre, candy-flecked, lost-planet appearance.

Over the years, as soon as the school holidays rolled around again, the pair would head north, up into the Central Highlands, the fertile, misty, red-dirt spiritual heartland of Kenya's biggest tribe, the Kikuyu, to visit Kinjah's parents in the tiny village of Kimbururu. Sometimes they'd camp overnight, and explore the surrounding hills on their bikes. Chris was usually the first to launch off on some daredevil prank on the cheap mountain bike he'd acquired in South Africa. 'Some of the hills we never dared to ride,' Kinjah says, 'but he would be the first to head off down them, often crashing into streams and then picking himself up laughing!'

'His [Kinjah's] parents were on a farm and I remember riding back and everyone had an extra five or six kilos of some kind of root and all kinds of vegetables for the next week's food,' Froome remembered of one special ride. 'I was amazed at these guys carrying so much extra weight on the way home. I was let off lightly because I was young but I was still struggling to keep up with them.'

On the journey back to Kikuyu, Kinjah would challenge Froome to ride as fast as possible to make it back to the village before dark. 'It was tough terrain, very hilly countryside and not easy for a young boy, but Chris always said, "OK, let's go!"' And they'd race each other home in the encroaching darkness, plummeting downhill toward Nairobi's cityscape and the vast expanse of the national park beyond.

'We had a great time riding together,' Kinjah says. 'But we still looked on Chris in a jokey way. He was fun to be with and we didn't think that one day he'd be ruling the world in the Tour de France!'

★

During term-time at St John's, when the familiar thwack of leather on a willow bat could be heard drifting across the playing fields and echoing through the cloisters, or when rugby practice was in full flow, Froome could be found otherwise engaged in his dormitory room, hammering away astride his racing bike mounted on a turbo trainer. If he wasn't studying – he had a particular aptitude for mathematics and Laing says he was 'a good, quiet student, bright and very diligent and never got into any trouble' – there he would be.

'I can remember he had one of those indoor trainers that he put in his dorm room and he would sit on this thing and cycle for hours on end while the other boys sat in the common room watching television,' Laing recalls. Froome would cycle hundreds of kilometres without leaving the room, a mark, Laing says, of his passion and dedication to his chosen sport.

At the relatively late age of seventeen he had become smitten with road racing – 'on bikes with thin tyres that went so fast,' he said – when one of his older brothers gave him his old road bike, which Froome recalled 'had a steel frame and friction shifters [gear control levers] on the down tube . . . I hadn't really been on a road bike until then, so it was a whole new thing for me.'

Around the same time, he had his first initiation into the remote, exotic world of the Tour de France. 'The first Tour I watched [2002] I saw the battle between [Lance] Armstrong and [Ivan] Basso in the mountains,' Froome said. 'It was on TV in the boarding house at St John's. I was seventeen and I was transfixed by it. I was in awe of the ambience of the crowd and the mountains. I had that "Wow, I'd love to do that one day" feeling. That was the pipe dream, but I never really, until recently, thought it'd come true.' Armstrong went on to win his fourth straight Tour.[2] The 24-year-old Basso rode himself into eleventh place overall in his second appearance in the race and claimed the white jersey for best young rider. Mesmerised by the young Italian's performance in the mountain stages through the Alps and Pyrenees, he became an instant idol of Froome's until years later; he gave up on cyclists as heroes after Basso was confirmed as another doping cheat when he was implicated in the 2006 scandal of *Operación Puerto*.[3]

In his final years at St John's, Froome would ditch the indoor rollers and head off in the late afternoon on long-distance rides, either solo or with his College friends and fellow cycling fanatics Matt Beckett and Gaetan Bolle, returning 'as the sun was setting and it was almost dark,' Laing recalls. 'We'd start worrying about him, wondering if he was OK!'

On Friday afternoons Froome would often ride home on his

2 Struck from the record books in October 2012 owing to Lance Armstrong's use of banned substances.

3 The code name of a Spanish police operation against the doping network of Doctor Eufemiano Fuentes, involving several of the world's most famous cyclists.

bike to spend the weekend with his father. 'I used to ride home on the highway,' he told *Cycle Sport* in 2009. 'It was the quickest way, sitting there, tailgating the rush-hour traffic in the outside lane at 50km per hour.'

One particular Friday, a traffic cop pulled alongside him, furiously flagging at him to pull over to the side of the road. 'He was pretty angry. He was saying, "What the hell do you think you're doing?" I told him it was quicker and safer to take the highway. I could keep up and wouldn't get mugged. He didn't buy it.'

★

David Kinjah started coaching Froome remotely, from his Kikuyu nerve centre. Froome would ask Kinjah questions via email, and his older friend and mentor would draw up a two-week or three-week training programme and advise him on what to eat. 'I emphasised the value of spinning on easy gears,' says Kinjah. 'I told him not to copy the other guys on big gearing because he needed to develop his leg speed, cadence and oscillation. I wanted him to work on getting a good riding rhythm.' Since Kinjah didn't have regular, easy access to the Internet, Froome, impatient for answers, brim-full of his own ideas, would call his mother and tell her to 'go and tell Kinjah to check his email'.

'It was basic coaching,' Kinjah says, 'and straightforward nutritional advice.' But when the pair went riding together in Kenya during Froome's school breaks it was for fun. Kinjah's logic was simple: 'I would never coach him like a Tour de France rider – just as long as he was fast and he could keep up with us, then he would be able to win a few races in South Africa.'

The man from Kikuyu is too modest to play on the profound influence he had on Chris Froome's career. He doesn't need to brag about it: Froome has done that for him, peppering virtually every interview with glowing references to his 'big mentor'. 'Kinjah is the one who first encouraged me to go and race,' Froome has stated frequently. 'He sparked my passion for cycling.'

'He was a big role model for me,' he made a point of telling the *Guardian*'s Donald McRae in January 2013. 'At the time he was the captain of the Kenyan cycling team. He had dreadlocks and he was incredibly welcoming and said to me, as a teenager, "Come and ride with us." I jumped at the opportunity to go training with the Kenyan national team.'

'It wasn't easy for him to be a cyclist in Kenya, especially in the villages,' Kinjah says. 'It was more of a survival stance with bicycles, and then he had to adopt a lifestyle. He got an advantage to have his head set right in the beginning; that it's not about the bike, it's about the rider. In South Africa he wasn't afraid of facing better bikes or better riders. He was himself and he still is a unique cyclist. He's not a copy of anyone.'

'Kinjah helped me to see you didn't need the best bike or perfect conditions,' Froome said. 'You can just get on a bike and go – no matter where you are.'

★

In 2003 Froome left St John's College and took up a place at the University of Johannesburg to study a BCom Degree in economics. While still at boarding school he had started cycling in a local Club Academy, named Super C, run by a local parent with a keen interest in cycling. It was an environment for young people of all abilities to ride their bikes together. They were ferried to cycling events in the Johannesburg area, and Froome competed in junior races with varying degrees of success. On Saturday mornings they hooked up with other bigger clubs, with older riders, to go on weekend club runs. Soon his university studies took a back seat to the central *leitmotif* of his life. 'Road cycling was very popular in South Africa, and I had the opportunity to race almost every weekend if I wanted to, so I just drew on that,' Froome said.

Froome was deeply serious about this cycling business, as Allan Laing had discerned. He possessed a burning desire to succeed, an ambition fostered during his untethered trips back to Kenya, out on long rides with Kinjah and his Kikuyu boys. Not long before he left the College, Laing's wife, who lived with him at the school, recalls Froome saying quite plainly to her, 'One day I'm going to do really well at cycling; I'm going to ride in the Tour de France.'

CHAPTER 3

A Tale of Two Time Trials

In his second year at the University of Johannesburg, some time in January 2005 – the tail-end of South Africa's summer – Froome was hanging out in Cycle Lab, a bike shop in the suburb of Fourways, not too far from his home in Parkhurst. The flagship branch of the national chain is located close to one of the best training runs in Johannesburg, making it a popular gathering point for the city's cycling community.

'At the time, the nineteen-year-old student was still taking part in Saturday-morning fun rides with the Super C Club Academy and competing in various junior races. Gareth Edwards, now an anchor on South African television, managed the Super C squad and recalled Froome as 'a fluffy creature who drove to races in his wreck of a car. He had long, straggly hair and wore more bangles than a girl. Chris was fluent in Swahili and he dressed in clothing, made from hemp, in the colours of the Swahili people. He did not look like a future Tour de France winner.' Due to the nature of the events – short distances over flat courses, ending in mass sprint finishes – Froome often finished in the middle of the pack, struggling to stay in touch with the front of the race.

Andrew McLean, a former competitive cyclist on the Johannesburg circuit, is co-founder of the Cycle Lab chain and manager of the Fourways branch. Cycle Lab already had a national cycling club, with around 6,500 members across the country. When McLean decided to launch an academy in Johannesburg using Fourways as the base, he enlisted a local coach, Robbie Nilsen, and merged the new Cycle Lab venture with the latter's small-scale enterprise.

'Robbie joined forces with us because we had a bit of money, infrastructure and a home for the new academy,' McLean tells me. 'It was through the academy that Robbie got introduced to Chris Froome . . . My impression of Chris was that he was too much of a nice guy. He went to an upmarket school, and kids from that kind of privileged background don't normally make it in a sport as hard as cycling. Chris is just the nicest gentleman you'll ever meet on a bicycle. I thought he had a lot of talent but lacked a killer instinct.'

A good friend of Froome's, Gavin Cocks, managed a Hi-Q franchise, in the north-eastern town of Nelspruit, a country-wide chain of car servicing and repair centres, similar to Kwik Fit in the UK. With cash sponsorship Cycle Lab's anonymous academy suddenly had a name: Hi-Q SuperCycling Academy. An Under-23 team was formed within the academy, and Froome became one of its first members.

★

South Africa has a deserved reputation for being a great country for so-called 'fun riders', explains Andrew McLean, but it is not an ideal breeding ground for serious talent. Cycling is hugely popular as a mass participation sport, and, as he says, 'we get thousands of people showing up for our big popular events – Cape Argus – but they're built around the weekend warrior. Each race is 100km, they're always quite easy and are ultimately designed for Joe Public to ride.

'It is the main reason why the standard of our pro racing is so poor. Guys like Robbie Hunter and Daryl Impey have bitten the bullet and gone overseas and flourished. If you're a sprinter and you stay here, you can win a whole lot of races and be a local hero, but you'll never get to the level that you need for racing in Europe.'

Competitive cycling events in South Africa were completely wrong for nurturing riders who could feasibly make the giant leap to a Pro Tour team in Europe. The races were too short, mostly 100km or less, and too flat, with no hint of a climb, resulting in predictable bunch sprint finishes. Riders with real all-rounder potential, like Froome, simply couldn't keep up and often became disillusioned, demotivated or lost to the system. The talented young Kenyan was in danger of slipping down the plughole into oblivion.

Froome had been left to his own devices, languishing in a club for social cyclists and competing in races entirely unsuited to his nascent abilities. He was an aspirant stage race rider. But such events didn't exist in South Africa. There were no races in which he could hone his skills as a climber or test his ability against the clock in a competitive time trial.

'The organisers of races in South Africa are not worried about pro riders,' McLean says, 'because they make their money out of the thousands of fun riders.'

The country boasts the two largest individually timed bike races in the world – Cape Town's Cape Argus Pick 'n' Pay Cycle Tour and the Pick 'n' Pay 94.7 Cycle Challenge in Johannesburg – with each attracting upwards of 35,000 riders. While still at St John's, Froome twice took part in the 94.7 Cycle Challenge, in 2001 and 2002. In essence, they are giant versions of those cyclosportives known as *gran fondo* in Italy – offering a challenge midway between racing and touring.

The problem in South Africa, McLean says, is that every 'big' race in the country serves as a qualifying event for the 109km Cape Argus – staged annually on the second Saturday in March – and is therefore restricted to an easy 100km, so that the masses of 'fun riders' can get good seeding times. It is a form of racing that seems to be unique to South Africa, where all sorts of people of all ages and abilities are put together in the same race, including the best riders in the country who race at the head of these events, in the same way that Olympic champion athletes jump-start the rest at marathons such as Boston, London or New York.

'A guy like Chris, who is by no means a sprinter, needed a hard 200km race with mountains to show what he was good at,' says McLean. 'I don't think he even ever won a major race in South Africa. The style of racing here didn't really suit him at all. It made Chris Froome look like a very average *domestique.*'

★

The first ever result recorded for Chris Froome as a Hi-Q SuperCycling Academy rider was for a race called the Berg en Dale Classic on 28 January 2005. He finished the 157km criterium race in 38th position out of 75 riders. In his first season with Hi-Q he competed in twenty South African races in 2005, without setting the veld on fire. The statistics read: twenty races, no wins.

However, the twenty-year-old did have one eye-catching result that first season and it hinted, for the first time, at an embryonic talent for stage racing and a bright future beyond the shores of Africa.

The Tour de Maurice, a six-day stage race held on Mauritius, started with a 4.1km prologue time trial in Tamarin, a picturesque old fishing village on the west coast of the island, on 30 August 2005. Froome didn't feature at the head of the race on either of the opening two days, but he made a big impression on Stage 2 when the race turned inland towards the elevated central plateau. The hilly 95km stage, around the town of Curepipe where the terrain rose 600m up the side of a dormant volcano, suited Froome's natural climbing ability, and he rode to the first proper victory of his fledgling career. It was a major breakthrough for Froome and it takes pride of place on his website as the first of his career highlights, the racing *palmarès*.

★

From the start of 2006, Froome's second year at Hi-Q, he still wasn't winning races, but he was placing higher in the longer, harder ones and playing a key role helping the team.

In March he was reunited with his old buddy and erstwhile mentor, David Kinjah, in Melbourne for the Commonwealth Games. Froome and the six-man Kenyan team showed up in Australia for the start of the 2006 Games on 15 March, with,

Kinjah says, 'our normal shit bikes', since the federation had failed to provide them with new ones. For Kinjah there were shades of his previous appearance at the Games, in Manchester in 2002. The Kenyan team had arrived without proper equipment – in fact without bikes. Legendary Manchester-based frame-builder, Harry Hall Cycles, whose bikes were graced by many top British pro cyclists, including Robert Millar, saved the day after they heard of the team's plight and loaned the Kenyans Specialized bikes to use during the Games. The company also generously launched an appeal to help out cyclists back in Kenya by donating second-hand race equipment.

At the Melbourne Games in 2006, Froome, Kinjah and the Kenyan cycling team could well have done with the help of a benevolent local bike shop, considering their intention, or at least Froome and Kinjah's, to enter every event going – including the men's road race and time trial, the mountain bike event and even some events at the velodrome.

'We were registered to ride the track too,' Froome said at the time, 'but couldn't get hold of enough equipment to race.' Perhaps it was just as well given they had zero experience of track racing. Bedlam might well have ensued: pile-ups, cartoon chaos.

Kinjah says that the Kenya Cycling Federation wanted to see them fail, even trying to sabotage his and Froome's chances in Melbourne. They'd had to scrounge and buy bicycles and parts because the federation failed to supply them with the proper equipment and, during the road race, he says the Kenyan cycling officials even hid their spare bottles and food. 'We had a cooler-box of supplies, which they took away from our support area on the course. I only had two half-filled bottles of water with me and had to try and get bottles from other teams to keep going,' says Kinjah.

In December 2010 Froome posted a link on his Twitter account to an article about his and Kinjah's exploits at the Melbourne Games, with the pithy comment, 'Politics in Kenyan cycling – it's a shame that the riders suffer for it. Managers hiding bottles is just the beginning.'

In their race report for the 2006 Commonwealth Games men's ITT, dated 21 March, *Cycling News* wrote, with no little incredulity: 'The first of 72 riders off recorded an impressive time which made a mockery of his ranking for the event. Kenyan Christopher Froome stopped the clock in 53:58:01, a time which kept him on top of the standings for almost an hour as the next 49 starters failed to better his effort!'

New Zealand's Logan Hutchings finally overhauled Froome, coming home two minutes quicker, but the twenty-year-old rookie had made his mark and eventually went on to finish seventeenth, 5:20:72 behind Australia's gold medallist Nathan O'Neill. Kinjah was a further three minutes back in 31st place.

Watching with growing interest from the sidelines was Doug Dailey, logistics manager at British Cycling, at the Games in Melbourne with the England cycling team. Dailey had enjoyed a long illustrious career as a national, international and Olympic road cyclist. Twice British road race champion, he competed in the 1972 Munich Olympics and, after his racing career was over, he became Great Britain cycling team's head coach during the lean years of the 1980s and 1990s. By 2006 he was at the vanguard of British cycling's thrilling resurgence on the world stage, at the Olympic Games in Athens and then Beijing, working alongside performance director Dave Brailsford, before retiring in 2012.

On a sweltering day in Melbourne, Dailey's interest in the lanky white Kenyan was suitably piqued. 'I was quite impressed with his riding,' Dailey tells me from his home in North Wales, a gentle Scouse lilt still strong despite over twenty years in the Vale of Clwyd. 'He was the first man off, but I noticed he was still in the hot seat at the finish for ages. And it took about 50 riders before he lost a podium place.

'I saw him in the road race too. The support was pretty chaotic. They kept on missing riders at the feed and dropping bottles.'

Froome's trademark *murungaru* posture on the bike was also instantly apparent to Dailey. 'He was all over the place. I think that was due to his formative years in Kenya, riding without the best equipment, on a bike that was too small for him – no one had tackled that problem. And he stuck with that style – but it seemed to work.'

The great Michael Johnson, the four-time Olympic sprint champion over 200m and 400m, earned the nickname 'The Duck' because of his style of running bolt upright with small steps. To the teasers he said, 'Well, maybe so, but I was the fastest duck out there.'

In an otherwise all-black Kenyan team, Froome's European roots were apparent. Acting on a hunch, Dailey went down to the Kenyan pit and had a brief chat with Froome on the subject of ancestry. 'I just thought, I bet he's a dual nationality, I bet he's got a British passport, and he told me that he did in fact have a British and Kenyan passport.'

Froome was a British passport holder from birth and had only recently acquired a Kenyan document to allow him to compete in Melbourne. It was a passport of convenience. 'They dangled a Commonwealth selection in front of him,' says Dailey. 'For a young kid like Chris it was beyond his wildest dreams that he would ride in the Olympics or World Championships. So he took the Kenyan passport and racing licence to ride the Commonwealths. And thank goodness he did because he caught my eye!

'We exchanged email addresses, and I reported back to Dave Brailsford and [British Cycling coach] Shane Sutton that this was a rider to watch,' Dailey says. 'I thought it would be a good idea to keep in touch with Chris. I always like a long shot; I'm a bit of a gambler. I knew in my own mind that if he was going to make any progress in cycling he was going to be up against it if he continued to ride for Kenya. They would never qualify for the Olympics. He would be far better off riding for Great Britain.'

Froome was up against the odds two days after the time trial. Riding in the men's cross-country mountain bike race at Lysterfield Park, Froome and his fellow Kenyans battled their way round the gruelling 53km circuit, eight laps of a narrow, snaking 6.6km course, but were lapped by the field.

In the road race on 26 March Froome and Kinjah were the surprise package, playing significant roles in the main break of the day. Kinjah tagged on to an early attack by Scotland's Duncan Urquhart and a five-man group which stayed out front for 122km before being reeled in by the chasing bunch with 44km remaining. At 22km to go, Froome tried his luck, exploding off the front of the main pack, but minutes later the gap was bridged by South Africa's Ryan Cox and several counter-attacks followed. Froome's daring attack had provoked ferocious jockeying at the front of the race, and attacks came thick and fast, including a failed attempt by a rider representing the Isle of Man, one Mark Cavendish. The peloton having been shot to pieces by Froome, Mathew Hayman made the race-winning move, jumping away on the last-lap to take another gold medal for Australia.

Froome told a journalist after the Melbourne road race how difficult it was to get funding from the Kenyan government and how he was 'going to put all my efforts into one day getting hired by a professional team in Europe'. It seemed a wild ambition at the time.

'It was really exciting for me to ride with Chris Froome in the Commonwealth Games for the Kenya team,' Kinjah says. 'I never thought we'd be able to have him. I always feared that he would disappear into South Africa and get absorbed there. But he stayed very loyal to Kenya, even when the federation was ignoring him.'

Kinjah says if Froome had depended on the support of the Kenya Cycling Federation he would be nothing right now. 'He's achieved everything because of his own hard work and determination. It didn't come from the federation; it came from him.'

★

Fresh from his experience of racing at an international level in Australia, Froome returned to the South African Under-23 circuit on April Fool's Day and took eighth place at the Speke Vasbyt Challenge, a one-day race covering 160km in Pretoria.

A smattering of middling results was followed on 22 July with second place overall at the Anatomic Jock Race, in Barberton, winning a one-off 7km hill climb time-trial challenge the day after the main 150km road race. In a country of flat races it was a rare opportunity for Froome to show his climbing prowess. There was more to come.

At the 2006 Tour de Maurice, starting in late August, the 21-year-old repeated his success of the previous year on the hilly Stage 2, climbing to victory up the volcano in Curepipe. And he sealed his first ever stage race triumph with a commanding performance in the short 15.4km ITT in the dramatic shadow of the basaltic monolith in Le Morne Brabant. Hi-Q teammate Alex Pavlov finished second on the final general classification (GC), with Christoff Van Heerden winning Stage 5. Hi-Q SuperCycling had taken the sleepy paradise island of Mauritius by storm.

In its weekly mailout to members and supporters, dated 7 September 2006, the Hi-Q SuperCycling Academy proudly led its Club Newsletter number 206 with the headline: 'WE WON THE TOUR DE MAURICE!!!'

★

On a high after his success in Mauritius, Froome saw that year's World Championships, to be held in Salzburg, as a prime opportunity to race in Europe for the first time. The only snag: Kenya weren't sending a team. Indeed, when Froome asked if they were, 'I was laughed at,' he said. However, Froome and Kinjah devised an ingenious way around this obstacle. It was like cycling's version of *Cool Runnings*.

'Back then we used to read all the Kenyan Cycling Federation's emails,' Kinjah says. Reading was one thing, but they could also write emails. Froome takes up the story. 'The Kenyans didn't have a team going into the Under-23 world championships but I had access to the Kenyan Cycling Federation's email account,' he told the *Guardian*. 'I remembered how to get into the chairman's Hotmail, and so I emailed the UCI saying, "We're going to send a cyclist to the U23 worlds.'" In a different version of the ruse, Froome told *The Times* he 'made up an email address – it was something like Kenyancyclingfederation@hotmail.com' to use to write the email to the UCI.

'So he actually sneaked his way into the world championships because the federation once again didn't support him,' Kinjah says, chuckling.

★

The email ploy worked, and the UCI granted Froome a place in the starting list for both the Under-23 ITT and the road race. He rolled into Salzburg the day before the time trial, 19 September, cutting a slightly eccentric figure.

'I had to take four buses and walk a couple of kilometres, carrying two bikes and a suitcase, to a little B&B outside Salzburg – in the rain,' Froome recalls.

With no fellow team members or support staff he improvised both parts. His Kenyan team manager hat on, he was due at a team managers' meeting that morning at the Salzburg Arena, the city's main exhibition and conference centre. Already horribly late, Froome meandered around Salzburg on his time-trial bicycle in torrential rain, lost in the maze of the city's winding streets and frequently consulting his sodden street guide in a frantic attempt to get to the Arena. 'The map disintegrated within minutes so I got lost in downtown Salzburg,' Froome said.

He finally arrived twenty minutes late and burst into the auditorium in the middle of an announcement by a UCI official on the subject of back-up vehicles in the race. Soaked to the bone, the dishevelled latecomer brought the meeting to a sudden, perplexed halt.

The hapless Froome couldn't have chosen a more conspicuous entrance; the door into the hall decanted him straight to the front of the proceedings. The room went silent. All eyes fell on the young man, drenched, carrying a time-trial bike and clutching a handful of wet mush that had once been a map.

'I was told, "No, no, this is a meeting for managers only." I said, "I *am* the manager. I'm the whole team, just me and my bikes." The guy gave me a strange look.'

With his managerial duties completed, Froome dashed off for another important appointment at 10 a.m. to confirm his participation in the two Under-23 road race events. Job done. Between 1 p.m. and 4 p.m. the time-trial routes were available for teams and individual competitors to recce, so he sped off to ride the 39.54km course.

The next day, Wednesday 20 September, Salzburg was bathed in glorious sunshine. Nine months earlier, all 35 of the city's churches had rung their bells in unison to celebrate the 250th anniversary of the birth of their most famous son, Wolfgang Amadeus Mozart. It was the beginning of a bumper year-long party. Tourists were out in force. Those not off visiting Mozart's residence or taking the *Sound of Music* tour – the Hollywood movie was partly shot on location in the city – lined the streets for the start of the 2006 cycling world championships.

On time and free of any last-minute mishaps, Froome arrived at the starting line, in the square outside the beautiful Mirabell Palace gardens. The start list showed that Chris Froome of Kenya would be the 34th starter from a field of 61, due off at 14:49:30.

By the time Froome was ready to go, Russia's Alexander Filippov had already set a blistering pace and was leading the way at the first time check. Froome readied himself on the start ramp. His red helmet gleamed in the afternoon sun. His tall frame was clad in a green, white-sleeved jersey with splashes of red. Black Lycra shorts completed the colours of the flag of his country of birth. Kenya's sole representative was primed for action.

It was a huge moment for the 21-year-old. Only a few months ago he was an undergraduate student in Johannesburg. He'd been racing road bikes for less than four years. Just seven years had passed since he was haring along dirt trails around Nairobi on his beloved BMX. Now he was about to ride one of the biggest events in the Continental cycling calendar: the UCI Under-23 world championships. His first ever race in Europe, rubbing shoulders with the sport's youthful elite. The field was liberally sprinkled with names that would go on to great things: future world time-trial champion Tony Martin of Germany, Norwegian wunderkind Edvald Boasson Hagen and Colombian climber Rigoberto Urán. Froome was the rookies' rookie.

5, 4, 3, 2, 1 . . . Froome rolled off the start ramp and accelerated into the opening straight. He was barely into any kind of rhythm before he was brought to a sudden, shuddering halt.

'After about only 150m I rode straight into a commissaire holding a bunch of papers which went flying up in the air,' recalls Froome. 'Both of us hit the ground. It was quite a start to European racing!'

In their report of the race *Cycling News* wrote: 'No major race incidents occurred, except for the crash caused by the only Kenyan starter, Chris Froome. In a right-hand-side bend, Froome left the line to the left and hit an official on the right shoulder, with both men going down. At the finish, the Kenyan felt deeply sorry for his mistake – which luckily didn't leave anyone seriously hurt.'

'It was my own fault, completely,' Froome said afterwards. 'I thought the road was going to the left, and as the man stepped to the left and raised his arm I thought he was showing me the way!'

Despite losing at least a minute recovering from the tumble, dusting himself down and remounting his bike, he still managed to finish in a highly commendable 36th place, 3:32:28 behind the winner, Dominique Cornu of Belgium.

Two days later, on the eve of the road race, an embarrassed Froome saw the unfortunate race official. 'His chest and ribs were black with bruises,' Froome said. 'He wasn't too impressed.'

By contrast, and likely much to his relief, Froome finished the road race on the Saturday in less dramatic fashion, coming home 45th in a large group containing Boasson Hagen, Cavendish and Urán, five seconds adrift of the winner, Germany's Gerald Ciolek.

The trip had been an illuminating voyage for the young African and a baptism of fire into the world of European racing.

After two seasons with Hi-Q Froome decided to move on. His coach Robbie Nilsen had left, and without his guidance there was no reason for him to continue at the academy. After his impressive, gutsy display in Salzburg it was time to take things to the next level. Europe clearly beckoned. At the beginning of 2007 Froome was introduced to an influential figure on the South African cycling scene, a man with the means and the know-how to provide him with his passage into the world of European professional road racing.

Bambi on Ice

John Robertson had never heard of Chris Froome. No one had, he tells me. Robertson runs the bizhub-FCF women's pro cycling team from his base in Centurion, Pretoria, with Conrad Venter, team mechanic turned sports director. In a long career, steeped in cycling, Robertson has served as South African national team manager and has been instrumental in nurturing a host of Africa's top cycling talent. Nowadays he says he also does hospitality work for Skoda at the Tour de France. For the last four years they've flown him in from South Africa to play host to special guests, driving one of their VIP vehicles at the race. It is easy to see why. A genial character with a vast knowledge and experience of bike racing, he is a natural storyteller – the perfect host.

In an earlier guise Robertson was founder and owner of the first incarnation of the now defunct South African-backed Team Barloworld, sponsored by a multinational brand management company headquartered in Johannesburg. He was at the helm of the team from its inception in 2003 until the end of season 2005, when he left to take up the reins of the second-tier Konica-Minolta, at the time Africa's only registered Pro Continental cycling team, with a temporary base in Belgium and a strategy of angling for invites to UCI-ranked races in Europe.

Robertson enjoyed a successful first season with Konica-Minolta – even beating Barloworld at the Giro del Capo in March 2006, with Peter Velits topping the overall standings.

'For me, with all the time I've had in cycling, I think that's one of my proudest moments,' he says. 'I went there with a small team, on a budget of €200,000 and beat a €3m team.'

★

Going into the 2007 season Konica-Minolta were reduced to starting with an almost clean slate. Only two riders, Herman Fouche and Travis Allen, remained from the roster that had brought them victory at the Giro del Capo. It was now an all-South African line-up. Robertson lost one of his most promising young riders, John-Lee Augustyn, to Barloworld but gained double South African national champion, Tiaan Kannemeyer, winner of the 2003 Tour of Egypt, and Jock Green, a stalwart on the South African cycling scene, from his old team.

As it stood, Konica-Minolta had seven riders confirmed for the new season. They needed one more to complete the eight required to register the team. Robertson was in negotiation with David George, an experienced rider from Cape Town, by then almost 30 years old, who'd ridden in Lance Armstrong's US Postal Service team in 1999 and 2000, for the final vacant spot. Under the auspices of Robertson at Team Barloworld, George had won the Giro del Capo two years running in 2003 and 2004. Robertson was keen to work with him again.

Robertson was asked if he'd be willing to meet a young Johannesburg amateur rider, Chris Froome, with a view to signing him up for Konica-Minolta for the 2007 season. Froome knew Konica-Minolta was one of the very few semi-professional teams in South Africa who had an overseas programme and, more importantly, a presence in the European racing scene. It would be the perfect stepping stone for Froome to get out of Africa. Since its formation in January 1998 Konica-Minolta had prided itself on providing a platform to develop young riders and had become something of an institution in South African cycling. It had won every major classic race in its homeland including the Pick 'n' Pay Cape Argus, the Amashova National Cycle Classic and the Giro del Capo, and had boasted several South African National Road Race champions in its ranks.

Riders who had successfully passed through the ranks included Augustyn, Jeremy Maartens, James Perry, Jaco Odendaal and Peter

Velits, who would be crowned Under-23 World Road Race champion in Stuttgart later in 2007.

Before Robertson's arrival Konica–Minolta had raced in Europe during the South African winter months. Robertson planned to raise their profile even higher on the continent by basing the team in Belgium – the move denied by Barloworld – and speculating for invites to major stage races, like the Tour of Britain.

Froome met Robertson at his Pretoria office at the start of 2007, and the Konica–Minolta boss was struck by the steely poise of this polite, quietly ambitious young man. Two things immediately impressed Robertson. 'First of all, he'd won the Tour de Maurice. I always believe that if someone wins a stage race then he has a winning mentality. You simply don't win a Tour unless you have something extra. And second, he had a pretty good result when he went to the 2006 Under-23 World Road Race Championships.'

Considering it was Froome's first ever time racing in Europe, Robertson was struck by the fact that he'd finished in the main chasing group, a mere five seconds behind the Belgian title winner Dominique Cornu, and alongside Robertson's talented *protégé*, Augustyn. 'I thought to myself, If this guy can come from nothing and go to the Worlds in Europe and finish in the top 50, then there's something for us to work with here.'

As the registration deadline loomed, Robertson was still waiting to hear from David George, who was mulling over several offers after leaving Spanish outfit Relax-GAM, with whom he'd ridden the 2006 Vuelta a España, finishing in 70th place overall. George or Froome? Who should Robertson plump for? The established pro or the unknown rookie? It was a no-brainer. 'Obviously if I'd had the choice then I would have gone with David George,' says Robertson. But Cycling South Africa, the sport's national federation, called Robertson one Friday afternoon with an ultimatum – submit his final list of eight riders for the Giro del Capo, starting on 6 March, otherwise they wouldn't be allowed to register for the 2007 season. 'So we went with Froome.'

The 21-year-old was literally last pick. They had to take a gamble and include him in the team in order to secure their participation in the first races of the season; this rough-and-ready amateur – from what Robertson refers to as a 'shirts and shorts' team – with no track record to speak of and racing with barely the right equipment.

'As far as his results in South Africa, well, up until then they were basically non-existent,' says Robertson.

From an experienced mechanic's perspective, Conrad Venter saw immediately that, while Nilsen had been a good coach for Froome, the partnership had paid scant attention to important details such as equipment. 'The biggest problem with Chris when he came to us was that he hadn't had the right guidance,' Venter says. 'Besides his training, everything was just wrong. The set-up wasn't very professional; no offence to those guys, they still did well to get that far.'

Robertson and Venter immediately set about making adjustments to the host of little problems which were holding Froome back from fulfilling his obvious potential. 'I like to take chances on people,' Robertson explains. 'I could see there was something there with Chris, but you have to be prepared to take the risk and roll the dice. Not a lot of people are willing to do that. They just want to take a big-name guy or a guy who's already got results. What myself and Conrad have done over the years with Konica was to take people no one's ever heard of, for example, the Velits brothers [Slovakian twins Martin and Peter] and turn them into professional cyclists.'

The challenge of working with Froome appealed to Robertson's spirit of taking a leap of faith. Indeed, in Froome's case, Robertson goes even further, claiming he might never have made it without their support. 'Looking back now, I can't say we made Chris but I don't believe Chris would even be riding a bike today if it wasn't for Konica-Minolta and the opportunities he had through us being based in Europe.'

★

Before Konica-Minolta's first long training ride together for the start of the 2007 season, Robertson encouraged his team to bring along the bikes they were currently riding. Froome pitched up with a bike that was clearly way too small for his gangly frame.

'I remember in the car turning round to Conrad and saying, "What are we going to do with this guy for the year? His bike doesn't even fit!"' Robertson says.

'Middle-of-the-range components on there,' Venter laughs. 'Everything was just horrible!'

A few of Froome's new teammates even cast aspersions on the wisdom of signing him, asking Robertson what he was planning to do with him. The guy had no results. What on earth possessed them to take him on in the first place?

When the team headed off to Clarens for a four-day training camp in the foothills of the spectacular Rooiberge and Maluti mountain ranges, Froome showed his sceptical compatriots why Robertson had taken a gamble on him. On the final day Robertson urged his riders to hit the gas and go full pelt up the tough finishing hill. Blithely unaware of any grumblings in the ranks, Froome glided away from the rest of his team. But it wasn't enough for Robertson. 'I went up beside him in the car, and it was obvious he wasn't going as hard as he could,' Robertson says. 'So I said, "Chris, fucking ride your bike!"'

Froome heeded Robertson's words, gave it some welly, and was first to the top of the climb by a street. At the summit Robertson told him that if he could produce that kind of form then he was capable of winning the Giro del Capo. At the very least Robertson predicted he would get on the podium.

In the event, Froome finished sixth overall at the 2007 edition of the Cape Town stage race, 2:39 behind the winner Alexander Efimkin, ironically of Team Barloworld, and another of Roberston's former pupils. The man whose place Froome had taken at Konica, David George, finished third with CSC Marcello, the team he'd opted for instead.

Froome was fitted for a new bike before the race, and Robertson was delighted with his debut for the team, especially on the climbs where he described his performance as 'unbeliev-able'. 'He was immediately on the up and up,' Robertson says. 'He was incredibly tough and phenomenally determined to improve. Then we got him into the UCI [Union Cycliste Internationale] centre in Aigle in Switzerland.'

★

The UCI Centre Mondial du Cyclisme, or World Cycling Centre (WCC), is housed within the grounds of the world governing body's headquarters in Aigle, a small, scenic town wrapped in the craggy embrace of the Swiss Alps, not far from Montreux. Since its doors opened in 2002, the WCC has become internationally recognised for its work in developing cycling talent, particularly from emerging nations and continents, like Africa and Asia, which are hampered by poor funding and a lack of top-quality facili-ties. Designated an official Olympic Training Centre, the WCC facilities include a 200m cycling track and an Olympic BMX track. In the space of a decade it has welcomed in the region of 600 athletes from 118 different countries and produced Olympic and world champions.

In addition to his day job running Konica-Minolta, Robertson was also in charge of the South African National Under-23 team. However, because the Kenya-born Froome didn't qualify to race with them in the upcoming Giro delle Regioni, one of Italy's most prestigious Under-23 stage races, Robertson suggested he apply to ride for the UCI development squad.

The deal Robertson struck with the UCI was that their man Froome would train and compete in WCC colours while Konica-Minolta continued to pay his salary. It was the perfect place for Froome to learn the ropes of European racing.

'The WCC was a great opportunity for me. It's an excellent school for the riders from smaller federations which don't have the resources,' Froome has said of his time at Aigle.

He began a ten-day training stint at the centre on 13 April. For the duration of the 2007 season he divided his time between living and training in Aigle and holing up at Konica-Minolta's European HQ, what John Robertson refers to as the 'Tim Harris School', deep in Belgium's Flemish cycling heartland.

★

Robertson had rented a house in Tielt-Winge, 45km east of Brussels, from a friend, former professional cyclist and 1989 British road race champion, Tim Harris. Neighbouring village Meensel-Kiezegem is the birthplace of cycling royalty, Eddy Merckx, no less.

In Robertson's opinion Belgium is still the best place to toughen up a young cyclist and introduce them to the strict discipline of being a pro. 'I've kind of got the philosophy in cycling that you can take any young rider to Belgium for six weeks and you'll know at the end of that period if he's going to make it or not.'

Belgium's terrain is largely flat, interspersed with short, leg-breaking climbs; many of the roads are cobbled, and the racing is frantic from the gun. This is the breeding ground of teak-tough northern Classics riders. In Flanders, the heartland of Belgian cycling, generations of legendary hardmen have grown up battling with the elements on stone-paved roads (known as *pavé* in French and, a touch grotesquely, in Flemish as *kinderkopje*, 'children's heads'). The featureless countryside – the battlefields of World War I – is battered by fierce crosswinds, which howl in from the North Sea. The masses that line the merciless roads of the famous Tour of Flanders have cycling etched in their wind-beaten faces and embedded in their souls. As a young rider, Belgium can make you or break you.

'All we did with those guys at Konica was give them opportunities. I can be a hard manager and I'm always straight down the line with the guys. Chris was one of the guys who just needed that opportunity – "Give me the chance, get me to Europe, put me in races."'

The entire Konica-Minolta team lived and trained together in

Harris's house in Tielt for six months. With frequent gales blowing across the drab polders, the displaced South African riders, spoiled by the all-year-round temperate climate of their homeland, were loth to head out on training runs, says Robertson, and would hide from the wild weather, preferring to spin on turbo trainers in the basement. But not Froome. He was never a fair-weather cyclist.

'Chris stood out to me,' Robertson says. 'He would go out on crazy rides for six or seven hours.' The man from Nairobi would tape food to his bike so he could ride without pause at a certain power for the entire marathon training run. He had to keep going to maintain the intensity. There was no time for pit stops, coffee breaks, anything.

'He knew exactly what power output he needed, hence the epic rides. The other guys did three hours, went to a coffee shop and then came home, but Chris was out to Liège and back.

'I never knew how he did it!' Robertson says, still incredulous at Froome's obsessive drive. 'He's one of the few guys I know who could do seven hours alone. Most people would go mental if they had to ride for that length of time on their own! Looking back, it's no surprise to me that he is where he is now.'

★

Froome kicked off his stint of racing with the UCI development squad on 21 April. He turned out for the first time in the UCI development squad's blue-and-white kit in the *espoirs* precursor to the traditional spring Classic, Liège–Bastogne–Liège, the third leg of seven UCI races – the Under-23 Nations Cup series – scattered through the 2007 season. His 150km training runs around Liège made him familiar with the race route and gave him an advantage over his fellow Aigle residents. He was first home of the UCI Mixed Team, in 28th position, in a small group just over a minute behind winner Grega Bole of Slovenia. And he beat all his South African buddies from the Tim Harris School.

A week later Froome recorded his first victory on European soil. As part of a six-man UCI mixed nation squad consisting of two Korean riders, one Chinese, an Algerian and a Colombian, Froome's breakthrough came at the Giro delle Regioni stage race on 26 April – a top-quality fixture in the Under-23 Nations Cup series.

Froome being Froome, his debut appearance in one of Italy's most reputable amateur races wasn't without incident, and, but for some schoolboy errors on the descents, he might well have challenged the overall. The problem was that he had no clue how to ride fast downhill. On the flat terrain of South Africa's Highveld there was little scope for practising technical descents.

★

Michel Thèze spent seven years as a senior UCI coach at the World Cycling Centre and was Froome's development team manager in 2007. 'It was the start of his career, his first proper racing experience in Europe,' he says. 'He had no idea how to ride on the road in a group.' Added to this, Thèze recalls, he was overweight and had lousy bike-handling skills, further hampered by an odd riding position on the bike. 'This bad technique contributed to him crashing a lot. It was a big problem for him when he first arrived.'

'He didn't know quite how to race,' Robertson agrees. 'Most kids get a racing bike for Christmas when they're thirteen, but he only started riding a road bike when he was seventeen or eighteen, which is one of the reasons he struggled initially going downhill.' On the mountainous first stage of the Giro delle Regioni, from Fornelli to Macchiagodena, the switchbacks of Europe bamboozled Froome. He was like Bambi on ice.

'We kept hearing on the commissaire's race radio, "Chris, Chris, crash, crash!"' Robertson recalls. Initially they thought it was one of their own South African team members, Froome's former Hi-Q buddy, Christoff Van Heerden, so they'd drive like maniacs to the front of the race only to find out it was a false alarm. There were three Chris's in the race. And the one who kept crashing wasn't Van Heerden – nor was it Austria's Christoph Sokoll.

'Chris Froome must have crashed at least three or four times on that opening stage,' Robertson says. 'I remember he missed one corner completely and went flying down a guy's driveway into his garage! He had to learn fast and he had lots of hairy moments. He had a lot of courage just to keep going. Most guys after three crashes would have thrown in the towel.'

But Robertson could see that each day Froome was getting better and better. He was narrowly pipped in a two-man sprint to the line by Slovenian Grega Bole at the Stage 2 finish. This time, misfortune rather than a self-inflicted crash denied Froome victory – his chain snapped metres from the line. Close, but no bouquet. Still, it left him well placed at eleventh, 37 seconds off the overall lead.

The tumbles, however, continued. On Stage 3, the longest, from Porto Recanati to Cignolo, he hit the deck on two crucial descents, losing over a minute to the leaders and ruining his chance of a tilt at overall victory.

'I was showing strength on climbs, but my technical ability was poor. I kept on crashing,' Froome recalled of this period racing with the UCI development squad.

★

Still, the raw neophyte was doing all right given he'd only been at the UCI centre for less than a fortnight before being hurled into the deep end at the Giro delle Regioni. The costly spills of Stage 3 aside, he was consistently finishing each stage at the front of the race.

After riding in with the bunch on Stage 4, it all came together for Froome on Stage 5, a 146km run out through the rolling hills of southern Tuscany, from the spa town of Chianciano Terme to the hilltop finish at Montepulciano.

Froome's explosive burst of acceleration up the final 1.5km climb from Porta al Prato to the finish line at the Piazza Grande splintered the chasing pack, including eventual overall winner, Rui Costa of Portugal. Only France's Cyril Gautier managed to stay with Froome to the finish line but he succumbed to a final lunge from the UCI's rookie.

Suddenly, out of nowhere, this Kenyan novice with the dodgy descending skills had won his first race in Europe. It was a remarkable display by Froome, given his lack of technical prowess or professional training, to beat riders like Costa and Dutch climbing specialist Bauke Mollema, both of whom would go on to become well-known names in cycling.

An incident-free last leg – a 130.5km circuit in the countryside surrounding Artena, on the outskirts of Rome – saw him end his first continental stage race in twentieth place on the GC, just 1:25 behind the top-placed man, Costa.

Watching Froome's performance with some degree of interest was Rod Ellingworth. He ran Great Britain's Under-23 academy from their base in Quarrata, Tuscany, and was at the Giro delle Regioni overseeing a strong Great Britain team, including young sprint sensation Ben Swift, future British National Road Race champion in 2012, Ian Stannard, and former British track champion, Jonathan Bellis from the Isle of Man. Ellingworth was instrumental in guiding another Manx rider, Mark Cavendish, through the academy and into the professional ranks in Europe. Cavendish was one of the first success stories to emerge from Ellingworth's Under-23 set-up. Meanwhile, in Italy, Swift had shown impressive form to take the final stage of the Giro delle Regioni and finished the race with the King of the Mountains jersey for best climber.

Ellingworth had a chat with Froome about the subject of nationality. 'Although I was riding under the Kenyan flag I made it clear [to him] that I had always carried a British passport and felt British,' said Froome. 'It was then that we started talking about racing under the Union Jack.'

It was a chance encounter and conversation that would have a significant impact on Froome's life and career. Froome had already spoken with Doug Dailey about the prospect of him racing for Great Britain after their similarly chance meeting at the 2006 Commonwealth Games in Melbourne. Dailey had kept tabs on Froome and asked him to keep in touch. Ellingworth and Froome agreed to do the same.

Despite having already represented Kenya at international level, Froome could still feasibly qualify to ride for Great Britain, on the condition that the, thus far, unreliable Kenyan Cycling Federation gave him the green light to do so. The International Olympic Committee rules state that an athlete cannot compete for a 'new' nation within three years of switching nationality, unless the 'old' nation, in Froome's case, Kenya, gives permission. It would mean handing back his Kenyan passport. The queues at immigration would be annoying, but a small price to pay, Froome said later.

★

Froome's apprenticeship with Konica-Minolta continued at the Tour of Japan, which gave him the chance to build on his burgeoning gift for stage racing. First held in 1996, the national cycling tour started in Osaka on Sunday, 20 May, the happy occasion of Froome's 22nd birthday. It was a race in which he came of age and, as in Italy the previous month, where he would attract more attention from interested onlookers.

Part of the UCI Asia Tour, the week-long race ostensibly, while a tour of the country, is more a series of circuit races taking place in and around major civic centres on Japan's main island of Honshu.

'That's where I first remember him really getting noticed, very early on in the race,' Venter says. 'We took him there as part of a strong team, but Chris really stood out.'

It was on Stage 6, the penultimate leg of the seven-day event, that Froome made his mark. He set the pace at the head of the peloton on a custom-built circuit in Izu, a mountainous penin-sula south-west of Tokyo. The stage started with a steady climb of 8.5km from the city's Shuzenji Stadium to the Japan Cycle Sport School. There followed fifteen laps of an undulating 8km circuit round a sprawling bicycle theme park. The stage profile, a series of jagged waves, resembled a child's drawing of mountains. It was clear early on that Froome had his climbing legs with him.

As Robertson recalls, Froome was part of an early break of around a dozen riders on the extremely technical and hilly circuit. Their lead reached three minutes when the peloton attempted to chase them down. 'One by one, each guy in the break was blown off the back until only Chris was left. The peloton rode themselves to pieces trying to catch him, but it was no use. He won by about 50 seconds – it was an incredible ride.'

By the end of Stage 7 and the promenade around the streets of Tokyo in front of an enthusiastic crowd of 120,000, Froome had finished sixth overall, 3:33 behind the deserving winner Francesco Masciarelli of Acqua & Sapone-Caffè Mokambo. His team boss, Lorenzo di Lorenzo, shared Robertson's view that Froome's Stage 6 ride had been impressive. He approached the Kenyan after the race to praise his performance, enquiring as to his availability for the following season. Was he fixed up with a professional team for 2008?

But Robertson already had plans to showcase Froome on a bigger stage. 'If we could swing an invite to the Tour of Britain [in September] and if Chris rode well there then I believed that Team Barloworld would snap him up.'

★

Before returning to Aigle for an extended two-month spell on 23 July, Froome had an appointment in Algeria on 14 July to represent Kenya in the 150km men's road race at the ninth All-Africa Games. He was part of an early seven-man break that stayed away until the finish. The winning group contained two South Africans, Hanco Kachelhoffer and Daryl Impey, with the latter outsprinting Eritrea's Frikalsi Oebesay for gold with Froome third. It was the first medal of any colour for Kenya at the quadrennial multi-sport event.

Back in Aigle, Michel Thèze noticed a difference in Froome's demeanour. In a short space of time, a matter of months, he seemed to have grown up, on and off the bike. 'He'd progressed a lot. His technique had improved greatly along with his tactical nous in races.'

This new maturity came to the fore in the Mi-Août Bretonne, a four-day UCI Category 2.2 stage race in France, part of the lower-rung UCI Europe Tour. Froome rode to a commanding overall victory against elite riders, again in the mixed-nation colours of the UCI development squad.

It didn't surprise Thèze that Froome had made such a rapid improvement. 'Chris is very intelligent, and he has a very calm but tough temperament.'

On fire now, two weeks later in the GP Tell in Switzerland, the second last round of the 2007 UCI Nations Cup, Froome finished nine seconds adrift of the winning time (tied with Tony Martin) in the opening 2.19km prologue in Lucerne. Again he showed his climbing strength on the hilly third stage, a 148.2km circuit around Zell in the upper Töss Valley. The man racing on a Kenyan licence tagged on to a three-man break on the final lap but ran out of steam to take fourth on the line.

Even better was to come on the gruelling final *étape reine* ('queen stage')[4] of the race. The only proper mountain test ran 137.9km from Chur, Switzerland's oldest town, to the final 30km ascent to the ski resort of Arosa, 1700m up in the Grison Alps. Part of the leading group all day, Froome single-handedly chased down eventual lone escapee, Swiss climbing specialist Mathias Frank, on the last 5km stretch to the summit, rapidly eating into his commanding lead, but ran out of road and was forced to settle for second place, 1:39 behind Frank.

It was another hugely encouraging performance by the novice and secured him eleventh place on the final GC, 4:10 down on Russian winner Anton Reshetnikov.

Michel Thèze wanted Froome in his team for the final leg of the Nations Cup due to start in Belle-Île-en-Mer, a picturesque island off the coast of Brittany. It was the 44th Tour de L'Avenir, a race dubbed 'the Tour de France of the future' and one boasting an illustrious roll-call of past winners, including Laurent Fignon, Miguel Indurain, Greg LeMond, Joop Zoetemelk and Felice

---

4   The road race stage which includes the highest point of the whole race; it is usually, but not always, the toughest stage of the race.

Gimondi, all Tour de France winners. Froome would surely have leaped at the opportunity to try to add his name to such a rich lineage of cycling stars.

'I wanted to take him to the Tour de L'Avenir, but the date clashed with another race, and I knew he was hoping to turn pro, so it was better for him to go to the UK,' says Thèze.

John Robertson had achieved his season-long aim: to bag Konica-Minolta a starting place at the Tour of Britain. A strong Barloworld squad would be there – including South Africa's Robbie Hunter, Ben Swift of England and Geraint Thomas, the Welshman. Robertson was hoping his man Froome would put on a good show and catch the attention of their experienced Italian team manager, Claudio Corti.

★

The 2007 Tour of Britain, the fourth edition of the race, opened on Sunday, 9 September, with a 2.5km prologue time trial in London's Crystal Palace Park. It then wound northwards in six stages, covering over 950km, taking the riders from the south coast of England into Somerset, on to Wolverhampton and the West Midlands, passing through Yorkshire and then Liverpool before crossing the border into Scotland and concluding in Glasgow the following Saturday.

Konica-Minolta took their place in the seventeen-team roster, which also included five British teams and three ProTour teams who had raced in that summer's Tour de France. Leading Barloworld's six-man team was Robbie Hunter who had so memorably outsprinted Fabian Cancellara to win Stage 11 in Montpellier at the Tour, the first ever Grand Tour stage win by a South African. The defending champion from 2006, the Dane Martin Pedersen, was also back. T-Mobile's selection included young Isle of Man sprint sensation Mark Cavendish, who had made his Tour de France debut amid a fanfare of expectation only to crash twice, on Stages 1 and 2, and abandon on Stage 8 as the Alps loomed. The Manx speedster started his home Tour with a bang, overcoming painful wisdom-tooth surgery to sweep to a narrow prologue victory at Crystal Palace and then scored back-to-back stage wins with a sustained 200m burst to the Stage 1 finish in Southampton.

Undaunted by the line-up of been-there-done-that-got-the-T-shirt pros, Froome was in the mix from the get-go, most notably getting himself into Stage 2's winning break, hanging tough over several vicious inclines, including the Category 3 climb at Wheddon Cross that split the lead group, to finish twelfth. He even managed to avoid a late crash when a dozen riders tumbled in the last 150m. Russian veteran Nikolai Trusov took the honours and the leader's yellow jersey.

'They only caught Chris and the escape group in the last two or three kilometres but they struggled I can promise you,' recalls Robertson.

Froome rolled into Wolverhampton the next day in the main peloton alongside race leader Trusov to move up to twentieth overall, and then finished at the head of the race again as Stage 4 arrived in Bradford. Trusov lost his yellow jersey to Adrian Palomares, the Spaniard who powered to victory in the stage dedicated to the gallant cancer fundraiser, Jane Tomlinson.[5]

Froome consolidated his GC place on the undulating road from Liverpool to Kendal before cracking on the last leg, in blustery conditions on long, hilly sections of Scottish countryside north from Dumfries to Glasgow, and in the thick of what *Cycling News* called 'some of the fiercest [racing] ever seen on British roads'. Froome lost over six minutes to Team Great Britain stage winner Paul Manning. He slipped to 31st on the final overall rankings.

Frenchman Roman Feillu won the race by the narrowest of margins – 0:49 seconds – over Palomares. No matter, Froome had made his mark. Robertson's faith had been justified. Barloworld's curiosity was suitably aroused by the young Kenyan with the unconventional riding style, huge engine and the ability to glide away from others on the steepest climbs.

---

5 Jane Tomlinson was an amateur English athlete who raised £1.85 million for charity by completing a series of athletic challenges, despite suffering from terminal cancer. She died in 2007, aged 43. See www.janetomlinsonappeal.com.

Froome returned to Switzerland to prepare for his last outing of 2007. His fruitful time at Aigle, training and racing with budding pros from around the world, had come to an end.

In Stuttgart he ended his first season in Europe with a mixed flourish at the UCI Under-23 World Road Race Championships. Again he was Kenya's lone participant, although happily without the mishaps of the previous year in Salzburg. He rode to a disappointing 41st place in the ITT on 26 September, 3:31 slower than Holland's rainbow-jersey winner Lars Boom. (Oddly he'd fared better in Salzburg despite colliding with the race official.)

Froome was in friskier form three days later in the Under-23 men's road race, a 171.9km circuit of the Swabian metropolis in Germany. On the fourth lap he launched a counter-attack to an existing two-man breakaway and made a spirited solo effort to bridge the gap, but his brave bid lasted only twenty minutes and he was quickly swept up by the peloton, finishing in the main bunch in 21st place. Peter Velits of Slovakia, another of John Robertson's discoveries, took gold.

★

Team Barloworld's manager Claudio Corti had been duly impressed by Froome's showing at the Tour of Britain but, ironically, it took a South African to finally smooth his passage out of Africa. Barloworld's top sprinter, Robbie Hunter, is South Africa's greatest cycling export and was the first rider from the country to compete in the Tour de France, in 2001. Hunter knew that Barloworld's Johannesburg-based sponsor was keen to enlist more African and South African riders to the team. One rider in particular had caught Hunter's attention, and he encouraged Corti to sign him for the 2008 season. 'You wouldn't know the money I spent on phone calls to Claudio forcing him to take Chris. He didn't see anything in Chris back then,' Hunter recalled. 'I said: "I don't care what you've got to say. I know what he's gone through to become pro, and that he's got something to give as a pro". I saw what Chris was doing, he deserved a chance and I gave him that chance.'

Back in Aigle after the Tour of Britain, Chris Froome fielded a telephone call from Hunter. 'He said Barloworld were looking for new young riders and, because of the whole South African connection, I was more appealing to them than other riders. I didn't really know Robert before that,' Froome said. He did now. They were about to become teammates.

On 19 September 2007 it was announced that Froome and Daryl Impey, a 22-year-old sprinter from Johannesburg, had signed for Barloworld. The team's statement described Froome as 'an eclectic rider who has also done well in mountain biking' and said they were pleased to have two African riders in the 2008 line-up because of the team's South African sponsors. 'Cycling needs to find new faces and new talented riders, and that's our strategy at Team Barloworld,' said team manager Corti.

New faces, new talent. Step forward, Chris Froome.

CHAPTER 5

A Brave New Barloworld

After spending winter at home in the pleasant summer tempera-tures of South Africa, Barloworld new boys Froome and Impey arrived for duty with the team in northern Italy in mid-January to the shock of proper wintry weather: sunless skies, clinging damp and sub-zero temperatures. Luckily they'd packed their winter woollies. 'It took a while to get used to having to go out in two or three layers of clothing,' said Froome.

Froome had signed a two-year deal with Barloworld. The team was sponsored by a South African multinational company, managed by Italians – with Italian as the *lingua franca* – but regis-tered in Britain. It was a mix of often conflicting new and old cycling traditions, although there was a strong sense of camara-derie within the team.

While not a ProTour team, in the premier division of the sport, Barloworld's status as a Professional Continental team meant they could manoeuvre for invitations to the prestigious spring Classics series in Belgium and the Netherlands, contest mid-level one-week stage races and vie with other second-tier teams to bag wild cards for the Grand Tours. Their case for securing last-minute entry to the three biggest stage races on the world cycling calendar – the Tours of Italy, France and Spain – had been strengthened by their exceptional Grand Tour debut at the 2007 Tour de France.

Little-known Colombian Mauricio Soler stunned the big guns of the climbing glitterati by winning the King of the Mountains' polka-dot jersey and taking victory on Stage 9's mountainous romp to Briançon. Hunter, the man instrumental in Froome's arrival at the team, made a huge impression at the race with his swaggering win in Montpellier. He also finished second overall to Tom Boonen, Belgium's classics specialist, and powerhouse *rouleur*, in the battle for the green points jersey for best sprinter.

The team's sports director, Claudio Corti, was an avuncular, wily old-school Italian, a former professional, silver medallist at the 1984 World Championships in Barcelona and Italian national road champion in 1985 and 1986. With the Supermercati-Brianzoli-Chateau d'Ax team in 1990, in his first role as a sports director after retiring from racing, he led Gianni Bugno to victory at the Giro d'Italia.

In the team manager's hot seat at Saeco, Corti forged his reputation as a latter-day cycling alchemist, guiding three more riders to the overall winner's pink jersey in Milan: Ivan Gotti (1997), Gilberto Simoni (2003) and Damiano Cunego (2004). Completing Barloworld's managerial line-up were Alberto Volpi (another ex-rider; tenth overall at the 1985 Giro d'Italia) and Valerio Tebaldi (a double Tour de France stage winner, in 1988 and 1989).

Corti had taken note of Froome's sixth place overall with Konica-Minolta at the 2007 Giro del Capo, when his own rider, Alexander Efimkin, had taken overall victory in the South African race. Froome's strong showing at the Tour of Britain confirmed Corti's opinion, with Hunter's endorsement persuading the Barloworld boss to offer the 22-year-old a deal.

'I saw him in some races in 2007 and I was impressed with his physical attributes and his ability to stay with the top pros on diffi-cult climbs,' the unassuming Corti tells me in staccato English. The 58-year-old, originally from Bergamo, is currently general manager of Team Colombia, a Professional Continental team consisting predominantly of riders from the South American country.

Froome struck Corti as a serious individual, albeit 'with a very nice character', single-minded about what he wanted to achieve in cycling and bent on doing whatever it took to succeed. He was always asking questions, Corti says, and he was also a bit of a loner, which was no bad thing in the Italian's opinion.

'Chris had the right attitude to live the life of a pro,' he explains. 'He was happy to live alone and not just hang about with the other South Africans. He wanted to be by himself. It seemed to me that he was used to it, and he preferred to solve problems himself.'

Operating on a meagre budget, Team Barloworld's set-up was slightly ramshackle, the training and dietary methods distinctly traditionalist, and, outwith training camps and races, the riders were largely left to their own devices, which suited the free-spirited Froome. But the pedigree of the team's management – Corti's reputation as a motivational man-manager was unquestionable – and riders was of a high standard, *and* they were riding the crest of a wave from the previous season. Added to that, the South African sponsors were ambitious for the future. Promotion from UCI ProContinental Team status to the top of the pile and a place in the eighteen-strong ProTeam division was Barloworld's ultimate objective.

In late January new recruits Froome and Impey joined the team's two other Africans, Hunter and John-Lee Augustyn, who, like Hunter, had been at Barloworld for one season already, at Marina di Bibbona on the Tuscan coast, for nine days of intense workouts at Barloworld's first training camp of the new season.

Having moved from Kenya to South Africa, Belgium and Switzerland, now Froome was to call Italy home. The typical nomadic lifestyle of a professional cyclist can be a lonely, austere existence, an unremitting round of training, eating, sleeping, travelling and racing. Months on the road spent away from friends and family can be an emotional strain and a psychological burden, often acutely so for those hailing from distant continents such as Africa, Australasia . . .

The adjustment for Froome was not without difficulty. 'Trying to set up in a new country, learn a new language – it was quite a shock in 2008. It was some first year as a neo-pro,' he said.

In February Froome and his then girlfriend of three years, Andrea, chose as their Italian abode a small apartment on the outskirts of Chiari, a sleepy hamlet in the province of Brescia. The pretty town retains the shape of the original eleventh-century village, with canals tracing the line of the ancient walls and an attractive central square on the site of the old castle. Two key factors made Chiari the perfect base for the couple: the nearby Lombardy hills provided ideal terrain for Froome's daily training rides, and its railway station enabled part-time model Andrea to chase work in the country's fashion capital, Milan, a one-hour hop away.

Corti was pleased to see his new signing embrace life in Italy. 'It showed he was a serious rider with clear ideas. I could tell he was content to stay and live in Italy. He rented a home and registered with the government, and he had a girlfriend.'

True to his lone-wolf instinct, Froome chose to live apart from the rest of the Barloworld riders, most of whom lived further north in Corti's present-day base of Adro. Froome intentionally wanted to put some geographical space between himself and the rest of the team. He occasionally hooked up with teammates for the odd training ride and would call on Valerio Tebaldi when he wanted to do some motor pacing, but living apart from the gang appealed to his solitary nature and penchant for long, punishing solo rides.

'I sometimes meet up with others but I honestly prefer to ride alone when I'm doing special workouts or even long rides,' Froome said at the time. 'It's a very satisfying feeling to do a six-hour or seven-hour ride on your own.' Those punishing solitary rides prompted Alberto Volpi to describe him as a 'training fundamentalist'.

His only company would be his iPod, loaded with pulsing electronic dance music, with mixes by the likes of Dutch super-star DJ, Tiësto. 'I don't listen to stuff like that at home, but it's good to have a beat to ride to when you're on the bike,' he said. Back in the village, the tall, pale foreigners were anonymous to the locals. No one knew Froome was a professional cyclist. The incognito lifestyle suited him just fine. 'Northern Italy is a great place for a professional cyclist to live,' he said. 'The food, roads and weather are fantastic.'

His 'special workouts' invariably took him north of Chiari, through fields of high sweet corn and fruit trees, under the Milan–Venice *autostrada* towards Sarnico, on the southern tip of Lake Iseo, and on to a 30km route, popular with pro and amateur cyclists from the Brescia area. He would circumnavigate the lake clockwise before taking a detour up into the hills. Through the foreboding darkness of the long tunnel between Predore and Gallinarga that skirts the edge of the lush Parco del Corno di Predore, Froome would habitually hang a left at the lakeside village of Tavernola Bergamasca and climb the squiggle of narrow, hairpin switchbacks, up through green fields to the tiny village of Vigolo, with its breathtaking views over the lake.

Intent on enhancing his climbing power, Froome would use these long intervals in the hills above Lake Iseo to form the backbone of his training programme. He would ordinarily push himself to his anaerobic threshold and beyond, riding the whole way up the 8km climb out of the saddle, hovering on the very edge of his limit. 'I try and do twenty-minute climbing intervals, riding at my heart-rate threshold of 150 until I get to almost the top of the climb and then I go over a little bit.

'I follow my training programmes very closely and build them around events and key races. I try and mimic key parts of the race, so that I can adapt to it and handle it when I'm in the actual race.'

Due to ride a packed spring schedule of hilly Classics, like Amstel Gold and Liège–Bastogne–Liège, Froome worked hard in the early months of 2008 to reach peak form for April with multiple repetitions of 2km and 3km climbs.

From Vigolo, Froome's regular early-season training run took him along the Strada Provinciale 78 to Parzanica and a spectacular descent to the glimmering water below, slaloming down a dozen zigzags, past Acquaiolo, to emerge finally at a cement works (the only blot on the beautiful landscape) back on the shore of Lake Iseo. The steep plunge to the lake enabled him to work on his, still wobbly, descending skills.

There would be no easing off on the final leg home, and he

would invariably hit warp speed back to Chiari, grimacing with pain as the dial reached 65kph. The hard toil and concentrated effort were necessary if he were to achieve the glittering goal he had pinpointed for his first year at Barloworld.

'I was told at the beginning of the year that riding the Tour de France was possible, but it was not 100%,' Froome said. Could the 22-year-old really hope to be selected for the biggest race in the world in his debut season as a pro? With this tantalising prospect prominent in his mind he combined the short, punchy climbs with long-distance rides up into the mountains east towards Lake Endine and even further north to Clusone, often totalling 170km, so he could maintain a solid endurance base beyond spring and into the summer months.

★

'Biff, bang, wallop!' read the 10 February 2008 headline in an online piece in the *Star*, one of South Africa's biggest daily newspapers. Team Barloworld chose to make the inaugural Intaka Tech World's View Challenge its first race of the season in early February. The UCI 1.1-ranked series was made up of five one-day races with different routes and distances each day, over 588km in total, through the rolling terrain of South Africa. The riders would enjoy a rest day between race days three and four. Having just got out of Africa, Froome, along with Hunter, Impey and Augustyn, was back in familiar territory. And it was a typically Froomean debut – a display of his entire racing repertoire from the sublime to the ridiculous.

The opening stage took place on an undulating circuit in and around Pietermaritzburg, 80km inland from Durban. In a frantic day of racing, which was marked by a peloton splintered by a series of breaks and dynamic intermediary sprints, Froome lost over seventeen minutes. On the second day he dropped out due to the tar-meltingly hot conditions, with temperatures hitting 48 degrees. He wasn't alone: 75 out of 99 starters wilted in the desert heat on the 127.4km Thornville–Polyshorts Circuit.

Froome found his racing legs on Stage 3, but then, not for the first, or last, time in his fledgling career, a tendency for space-cadet behaviour emerged in a bizarre finish. It had all been looking so good for Froome on the third day of hard racing through the lush countryside around Wartburg, New Hanover and Dalton. He launched an attack 60km into the 108km stage and was joined by Milram's Martin Velits and MTN Energade's Ian McLeod. The trio built up a lead of three and a half minutes on the bunch, before Liquigas put six riders on the front of the peloton to crank up the pace and haul back their advantage.

Barloworld boss Corti gave Froome instructions not to work with Velits and McLeod and save his legs for the final climb, 10km from the finish. The plan worked a treat as Froome took flight, dancing away from his break partners over the summit of Copes Folly before descending from the lush upland savannah down to Pietermaritzburg. It was a bold move, tactically astute – the pursuing peloton were running out of road – and now Froome was about to reap the rewards of a satisfying day in the saddle. With Velits and McLeod blown off his back wheel, all he had to do was stay on his bike in the final stretch and the stage win was surely in the bag.

With less than 100m to go, Froome sat up in the saddle to zip up his jersey – it was flapping open to cool his sweat-soaked torso in the late-afternoon heat – to ensure the sponsor's logo, Barloworld, was visible to the gaggle of photographers eagerly waiting to snap him as he crossed the finish line. But, at the exact moment he was making himself presentable, there was an almighty *whooosh*, as the head of the chasing bunch, a furious blur of legs and pedals engulfed in a dust cloud, conjured itself out of nowhere. In the final kilometre someone in the crowd had shouted to Froome that he had a two-minute gap on the bunch. With 100m to go, the gap had vaporised.

Teammate Robbie Hunter must have given Froome the fright of his life as he hurtled past to win the sprint ahead of Milram's Björn Schröder and Konica-Minolta's Christoff van Heerden. Daryl Impey crashed in the *mêlée* as three riders sought to avoid hitting Froome, hogging the middle of the road – 'Look, Mum, no hands!' – and dawdling towards the line. The startled Froome rolled over the finish line in seventh. 'Yes, I thought I had won and I sat up in the final hundred metres,' said a sheepish Froome afterwards. 'I got a big shock when they came around me.'

'That would have made a great picture: three guys from the same team in the finish straight – one zipping up his jersey too soon, another celebrating a win and another flying through the air as he crashed,' Impey said with a laugh afterwards, his injuries fortunately not too serious.

Froome took the King of the Mountains jersey but he knew he had just blown the chance to win a UCI-ranked 1.1 race on his professional debut. It was a lesson learned. After a quiet day on Stage 4, he skipped the final stage of the series from Edendale to Cedara.

★

Looney Tunes-style cartoon antics aside, it had been a promising start to the 2008 season for Froome, and Barloworld were back in South Africa in early March, and in Cape Town to defend their Giro del Capo crown, won the previous year by Efimkin, the Russian who had since departed to Quick Step.

Despite the searing heat, Froome rode consistently from seventh place on the opening stage in Wellington on 4 March all the way through to the final short time trial in Camps Bay. He even fulfilled *domestique* duties for teammate Christian Pfannberger on Stages 2 and 3, again in sweltering conditions that would have floored a camel, to help the Austrian champion protect the narrow race lead he had established by winning Stage 1 in Wellington.

Froome diligently ushered Pfannberger through the penultimate leg around Stellenbosch, taking in the tricky climb of Helshoogte Pass, to all but seal victory for his teammate. Only 5.5km of racing remained in the final day's time trial.

Barloworld swept the board in Camps Bay – Pfannberger took third behind Team MTN's David George in the ITT to clinch the team's second consecutive overall victory, picking up the points jersey in the process. Froome's seventh position in the race against the clock catapulted him into second on the GC.

Victory in the team classification and an unlikely King of the Mountains prize for sprinter Hunter rounded off a highly successful week for Corti's men.

★

Froome's heady debut pro season continued apace in March with another encouraging performance in Portugal at the Volta ao Santarém, where he claimed the young rider's jersey and sixth place overall. There then followed a below par showing at the Critérium International, where he trailed home in 46th place, 9:07 behind the winner Jens Voigt.

A daunting, jam-packed racing programme awaited Froome in April. He was about to be pitched headlong into the deep end of the toughest, most prestigious, most historic series of one-day races in the cycling calendar, the Spring Classics.

Claudio Corti sent a team to the Tour of Flanders, the traditional curtain-raiser of the run of six Classics, but Froome was not selected. The Italian decided Froome's introduction into a world of uncompromising hardmen careering over perilous cobbled roads would begin at Gent–Wevelgem, inserted between Flanders and Paris–Roubaix. The race is not officially a Classic; it's ranked one below, but in the *hors catégorie* class. At 209km it was over 50km shorter than the Tour of Flanders, although often run along many of the same roads as its more illustrious cousin.

At the 8km mark Froome had the chance to wave to his old Konica-Minolta barracks as the race passed through Tielt. After that, Óscar Freire became the first Spanish winner of the race, sprinting clear of the bunch in the final 250m. Froome negotiated the dastardly obstacles of his first major Belgian race – including the cobbled, brutally steep incline of the Kemmelberg, climbed not once, but twice, and the double ascent of the equally nasty Monteberg tossed in for good measure – and came home in one piece, in a large group nearly five minutes down on Freire, in 121st.

★

Next up was the most coveted and most brutal one-day Classic of them all. Paris–Roubaix had garnered many nicknames since it was first staged in 1896 to publicise a newly built velodrome in an industrial suburb of Lille: the 'Queen of Classics', *La Pascale* (the Easter race) or simply the 'Hell of the North'. Miguel Indurain, the Spanish champion at the height of his powers, steered well clear of Paris–Roubaix's fierce inquisition. 'Cycling's last bit of madness,' according to former Tour de France organiser Jacques Goddet. Chris Boardman preferred to be a spectator, saying, 'I think it's a circus. I can see why people enjoy watching it, but I don't want to be one of the clowns.'

Steve Cummings, one of two British riders at Barloworld in 2008, along with the Welshman Geraint Thomas tells me that Froome had a sketchy grasp on the sport's history: 'Chris was really naïve and didn't know that much about the Tour of Flanders or Paris–Roubaix.'

Froome was about to find out. History lessons aside, in the real world he was a natural stage racer, not a one-day rider. Still, he went along to the start line in Compiègne on 13 April to join 198 fellow riders under a suitably brooding sky, the road slick from an overnight drizzle.

There is no mention of Froome throughout the live rolling report of the 106th running of the race on the *Cycling News* website. In fact he didn't even make it as far as the finish at the famous velodrome in Roubaix. The Hell of the North is merciless. An ability to suffer and absorb still more suffering is vital at Paris–Roubaix because the dreadful pounding on man and machine is relentless, the punctures frequent, the cobbles notoriously unpredictable to negotiate, pluming dust in dry conditions and mud when north-eastern France is at its most sullen.

Froome was there to help Barloworld's two main hopes for

success: Robbie Hunter and the Australian Baden Cooke, a sprinter and one-day race specialist. In his role as *domestique* he was obliged to sacrifice himself for his two teammates. This involved, among other things, stopping on several occasions to give replacement wheels from his own bike to Hunter and Cooke after they'd punctured.

In the dark depths of the Arenberg forest, the crooked *pavé* looks as though a madman has set upon it with a sledgehammer. On a wet day, the cobbles resemble giant polished ice-cubes encased in glutinous mud as thick as porridge. Navigating a safe passage over them on a racing bike is a unique skill, based on pushing a big gear, to smooth out some of the vibration, skimming across the surface like a pond-skating insect, for as long as your strength lasts, while trying to avoid the potholes and crashes, as riders all around come a cropper. A single rider losing control can cause an instant pile-up; if a rider punctures it can take several minutes to get a wheel change, because team cars get left way behind on the narrow *pavé* sections as the race gets strung out.

Each time Froome gifted a wheel to Hunter or Cooke, he'd have to hang about at the side of the road waiting for his team car to catch up. Then he'd take flight again to try and bridge the gap to the front of the race. His race came to an abrupt end, within 50km of the finish and while in a select group alongside Cooke (Hunter had by then dropped out; Cooke would go on to finish 31st, 11:08 behind second-time winner Tom Boonen), through a Froome-esque stroke of bad luck. Forced again into offering Cooke a wheel, and after getting a replacement for himself, he set off to give chase only to swing round a sharp corner and crash headlong into the back of a stationary commissaire's car, snagged in a race-traffic jam.

After the race Froome had bruises and welts on his hands from the cobbles buffeting his bike, like a road worker doing an eight-hour pneumatic drilling shift without gloves. Years later, when asked to name his favourite race he replied, 'Although it doesn't really suit my style at the moment, I'd have to say Paris–Roubaix.'

Three days later, wounds barely healed, Froome was in the thick of it once more at the Scheldeprijs Vlaanderen, the oldest cycle race in Flanders, a 207km career round Antwerp including seven treacherous cobbled sections. This is the last race for many of the Classics riders who build their season around the Tour of Flanders and Paris–Roubaix. Froome stayed out of trouble to finish a creditable 22nd, in the main peloton. Mark Cavendish spoiled Paris–Roubaix champion Tom Boonen's party on the finishing straight in Schoten, making a late lunge to steal the win.

Froome and Barloworld left the cobbles behind them, probably with some relief, and headed to Holland for the first in a trio of races dubbed the Ardennes Classics: Amstel Gold, La Flèche Wallonne and Liège–Bastogne–Liège. Considering the punishing schedule of six energy-sapping races in the space of nineteen days, Froome fared worse over the hilly courses of Limburg and Ardennes.

The three classics are shoe-horned into a week, Sunday to Sunday, Flèche Wallonne on Wednesday, sandwiched between the newcomer Amstel, established in 1966, and the race known as *La Doyenne*, Liège–Bastogne–Liège, the oldest in the spring Classics calendar, dating from 1892. The Amstel *parcours* (course), through the Dutch Limburg, 257 twisty-turny kilometres, 30 inclines, innumerable geometry-defying bends, did not suit Froome's climbing abilities. He crawled to the finish up the final climb of the notorious Cauberg in 139th place, in an eleven-man *gruppetto*[6] nearly twenty minutes behind surprise winner, the Italian Damiano Cunego.

In their preview of Flèche Wallonne, *Cycling Weekly* magazine gleefully announced that 'Chris Froome, the 22-year-old Barloworld climber who used to ride for Kenya is now a bona fide Brit. He's even listed on the official start sheet as a British rider. So hands off him, he's ours.'

---

6 An Italian term meaning 'the little group', similar to the French term *autobus*, to describe the backmarkers in a race.

It appeared that in the short window of three days between Amstel Gold and Flèche Wallonne the paperwork had finally come through, thanks to the diligent efforts of Doug Dailey at British Cycling, for Froome to officially trade his Kenyan racing licence for a British one.

Before he could be granted a British racing licence by the UCI he had to officially hand back his Kenyan passport. This proved to be a trickier proposition than Froome first imagined. Initially the Kenyan authorities wouldn't accept it, claiming they didn't have the correct paperwork (what amounted to a simple receipt). But he didn't want to surrender his passport without the proof he required for the UCI. Again, Froome found an ingenious solution to the problem when he was back in South Africa over the winter of 2007/08.

Dailey chuckles at the memory: 'He's a bright, resourceful guy, so he actually drew up his own affidavit, went along to the Kenyan embassy in Pretoria, handed in his passport and then gave them the paperwork to sign.'

With Froome's British racing licence in place at the start of the Olympic year, undeniable proof that he was eligible to ride for Great Britain, Dailey set in motion the tedious process of getting the British Olympic Committee to negotiate with their Kenyan counterparts to waive the three-year rule[7] and allow Froome to be available for selection for Team GB at the 2008 Beijing Games.

Cycling Weekly's Flèche preview also mentioned the hilltop finale of the race, the Mur de Huy, a fearsome 1,300m climb with an 18% gradient, describing it as being 'like the equivalent of a Tour de France sprint finish in super slo-mo'. The winner is normally a punchy climber, nimble on the steep Ardennes

---

7 By-law to Rule 41, Nationality of Competitors, of the Olympic Charter: A competitor who has represented one country in the Olympic Games, in continental or regional games or in world or regional championships recognised by the relevant IF, and who has changed his nationality or acquired a new nationality, may participate in the Olympic Games to represent his new country provided that at least three years have passed since the competitor last represented his former country. This period may be reduced or even cancelled, with the agreement of the NOCs and IF concerned, by the IOC Executive Board, which takes into account the circumstances of each case.

hills, but forceful on the flat and possessing enough zip in their legs to accelerate up the Mur – the kind of rider the Italians call a *scattista*. The kind of rider that wasn't Chris Froome, with his preference for longer, steeper Grand Tour-style climbs. He finished just ahead of the dreaded broom wagon that sweeps up the laggards at the back of a race, in 115th position, 9:56 adrift of Luxembourg's Kim Kirchin.

Froome's friend and Barloworld teammate, the South African climbing specialist, John-Lee Augustyn, who rode with him throughout the 2008 Classics season, recognised that Froome was more than a little shocked and unprepared for the arduous slog of riding such long distances over rough terrain while getting battered by fierce crosswinds from the North Sea. 'And then when you get to 200km they start racing!' says Augustyn. From a mountain-bike racing background, Augustyn was used to extremely tough, aggressive racing and therefore unfazed by the Classics. 'The harder the better for me. I liked the Classics,' he says.

By contrast, his African buddy Froome had a lot to learn – not just about how to prepare for such a stern test on the bike but how to read the mysterious hierarchy and learn the peculiar etiquette of the peloton, how to nuzzle your way into the bunch or earn the right to be at the head of the race.

In the beginning, especially when you are an unfamiliar face, Augustyn explains, it's hard to break in, be accepted or to get a handle on the esoteric rules. No new rider is permitted to ride at the front until he's proved himself worthy of notice. Especially in Flanders.

'After the first year, they make space at the front, they open the gaps for you,' says Augustyn. 'It was very hard for Chris at first, because he's quite an aggressive rider and his lines are not always the best, so the guys never gave him a gap; they shut him down. After you've had a few good results, they respect you a bit more so it becomes easier.'

Steve Cummings agrees with Augustyn's assessment of Froome's early months at Barloworld, adding that 'he was unlike other riders and obviously came from a very different background to everyone else. As a bike rider he was pretty raw, and we just thought, Who is this guy? Chris has got the kind of style where he always looks flat out but he's not. When people said that he won this race and that race and he was really strong as an amateur, we thought, Really? This guy? I found it quite hard to believe!'

Initially perplexed by his attributes as a cyclist, Cummings liked Froome a lot as a person. 'We always had fun with him. He was a bit different and liked a laugh. At Barloworld we were always joking around. It maybe took him a while to get the dry British sense of humour, but once he did, that was it.'

★

Liège–Bastogne–Liège's *palmarès* reads like a roll call of cycling's pantheon: Eddy Merckx, Jacques Anquetil, Michel Bartoli, Sean Kelly. One of the five Monuments of cycling,[8] in the past *La Doyenne* has found favour with both Classics specialists and the giants of the stage-race season alike. For one day in late April flyweight climbers lock horns with the hulking powerhouses of Belgium and northern France. The race, at over 250km, is dotted with a succession of small but tough climbs through the Ardennes hills, where American and German forces fought the Battle of the Bulge in the terrible winter of 1944. The hills start well before halfway at the town of Houffalize; the final phase begins with the toughest climb on the course, the Côte de la Redoute. This could have played to Froome's strengths, but it wasn't his day and he finished 84th, far behind Spanish winner Alejandro Valverde.

Chronic fatigue after six races in quick succession must have been a factor in the end. It had all proven to be a bit too much too soon for Froome. 'That was some race. I ended up absolutely exhausted. I was almost blacking out with the pain,' Froome said of his experience of *La Doyenne*. 'Maybe I didn't eat enough. But at least I finished.' His forgetfulness when it came to refuelling,

---

8   The five greatest one-day races in the sport are often referred to as the 'monuments' from season's start to finish: Milan–San Remo, the Tour of Flanders, Paris–Roubaix, Liège–Bastogne–Liège and the Tour of Lombardy.

an understandable lapse on the part of a novice, would return to haunt him a few months later in the biggest race of his life to date.

'Recently I've done a lot of races that haven't suited me – flat races in Belgium. It's not been so good,' Froome said, with a weariness that suggested he was glad to see the back of April. 'I'm a long-distance time triallist and climber; I'm best in stage races. Short prologues are definitely not my thing. I need time for my legs to warm up properly. I'm hoping to start doing races that are more my kind of thing.'

★

The five-day Vuelta a Asturias, starting in Oviedo in northern Spain on 3 May, was a race more to Froome's taste. On Stage 2b's rain-soaked time-trial course, 17.2km from Nueva along the Costa Verde to an awkward, twisting finish into Llanes, Froome posted a tremendous time to finish fifth, just 26 seconds slower than local boy Samuel Sánchez. The performance was made even more impressive when Sánchez went on to take the gold medal in the Olympic men's road race in Beijing in August.

Unfortunately Froome followed up this fine showing with a collapse on the penultimate queen stage (4) – an extremely taxing 180.2km route over three categorised climbs, from Pravia to the *hors catégorie* mountaintop finish at Santuario del Acebo. He came in over 26 minutes behind stage winner Tomasz Marczyński.

The day after the Vuelta Asturias came full-circle to its final conclusion back in Oviedo, a stage that Froome didn't start, drained by his previous exertions, the team was boosted by the news that Barloworld were to extend their sponsorship into season 2009.

★

At the start of May Barloworld boss Claudio Corti sent a strong wildcard team to Sicily for the start of the Giro d'Italia, but

Froome didn't make the cut. While his South African teammates Augustyn, Hunter and Impey – also omitted from Corti's Giro squad – raced in France at the Tour de Picardie, Froome took a well-earned break from competitive action and headed back to Chiari to train in the hills of Lombardy. The Tour de France was once more in his thoughts as he embarked on another of his epic 'special workouts' to Lake Endine and beyond, climbing high into the mountains around Clusone.

His main ambition for his debut pro season was no secret. He stated it loud and clear in an interview with *Cycling Weekly* on 3 June – to secure a place in the Barloworld line-up for the Tour de France in July. It would be a tense few weeks waiting for Corti to finalise his nine-man team.'

★

Within days of the interview his mother, Jane, passed away after a short battle with cancer. 'It was basically a bone marrow cancer, and she was only diagnosed a few days before she died,' Froome said. He was racing in Spain's Basque country at the time of her death, at the Euskal Bizikleta. Understandably out of sorts for the opening two stages of the three-day event, he stepped off his bike on the road to Arrate on 8 June when he heard the dreadful news. He immediately packed his bags and flew to Kenya to be with his family.

Less than two weeks later, on 25 June, Team Barloworld announced the pre-selection of their Tour de France line-up. Final confirmation of Corti's starting nine took place after the Ster Elektrotoer stage race in the Netherlands, Barloworld's final preparation before the Tour de France started on 5 July in Brest. Froome didn't travel to the start in Schijndel with the rest of the team. He was so shattered by his mother's death that he barely touched his bike for three weeks. However, selection for *La Grande Boucle* (a French name for the Tour de France meaning 'the big loop') proved to be a tonic for him after such a personal tragedy. Mental anguish perhaps could be alleviated, at least to a certain extent, by a different form of mental and physical stress.

'While I loved the time I spent with my family [in Kenya], having the Tour coming up was a welcome distraction,' said Froome. 'But there are regrets. I'd basically been away from home for two years, and when you look back it's easy to regret not spending more time with your loved ones.'

He arrived in Brest for the start of the 95th edition of the Tour de France stricken with grief. 'It was hard for me. I hadn't seen Mum for a long time so I went home for the funeral – only to get a call, two weeks before the Tour, to say I was riding. That pulled me back to reality. I had to carry on with life. I went straight to the start in Brittany with the only goal of finishing the Tour.'

When his place at the Tour was finally confirmed in late June, a journalist asked Froome if he would take any good luck charms along to the race. 'No lucky charms,' he replied, adding poignantly, 'but I recently lost my mother. Since then I like to think that she is watching over me whenever I race.'

CHAPTER 6

In at the Deep End

In the weeks following the end of the 2008 Tour de France, sometime in August, David Kinjah received a large package in the post at his Safari Simbaz headquarters. It was a goody bag from Froome ('He's always been generous,' Kinjah says.) The treasure chest contained all Froome's Barloworld kit that hadn't been taken back by the team: red team jerseys; time-trial skin suits; a zebra-striped Suomy helmet; the pedals from his celeste-blue Bianchi racing bike and the silver-and-white Diadora cycling shoes that he wore throughout his debut Tour de France.

Froome and his shoes had covered a fair old distance together: 3,559km to be exact, from Brest to Paris, on a dizzying anti-clockwise loop of France, up the Pyrenees and over the Alps, 21 stages in the space of three weeks. Over 90 hours in the saddle, pushing the pedals round and round, over and over again – a mind-boggling number of revolutions. Those shoes were special. Who knows, perhaps one day they might be as valuable as having a pair of shoes worn by Eddy Merckx, or Bernard Hinault or Miguel Indurain? What a journey they'd been on.

'Where are they now?' I ask Kinjah. In a presentation case, placed prominently among his collection of cycling memorabilia?

'Actually, one of the young riders wears them when he's riding in races,' Kinjah says. 'We keep telling him, "Hey, those are Chris Froome's shoes! He wore them in the Tour de France!"'

The young lad should be keeping them safe, locked away, or in a glass jar, Kinjah says. 'We tell him he's so lucky that we just let him destroy the shoes like that!' It's better that the boy gets wear out of them, Kinjah says. What use are they sitting in a glass cabinet? Chris would no doubt prefer it that way. Back in the villages, Kinjah explains, the Tour de France is still not a big deal to the Safari Simbaz youngsters. 'They have their own small local races, which mean more to them than the Tour,' he says. 'It's the same as for Chris when he was younger. He didn't know anything about the Tour.'

★

Almost exactly ten years had passed since his first encounter with David Kinjah. Now here he was, Chris Froome, the *kijana* from Nairobi, about to make his Tour de France debut. He would be the first Kenyan ever to start the most famous bike race in the world.

Froome and his Barloworld teammates joined the other nineteen teams on the stage in the centre of Brest on 3 July for the traditional pre-race presentation. In stark contrast to the previous year, when tens of thousands packed Trafalgar Square in London in anticipation of the first ever *Grand Départ* on British soil, only a few hundred hardy souls showed up on a cold and blustery evening in the harbour town on the coast of Brittany to greet the teams. After an emotional month, Froome was just happy to be there.

In the days building up to the big event he was characteristically frank. 'My results haven't been great this year; I've had some ups and downs. My mother passed away last month. That set me back a bit.'

'It makes this all the more emotional,' he said, on 4 July, the eve of the race start in Brest, when asked by *Procycling* magazine how the loss of his mother would affect the way he approached the coming three weeks. 'My mum was a big reason why I wanted to do this race. She always followed my cycling closely, and I wanted to ride the Tour to make her proud.'

In fact, following his mixed form in the opening half of the season, Corti had given Froome no indication that he would even pick him for the Tour. If anything, the vibes were to the contrary.

Most riders get the opportunity to recce the route and ride some of the key stages, especially in the high mountains. Froome just showed up, ready to roll – not a million miles removed from his first foray into European cycling at the Worlds in Salzburg.

At least this time he had a team, a team car and a manager dedicated to his performance in the race. He seemed unruffled, at least on the surface. It had been a horribly eventful month. He had bigger things on his mind than worrying unduly about a bike race; even if it was the biggest one on earth, the third biggest sporting event after the Olympics and World Cup, and watched by a cumulative audience of around 4.5 billion people worldwide. He was looking forward to getting the show on the road.

'I'm quite confident,' he said. 'Generally speaking, the longer the race, the better I go. [He added, somewhat naively:] All I need to know about the Alps and Pyrenees I'll get from the road map. Hopefully it'll get me through to Paris.'

The 2008 Tour de France kicked off without a short prologue time trial, the first time since 1966. It started instead with a rolling 197.5km road stage from Brest to Plumelec. The newly crowned Spanish road champion, Alejandro Valverde, claimed the stage win and the first yellow jersey of the race.

Most of the race favourites – Cadel Evans, Frank Schleck, Denis Menchov – finished comfortably in the main bunch, but Barloworld team leader Mauricio Soler had a disastrous start. He crashed inside the final 10km. Froome held back with teammates Cárdenas and Chuela to nurse him [Soler] to the finish, but they all wound up losing over three minutes. More worrying for the Colombian, the damage was inflicted on the same wrist he broke in the Giro d'Italia.

Meanwhile it took five days until Froome – with the Kenyan flag on top of his *dossard*[9] – even finished with the main field. That same day, on the flat road out of Cholet on Stage 5, the hapless Soler fell in the neutral zone, further aggravating his

9   The race number pinned to the back of a cyclist's jersey.

troublesome wrist injury and forcing him to abandon the race after only 12km.

It was a huge blow for Barloworld. They had lost their designated team captain for the Tour. One of Froome's main tasks had been to help Soler in the mountains. Who could fill the departed team leader's shoes as the roads headed upwards into the high mountain passes? Soler's fellow Colombian, climbing specialist Félix Rafael Cárdenas, was the obvious choice. He had won the mountainous Stage 12 at the Tour de France in 2001 and was a three-time stage winner at the Vuelta a España. Or what about Moisés Dueñas? Riding for Agritubel, he had taken overall victory at the 2006 Tour de l'Avenir, the junior Tour de France.

'Losing Soler is a big disappointment for the team,' Froome said. 'But we have to continue and do our job. Hopefully there's still time to achieve something with Robbie Hunter, Baden Cooke or Moisés Dueñas.'

The day before Soler's retirement, on the shorter than usual first ITT, Froome fared well on the flat 29.5km run in and around Cholet, finishing a respectable 33rd. With his rangy, long-legged style working the huge powerhouse engine more suited to longer tests against the clock, Froome frustratingly ran out of road. 'I was just getting right into it and then I realised that I was near the finish,' he said ruefully. 'Hopefully the time trial at the end of the race will suit me better because it's a bit longer.' He would have to learn how to manage such fluctuations in the mental and physical demands of the Tour, essential in the blooding of a newcomer. He confessed he was still a little overwhelmed by the scale of the race. 'I can't believe how big it is,' he said. 'The crowds are huge. I'm just trying to enjoy it.'

As Froome ran out of tarmac in Cholet, on 8 July British Cycling's Doug Dailey confirmed they had ran out of time in their own mad dash to get clearance from the Kenyan Cycling Federation for Froome to represent Great Britain at the 2008 Beijing Olympics in August. He'd swapped his Kenyan racing licence in the spring for a British one.

The problem was that Froome had already represented

Kenya at international level at the World Championships, the Commonwealth and All-Africa Games. When the approach was first made for Froome to ride the Olympics, Kenya blocked it. It was then pointed out that they hadn't qualified for a single place in the road race or time trial. To deny Froome the opportunity of riding for Great Britain in Beijing in August amounted either to complete incompetence or else to spoilsport petulance.

As the deadline for registration approached, the Kenyan authorities continued to drag their heels about releasing Froome until it was too late. In desperation, Froome had even tried to phone their head office from the Tour, but he couldn't get a connection. After the British Olympic squad was announced, Froome said, 'They have not been helpful at all, it has been really disappointing. I did a lot with Kenyan cycling, and to have them deny me the opportunity to ride in the Olympics leaves a bit of a sour taste in my mouth.'

'We fell at the last fence,' Doug Dailey tells me, still sounding deflated at the memory. 'Kenya hadn't qualified for the Olympics, but they blocked Chris and scuppered his hopes. I am confident we would have selected him for Beijing.'

Dailey says the hilly course in Beijing, with a big wall climb, rare for a city-based circuit at an Olympic Games, was 'made for Chris Froome with his climbing abilities. We didn't have any riders who were suited to the demands of that course. I felt it was a tragedy for Chris because you only get these freak courses every now and again.'

★

After a flat opening five stages, the Tour route took a decidedly hillier turn on Stages 6 and 7 as the race wound south across the baking hot intermediate climbs of the Massif Central. Froome lost touch with the peloton on both days losing a hefty fifteen minutes on the road to the Super Besse ski station before dropping even more time on the twisting and rolling roads of the region, on a day of heavy winds, incessant attacks and multiple crashes.

Froome arrived in Aurillac, ancient capital of the Auvergne, with teammate John-Lee Augustyn in a small group, 21:53 down.

As the race entered the high mountains for the first time on Stage 9, snaking up into the Pyrenees from the spa town of Bagnères-de-Luchon, Froome found his climbing legs and made it to the stage finish at Bagnères-de-Bigorre less than two minutes behind stage winner Riccardo Riccò, in 51st place. The Kenyan rookie had leaped ahead of a group behind Riccò on the Category 1 Col d'Aspin, giving an indication for the first time of a bright future in the mountains of the Tour. 'It wasn't as steep as I expected,' Froome said. 'It was great for me.'

However, the effort had made heavy inroads into his reserves. He cracked the following day on the 17.2km ascent of the fabled Col de Tourmalet, over 2,000m in altitude and with an average gradient of 7.6%, struggling to the mountaintop finish at Hautacam over 33 minutes behind stage winner Leonardo Piepoli, as an emotional Cadel Evans became the first Australian rider since Robbie McEwen in 2004 to pull on the famous *maillot jaune* of the race leader.

By contrast, Moisés Dueñas finished eleventh, soaring into the top 20 overall. Following the loss of Soler, the Spaniard's performance thus far provided some encouraging news for Barloworld. Unfortunately that news would soon turn sour.

On the first rest day in Tarbes on 15 July, enjoying a well-earned breather, Froome outlined his personal goal as simply 'to arrive in Paris and maybe pick a few stages to be up there to help my teammates'. And on the frantic nature of the first week of racing, a fraught ordeal for any newcomer, he said: 'It amazed me. I remember thinking how quickly everyone went and thinking, If I'm a climber, I've got to seriously work. How am I going to get through 21 days?'

Unfortunately Moisés Dueñas's strategy for making it to Paris was somewhat less innocent than old-fashioned grit and determination. The headline in *Cycling Weekly* on the morning of 16 July said it all: Dueñas Caught With Banned Drugs At Tour de France.

French police raided the 27-year-old Spaniard's hotel room following the announcement that he had failed a doping test for EPO[10] after the Stage 4 time trial in Cholet. When the cops unearthed a cache of assorted drugs – one police source described the haul as resembling 'a mobile pharmacy' – Dueñas was taken to the police station in nearby Tarbes. Under French law doping is a criminal offence. It was the second doping scandal of the race. The first involved another Spaniard, Manuel Beltrán of Liquigas, who had tested positive for EPO after the opening stage.

Dueñas's downfall was a humiliating catastrophe for Barloworld. He was immediately suspended by the team and withdrawn from the race. Corti and team doctor Massimiliano Mantovani were at pains to point out they had been completely oblivious to Dueñas's actions.

Froome was disgusted with Dueñas, furious that his selfish actions would not only damage the good reputation of Barloworld but perhaps even threaten the cycling team's entire existence. Unlike most riders, nervous of commenting on a teammate's extracurricular activities, the 23-year-old pulled no punches when asked for his opinion on the matter. 'I'm really pleased he got caught, because it's people like him who are ruining the sport and making racing that extra bit harder.' Journalists were asking the obvious question: did Barloworld have a doping programme in place? 'Obviously there isn't – if there were, he [Dueñas] wouldn't have hidden it in his bags,' was Froome's tart riposte. For a rookie, he was speaking like a rider of some maturity, and with refreshing candour. A sign, perhaps, that a new generation of young cyclists was coming through to challenge the old culture of *omertà*.

The dope bust had punctured the close-knit atmosphere within the Barloworld camp. And, of even more pressing concern, would be the response from the sponsors. How would Barloworld react? It was horrendous publicity for the South African corporate giant. Would they wash their hands of the whole sorry affair?

10 Erythropoietin, a hormone originally developed for leukaemia sufferers and then used as a performance-enhancing drug.

And would the team immediately be thrown out of the race? It was a mess, one that Froome could never have envisaged for his debut Tour de France. Everything – the present, the future – was uncertain, up in the air, for the entire team.

'Sadly he's put the future of a lot of people at risk. Barloworld said they were going to immediately pull out, but now we just don't know what's going to happen,' Froome said. 'The team was on the up and up, and he's ruined everything.'

Because Dueñas had apparently acted alone, the remaining seven Barloworld riders were allowed to start Stage 11 in Lannemezan, but things went from very bad to a lot worse for the team when Paolo Longo Borghini crashed on the descent of the Category 3 Col de Larrieu and abandoned the race with a broken collarbone.

Then Cárdenas was forced to abandon 30km from the finish in Foix with a muscle tear in his right thigh. Suddenly Team Barloworld was down to five riders. In light of Dueñas's tawdry departure, cynics might have construed that Borghini and Cárdenas's withdrawal from the race was rather too convenient, and also highly suspicious; especially since the pair had reportedly crashed into each other mid-stage.

After a horrendous day at the office the decimated and disillusioned quintet limped home in assorted states of disrepair, all some distance behind the stage winner, Norwegian champion Kurt Asle Arvesen.

On 17 July Stage 12 left the Pyrenees, and Dueñas's shame, behind on a 168.5km run from Lavelanet, descending steadily from the heart of Cathar country, with its hilltop castle ruins, towards the Mediterranean Sea and the finish in Narbonne. But Dueñasgate was just the tip of the doping iceberg at the 2008 Tour de France.

'Today's biggest news,' *Cycling News* announced at the opening of their rolling live report, 'is the positive A sample for EPO[11]

---

11 According to *L'Equipe*, one of the Italian climber's urine samples collected by the French Anti-Doping Agency showed traces of the (previously untraceable) third-generation EPO called CERA (Continuous Erythropoietin Receptor Activator). Cycling's drug war had reached a new frontier.

returned by Riccardo Riccò (Saunier Duval).' Days before, the young Italian climber had raised some eyebrows when he won the Super Besse (Stage 6) and Bagnères-de-Bigorre (Stage 9) mountain stages in devastating style.

Riccò, lying ninth on GC at the time, was ejected from the race, taken into police custody and sacked by Saunier Duval the next day. The Spanish-based team voluntarily pulled their entire team out of the Tour.[12]

Meanwhile, there was still a race going on. Stage 12 provided sprinters with an opportunity to flex their muscles and reopen their accounts after the tough slog through the Pyrenees. The pace was ultra-fast right from the start, and Baden Cooke crashed in the early, jittery phase. The Australian abandoned a short while later. And then there were four. Barloworld's remaining riders kept calm and carried on, tucked safely in the main bunch, as Mark Cavendish rocketed to his third stage victory. One small consolation for Barloworld's fab four was that there was no team time trial (TTT) in that year's Tour.

Two days later Froome and co. received the news they'd all been dreading. Barloworld were ending their sponsorship deal. A statement had been posted on the team's website as the race left Nîmes to cross Provence and the Luberon wine area, before arriving in Digne-les-Bains. This old spa town is the starting point of Victor Hugo's famous novel *Les Misérables*, an apposite coincidence for the survivors left behind miserably to pick up the pieces from Dueñas's wrongdoing. Barely two months had passed since a Barloworld spokesman talked proudly of the company's pleasure at extending their six-year association with their successful cycling team into 2009. Those words now evaporated in the hot midsummer Provençal air.

Froome seemed sanguine about the massive blow delivered by the sponsor's statement. 'I'm convinced the team will find the best solution for us all,' he told *Agence France Presse*. 'I know that for 2009 the sponsorship is still confirmed. It's not a good way

12 Six days later, team sponsor Saunier Duval, a French heating and home comfort technology brand, terminated their involvement with cycling.

to end things, but I can understand the sponsor's point of view, that they don't want to link themselves to doping in any way.'

Froome was also concerned that by being a member of Barloworld he'd be tarred with the same brush as Dueñas. 'People put us all in the same boat now. They see someone in the Barloworld kit and think, Oh, he is probably doping,' he added. 'It makes me angry, but what can you do about it? The best thing for me to do is not see [Dueñas] or I may get assault charges against me.'

Meanwhile team boss Corti attempted to put a brave face on his team's numerical handicap at the start of Stage 14. 'We will try for an escape with Robert Hunter and Giampaulo Cheula – we have only four riders!' the affable Italian said. 'The other two riders – John-Lee Augustyn and Chris Froome – we are saving for the mountains tomorrow.' There was an early escape, but it didn't include Hunter, and Óscar Freire took the honours on the line in Digne.

Despite the team's low morale, Froome was still able to see the funny side of their plight. 'It's a compact unit,' he joked. 'There's a lot more space in the bus and you don't need to wait to get a shower.'

The race crossed the border into Italy on Stage 15, descending from the vertiginously high Col Agnel into the Piedmont province of Cuneo. Unfortunately for Froome, the brief sortie into his adopted homeland proved to be the scene of his unravelling. It was no joke to be strung out and stressed in the so-called 'laughing group'; Froome's *gruppetto* came in 25 minutes down at the finish.

If the Pyrenees had proved to be less steep than he'd imagined, the Hautes-Alpes were taking their toll on his already leaden legs. Froome's teammate Augustyn went over the top of the Agnel in ninth spot, a sterling effort, but faded on the Prato Nevoso finale.

The Col de la Bonette, at 2,802m, is the highest paved road in Europe, the highest mountain pass and the furthest above sea level the Tour de France has ever ventured. As the race returned to France for Stage 16 following its sojourn into Italy, Barloworld's talented climber Augustyn crossed the rudely exposed, wind-blasted summit of the Cime de la Bonette, the day's second huge climb – having already scaled the Col de la Lambarde – on his own after attacking his leading group 500m from the road's top. At the start of the descent he misjudged a right-hand bend at full pelt, dived into the thin blue air over the edge of the mountain and belly-flopped onto the scree slope, sliding 50m down the mountainside with his bike somersaulting ahead. A gallant spectator slid gingerly down to his rescue and helped Augustyn clamber up the treacherous gravel slope to the safety of the roadside, feet splayed sideways in his cycling shoes, like a penguin trying to climb the face of a cliff.

Shaken but miraculously unscathed, the young South African jumped on a replacement bike and made it safely to the finish in Jausiers, five minutes down on stage winner Cyril Dessel. At least Barloworld's four hadn't become three. Froome missed all the drama, coming in almost 30 minutes later; his membership of the Tour's stragglers club deserved of a free upgrade to gold status. 'I was in the *gruppetto* most days but I thought to myself, I'd love to be up at the front one day,' he said.

The very next day Froome's aspiration was realised – on the queen stage of that year's Tour de France, the long, brutal seventeenth, a 210.5km epic that tackled the Cols du Galibier and Croix de Fer before going through the village of Le Bourg d'Oisans to begin the fearsome ascent up 21 hairpin bends to the ski resort of L'Alpe d'Huez, a Mecca of cycling. Since its introduction to the Tour in 1952 as the first high-altitude finish in its history, L'Alpe d'Huez is synonymous with *La Grande Boucle*. It is the stage that all climbers want to win, and a Tour de France without it always seems to have something missing.

Froome excelled over the first climb of the day, a half-marathon haul up the 2,645m Galibier, making its 57th appearance in the race since 1911. Fausto Coppi, Charly Gaul, Eddy Merckx and Marco Pantani are among the famous names of the past who were first over the top of the legendary mountain. The paint-daubed graffiti of their names on the narrow, winding road had long since faded from the burning asphalt as Froome followed in their illustrious tyre tracks.

He stayed with the race leaders, cresting the peak almost five minutes adrift of a four-man break, headed by Stefan Schumacher. The plucky young Kenyan hung on to the elite group's coat-tails all the way into the valley, over the Col du Télégraphe and down to the town of Saint-Jean-de-Maurienne, riding west towards the majestic, jagged skyline dominated by the Belledonne mountain range.

At Saint-Jean they turned left and climbed relentlessly for 30km to the 2,067m summit of the intimidatingly named Col de la Croix de Fer (Pass of the Iron Cross). 'I was surprised how well the climbs suited me,' Froome said. 'They weren't too steep but they were long, and I like that kind of climb.'

He might have liked the uphill switchback helter skelter ride of L'Alpe d'Huez too, had he not committed a novice's error. Just past Le Bourg d'Oisans, on the horribly steep opening 2km of the corkscrewing climb, a rude introduction to the Alpe, the race favourites gathered, bang on time as if by pre-appointment, for a battle royal: Frank and Andy Schleck, Bernhard Kohl, Cadel Evans, Carlos Sastre and Denis Menchov. Froome found himself riding in the slipstream of Menchov, the reigning Vuelta a España champion.

Sastre attacked on the first metres of the ascent, blowing the group to pieces. 'I was on Menchov's wheel after the first part of the climb,' Froome said. 'I thought I could perhaps get back on [following Sastre's sudden burst of acceleration] by following him, but I just didn't have the legs.'

In his excitement he'd forgotten to eat and had even, fool-ishly, refused the offer of sustenance – 'an amateurish mistake,' he reflected ruefully at the finish. Corti had called Froome back to the team car to pick up more energy gels, but he'd told him, 'No, no, I'm fine.' He had almost 10km of laborious climbing to ride with one energy gel left in his back pocket when he fell victim to the dreaded 'hunger knock' or *fringale*.[13] 'I blew completely, had no sugars left and lost a lot of time. That hit home how

13 A slang term from around 1945, meaning 'to hit the wall', describing when a cyclist is completely drained of blood sugar and energy. The French call it 'the wolf' starvation.

important energy is, that taught me a lesson. Corti said, "Why didn't you come back? You needed about ten gels, not one!'"

It was an error born of Froome's youthful inexperience, and yet he still managed to cross the line in 31st place, 11:41 behind new race leader Carlos Sastre, the Spaniard sealing what would prove to be a decisive stage victory.

Hinting at future untapped reserves of recovery, Froome kept his best form for the last week and followed up his fine showing on the famous Alpe with a highly creditable sixteenth place in the final long time trial, a 53km 'race of truth' from Cérilly to Saint Amand Montrond.

Unlike the shorter TT on Stage 4, Froome had no need to berate his performance on the penultimate day of the race. And this time he had plenty of road on which to unwind his long legs and let rip. Three weeks before, he had said his dream would be 'to set a good time in the long time trial of the Tour. To me that is the ultimate test, having to ride nearly 60km individually, at an average speed close to 50km/h. There is no place to hide when you are doing an individual time trial!' Froome set the second best time of the day by a young rider; Team Columbia's Swedish time-trial prodigy, Thomas Löfkvist, topped him by just 31 seconds. It was a highly satisfying way to top off his first Tour de France.

On the annual hell-for-leather circuit, up and round the Champs-Élysées in Paris, after joining a short-lived four-man break on the cobbles of the most famous boulevard on earth, Froome earned the cycling equivalent of a window seat with a view, trailing in 145th and last on the stage, due to him having to give up a wheel for teammate Robbie Hunter who'd punctured, but able to enjoy the glorious cityscape of Paris as the final stage circuit wheeled past the Arc de Triomphe down the Champs along the riverside and back, across the Place de la Concorde and up the Champs to the finish line.

Quickstep's Gert Steegmans galloped to victory; Froome savoured his own sweet taste of success: 84th overall on his debut Tour de France, in his first season as a full professional. He had measured himself against the best cyclists in the world in the hardest race in the sport and set a yardstick for the future. By way of comparison, it took the five-time Tour winner Miguel Indurain three attempts before he completed the race for the first time, coming 97th in 1987.

'It was a great feeling getting to Paris and finishing the Tour. Now you know the Tour is in your legs and the experience is there for the year after. I know what to expect next time. The adrenaline of it all keeps you going, but that can be dangerous as well as helpful. It helps you dig deeper than you normally do, but then you can also blow much bigger when you run out of legs. I had some good days when I performed well, such as on the stage to L'Alpe d'Huez, but there were other days when I struggled and almost didn't finish the Tour.'

Team manager Claudio Corti was glowing in his praise for the debut Grand Tour of his young African duo of Froome and Augustyn (a fantastic 48th overall). 'Without a doubt it's been a difficult and unlucky Tour de France for us, but we're very proud that Chris and John-Lee have emerged and shown their talent for stage racing despite both riding the Tour for the very first time. They've both got a great future ahead of them.'

Froome in particular caught the attention of the media, due in part to his Kenyan background but also because of his ability to stay with the best riders on the toughest climbs, the inner steel that seemed at odds with his self-effacing manner. It was, now, obvious that he had what it took to succeed in major stage races.

Corti went even further, he tells me, with a bold prediction: 'I caught Chris off guard when I told him that one day he could finish in the top five of the Tour de France. He thought I had gone crazy!'

★

Back in the relative calm of Chiari, Froome spent August combining recovery rides with a few one-day races in Italy and harder, longer days to Clusone and the foothills of the Alps, to hang on to the climbing strength and endurance he'd gained during the Tour. 'I'm trying to capitalise on my suffering in the Tour,' he said.

Simply riding so brutal a race as the Tour depletes any rider markedly. 'You lose a lot of muscle at the Tour de France and you need to recover that at first with one-hour or two-hour rides at a recovery rate and some strength work. I've got a lot of intensity in my legs from the Tour, so now I just need to use it.'

The extra work paid off when he recorded his best ever result in a professional race on 3 August taking third place in the Giro dell'Appennino, a one-day semi-classic. Froome was in the mix from the off, staying with the leaders on the final climb in the Appenine Mountains over the Passo dei Giovi before descending to the finish in Pontedecimo, for a place on the podium, ten seconds behind Alessandro Bertolini. Froome was delighted with the result but still craved a first professional victory in his debut season with Barloworld. 'I know my form will fade over time but hopefully I'll get a win before the end of the season and have a bit left for the World Championships,' he said.

★

The Beijing Olympics came and went without his participation. He would just have to wait until the three-year embargo on competing for Britain elapsed – perfect timing for the next Olympics, the 2012 Games in London.

But at least he didn't have to wait long, or travel far from his Italian abode, to finally don the colours of Great Britain for the first time with the World Championships road race due to be staged in Varese on 28 September. Froome was not one of the 77 finishers led home by Italy's Alessandro Ballan, but it was another box ticked in a year-long learning experience. He dropped out with a lap to go, later saying: 'I got to the 220km mark and my legs were just like *ufff* and they couldn't go on any more. I tried to sit at the front as much as I could and when I blew, I blew – that was it.'

Before the Tour de France he was 'Chris who?' Now the cycling world knew his name. 'I've heard that other teams were impressed by my ride in the Tour but I'm perfectly happy with Barloworld,' Froome revealed.

Rumour abounded that an offer had been made by Silence-Lotto for Froome to ride for Cadel Evans in the 2009 season. But he remained under contract to Barloworld, and Claudio Corti, now even more confident of his all-round potential, was determined to hang on to the talented novice.

'My main goals this year were not purely based on results but rather to look at the bigger picture and develop properly as a professional cyclist,' Froome said. 'I hope to have bridged the gap from riding at an amateur level to a professional level.'

He could consider the gap well and truly bridged. But he also knew that the real hard work lay ahead. It was over the winter months that satisfied reflection gave way to serious contemplation of the challenges ahead. It wasn't a time for hibernation but for transition. It was all very well finishing 84th at the Tour de France, but that had no meaning unless he followed up that result with better ones. He was nowhere near where he wanted to be yet.

★

Luckily he could leave the frosty north of Italy behind and fly south for the winter. Forget training in the interminable cold and torrential rain of northern Europe. He would follow in the flight path of the estimated 500 million birds whose annual migration took them thousands of miles from the harsh northern hemisphere winter to warm southern climes.

Froome's itinerant lifestyle was taking him 'home' again, back to Africa, and he would need plenty of his feathered friends' endurance to make it big in 2009.

CHAPTER 7

Fast Learner

Cauberg, Mur de Huy, La Redoute, Cols de Peyresourde, d'Aspin, Tourmalet, Hautacam, d'Agnel, Lambarde, Bonette, Galibier, Croix de Fer, L'Alpe d'Huez. All the list needs is an imaginary Kraftwerk backing track. In the space of a year Froome had scaled some of the greatest, most iconic climbs in cycling history. These climbs were now part of him. He had them in his legs, like growth rings in a tree trunk. Experience is necessary in all sports – and naturally comes with the wisdom of age, practice and competition – but especially in cycling where detailed knowledge of climbs and race routes is vital to any rider's enduring success.

For a natural climber like Froome, with aspirations of Grand Tour glory, this initiation into the geography of European professional bike racing – the twists and turns, cruel gradients and death-defying descents – would help immeasurably in his development as a stage race contender. Muscle memory. It would stand him in good stead for the years ahead.

To these monument climbs he could add the western flank of Mont Faron, the *pièce de résistance* of the Tour Méditerranéen, the opening race for Froome of the 2009 season. The six-day stage race started on 11 February in Béziers and ran along the Languedoc coast to Marseille and on into Provence, before coming to a spectacular conclusion on the summit of Mont Faron, overlooking the bay of Toulon. Barloworld's third spot, behind Caisse d'Epargne and Garmin-Slipstream (home to David Millar and Bradley Wiggins), in the 25km TTT left sports director Alberto Volpi's men ideally placed for a tilt at the overall.

Robbie Hunter had almost given them a dream start on the

opening day but lost out in a tight sprint finish in Narbonne to the Belarusian Yauheni Hutarovich of Française des Jeux. Daryl Impey was next to miss narrowly grabbing a stage victory in Istres on Stage 3, Kevin Ista taking the honours on the line, but it was a solid start for Barloworld. The gritty South African Hunter then notched his team's first stage win of the new season on Stage 4's 155km run from Greasque to Bouc Bel Air. On Stage 5 Hunter lost a photo finish, again to Hutarovich before Froome's chance to shine came on the final leg from Nice to Toulon.

He'd spent the off-season training at high altitude, first in Kenya on his mountain bike, where the roads were too bad to even consider bringing a road bike, then in South Africa. These annual winter trips home were clearly paying off. On his return to Europe, team tests revealed he'd gained a small but significant increase in power.

Froome climbed the rack of sharp hairpins of the majestic Mont Faron, slashed across the limestone rock face like the blade of Zorro, with Colombian teammate Mauricio Soler in tow. Soler had launched a solo attack at the foot of the climb to form a gap between himself, Froome and Frenchman David Moncoutié. The final stretch of the 9km climb meanders through a forest of cedars, Aleppo pines and oaks fragrant with the odours of warm resin, earning it the local moniker Toulon's *Poumon Vert* (Green Lung). Froome and Moncoutié caught Soler in the final kilometre only for Moncoutié to hit the Barloworld duo with a sucker-punch acceleration in the final 300m and steal the stage win from under their noses. At the summit Soler squeezed out Froome for second place.

Nevertheless it was a fine effort and enough to lift Froome into thirteenth place behind overall winner Luis León Sánchez. Froome's recent altitude training in Africa had set him up nicely for the first race of the year, but he was still surprised to perform so well after doing few high-intensity interval workouts. 'It shows my base fitness is there for the first race of the season and hopefully the rest of the season,' he said.

Froome traded one scenic coast for another, leaving the glistening Mediterranean behind and heading to the narrow coastal strip of Liguria for the Trofeo Laigueglia, the first race in Italy for the 2009 season. The semi-Classic started in Alassio on the scenic Riviera di Ponente and headed west to the finish in Laigueglia, taking a long, looping 170km detour inland to cover a trio of small but tricky climbs. It was Froome country, and he continued his early season form, with a solid 23rd, finishing in the leading main group of race winner Francesco Ginanni.

★

March took Froome back to South Africa once more for the familiar terrain of the Giro del Capo. Hunter got Barloworld off to a flyer on day one, sprinting to victory in Wellington. In Race 2 Froome made amends for his Intaka Tech blunder the previous year to claim his first win as a professional. In a blazing heatwave – several forest fires had rampaged in the Cape Town region during the week of the race – Froome jumped clear from a six-man breakaway on the 145km circuit of Durbanville to ride solo for the final 30km. As everyone wilted in the intense heat, Froome powered to the finish with the chasing group floundering home some three minutes in his wake. It was a commanding performance from the 23-year-old, who admitted he wasn't immune to the 40-degree temperatures. 'It was seriously hot out there,' he said. 'Almost as hot as Kenya! I don't know anyone who likes riding in the heat but I guess others might suffer more than me.' Pale-faced Brit Steve Cummings climbed off his bike along with Race 1 winner Hunter with a lap to go, their job done having got Froome and Daryl Impey into the break.

Afterwards Froome was mightily chuffed to get a first pro win under his belt with a jovial nod to his premature celebration at Pietermaritzburg. 'Yeah, I made sure I had the win well before

I went over the line,' he said with a beaming smile. 'I made sure the zip [on my vest] was up, there was no one near me who could come close and I had been told by Claudio [Corti, the team manager] that I had over two minutes on the rest of the break.' This time the two-minute gap was real.

★

Compared with 2008, Barloworld's racing schedule for the new season was relatively sparse, partly a consequence of the fallout from the Moisés Dueñas doping affair at the Tour de France. Race organisers Amaury Sport Organisation (ASO) deemed Barloworld unfit for a wildcard to *La Grande Boucle*, and so Corti had to plan his team's season around the earlier Giro d'Italia in May.

However, the team did receive late invitations in time to enter both Tirreno Adriatico and Milan–San Remo, and then, on 8 April, race organisers RCS Media Group announced they'd also made the cut for the Giro d'Italia. Barloworld boss Corti had always been quietly confident of securing a place. But the uncertainty had a detrimental effect on the riders' preparation for the second biggest race on the annual calendar. 'It was hard for us,' recalls John-Lee Augustyn. 'We didn't have too many races on the schedule so we had to do a lot of training to prepare for the Giro.'

Augustyn and Impey would join Froome on runs to Lake Iseo when their racing and training schedules synched. Otherwise, says Augustyn, Froome indulged his obsession for solo forays into the back of the Lombardy beyond. 'He would load his backpack with sandwiches and then off he'd go on his bike. Eight hours later he would phone me, completely lost, saying he didn't know where he was or where to go and I would look up Google maps to give him directions home.'

★

A more promising ride – ninth place, behind Slovenian winner Grega Bole – in the one-day GP Nobili Rubinetterie in Arona, on 18 April, was the springboard Froome needed as he readied himself for a second assault on the dreaded Mur de Huy, Flèche Wallonne's double-tiered stairway to heaven ... or hell, depending on how your legs were feeling. At least this time Froome knew what was coming.

The knowledge was tempered by the fact that the 2009 race would test the resolve of all but the toughest of Ardennes hardmen with a triple ascent of the Mur. The 'wall' is only 1,300 metres long but it packs a devastating punch, thanks to an average gradient of 9.3% that maxes at 25% on the inside line of the two corners. At these points, merely staying upright on your bike is a serious challenge.

Pre-race, Froome told *Cycling News*: 'My legs felt good the other day in Italy, in Arona. I am not sure about the Mur though; it is more of a puncher's type of climb.' He was referring to the French cycling term *puncheur*, meaning the kind of rider who specialises in rolling terrain with short but steep climbs, like the ones in the Ardennes Classics. In other words, the type of rider – such as Philippe Gilbert, Danilo Di Luca and Paolo Bettini – that wasn't Froome.

Asked if breaking his professional duck at the Giro del Capo had instilled him with fresh confidence, Froome replied, 'I think so. I know what I am getting myself into, whereas last year I was going blindly into these races.'

From Charleroi, in the heart of the predominantly French-speaking southern region of Belgium, the peloton navigated its way along a mazy chain of roads through the wooded mining valleys of the Belgian Ardennes and on to Huy for the start of a small closing circuit at the 67km point of the 197.5km *parcours*. Six *côtes* were spread along the second circuit, while the penultimate of the day, Côte de Ben Ahin, was often the catalyst for early attacks with the strung-out leaders anticipating the final ascent of the Huy to the summit at Notre Dame de la Sarte. This – the last of seven chapels dotted up the Chemin des Chapelles, was, according to folklore, the scene of a miracle in 1621 and a final destination for pilgrims to the city. The riders would experience their own miracle when they caught a glimpse of the chapel steeple, heralding an end to their torture.

A flurry of attacks punctuated each of the *côtes* on the city circuit after Christophe Moreau's all-day solo move ended on top of the Bohisseau, 162.5km after he began and with 25km left to race. When the peloton came together *en masse* for the last hectic scramble up the Mur de Huy's shocking incline Froome was poised, neck and neck with teammate Augustyn. Frenchman David Lelay immediately launched a kamikaze attack, blowing the bunch to smithereens. The Barloworld pair hit their own physical version of 'the wall' and started to slide back down it. Cadel Evans towed an elite group up Chapel Way past Lelay, but when the Australian suddenly crumpled Davide Rebellin pounced to nab victory for the third time in his career ahead of Andy Schleck and Damiano Cunego. Froome dug deep and reached the line in 34th place. It was a gritty display and a huge improvement on his first attempt at Flèche when he crept up the Mur for the last time almost ten minutes behind Kim Kirchin. He was proving to be a fast learner.

★

Further evidence of this took place four days later on 26 April, at Liège–Bastogne–Liège, with its own totemic ascent, *La Redoute*. At 1.7km long, the 9.8% bluff has been hoisted to legendary status by its inclusion since 1975 in cycling's oldest one-day Classic. Not as fearsome as the Mur, but at 34km from the end of a 261km route, which has already sucked the last reserves of energy from the field over a succession of small but tough climbs through the Ardennes hills, it delivers less a two-pronged rabbit punch and more a long, drawn-out uppercut to the belly.

Barloworld were prominent at the front of the peloton for the first half of the race. Froome was first home from his team in 45th, 2:54 down on Luxembourger Andy Schleck who soloed to victory after catching and unceremoniously dropping lone escapee Philippe Gilbert with 17km to go.

★

On the last day of April *Cycling Weekly* published an interview with Barloworld's British contingent – Froome, Cummings and Thomas – otherwise known as *il trio Britannico* to one of the team's Italian *soigneurs*, Mario Pafundi. While Scouser Cummings and Welshman Thomas had come through the established British Cycling system, Froome betrayed his African roots and late arrival on the British scene by struggling to understand Thomas's dry sense of humour and displaying a lack of British cycling knowledge in a tongue-in-cheek quiz.

Rumours had already circulated through the European peloton in 2008 about a planned British professional cycling team. These whisperings were confirmed in February 2009 when satellite broadcaster BSkyB announced the formation of Team Sky to be managed by Dave Brailsford, the British Cycling performance director and track guru.

Brailsford's vision of leading a British-backed team, riding clean, into the world of elite Continental cycling – and winning the Tour with a British rider within five years – was roundly pooh-poohed at the time. Now that dream was about to become reality with Team Sky's launch feverishly expected to take place in late 2009. 'It sounds like it's going to be a great option for the British riders,' Froome said.

With their contracts expiring at the end of the season and the uncertainty of whether they could find new sponsors when Barloworld exited, the trio was eager to embrace a British set-up. 'It seems that for the first time the British riders will have a team they can call home,' Froome continued. 'We're riding for an Italian-run team at the moment and so we do things the way they want them and on their terms. In a British team it would be easy to communicate, so things would run so much better. I've quickly realised that Great Britain has one of the best set-ups in the world and how they do things does make a difference to your performance.'

Asked if he felt British Froome answered, 'I honestly do. I was born in Kenya and lived in South Africa since my teens, but my family is British and my roots are in Britain. My grandparents and my brother live in Britain.' On the subject of future aspirations, he said his entire perspective of how much he was able to suffer altered after finishing the 2008 Tour de France and he expressed a desire to ride another Grand Tour 'with a goal of more than just making it to the finish'.

He wouldn't have to wait long for his second opportunity, which presented itself in the shape of the centenary edition of the Giro d'Italia due to get off to a spectacular start on 9 May at the famous Lido di Venezia in Venice.

The 2009 Giro d'Italia saw the famous three-week stage race celebrate its 100th anniversary with a spectacular and surprising route. While there were no stages featuring the massive, legendary mountain passes synonymous with the race's history (Mortirolo and Zoncolan were conspicuous by their absence), with six summit finishes, two in the opening week – at San Martino di Castrozza and Alpe di Suisi – it would be a constant battle right from the gun.

In another break with tradition, Rome would play host to the final stage with a short time trial starting and ending at the Forum. It was the first time since 1989 the race hadn't finished in Milan. Tossed into the middle of the heady mix of racing was the longest time trial in seventeen years, the second and toughest of three tests against the clock. The race kicked off in Venice on 9 May with a TTT that skirted the famous Lido di Venezia, scene of the annual Venice Film Festival.

Pre-race favourite Ivan Basso, returning to the race he won in 2006 for the first time since serving a two-year suspension for 'attempted doping', said the 60.6km Stage 12 ITT through the rugged coastal countryside of the Cinque Terre on the Italian Riviera, would be the key to the race. With this in mind, Froome and teammate Mauricio Soler went on a detailed reconnaissance of the stage's unusual route whose *menu del giorno* took in two tricky climbs – the Passo del Bracco and Passo del Termine – each with technically difficult descents.

A fraught affair on dry roads, it was a potential nightmare if rain clouds were to gather over the Cinque Terre on 21 May.

With climbing from the start, and virtually no flat stretches, there would be little chance for moments of recovery. Its abnormal *parcours* was like nothing Froome or his teammates had ever encountered. 'Rather than a time trial, it's like a stage,' Froome said. 'It'll be very important to judge your effort right from the start and eat and drink enough.' He wasn't about to get caught out on that front again. Alberto Volpi advised the riders to treat the stage 'more like a long breakaway than a time trial'. In the week leading up to the race start in Venice, Barloworld staff drove behind Froome and Soler and filmed the entire course from Sestri Levante to Riomaggiore. The team would watch the footage in preparation for the stage hoping to gain any small advantage over the rest of the field.

★

In the past year, a common reaction to Dave Brailsford's much-vaunted plans for an all-British pro team – confirmed in February as Team Sky – had been a question of numbers. Britain didn't have enough riders. He could have been forgiven for having a sly smile to himself on scanning the start list for the 92nd Giro. A quick calculation would have told him that nine British riders were set to roll off the start ramp in Venice on Saturday, 9 May 2009 – a record number of British starters in the Giro d'Italia. Nine. Exactly enough for an entire Grand Tour team.

The Brit Pack was spread across seven teams. Columbia-Highroad's ace sprinter and winner of the Milan–San Remo in March, Mark Cavendish, was the most high-profile among them, hoping for at least one, but feasibly multiple, stage wins. His team were also good bets for the opening team time trial at the Lido di Venezia – if they let him cross the line first he would become the first British rider to pull on the race leader's *maglia rosa* (pink jersey).

Barloworld even omitted two of *il trio Britannico* but for different reasons. Corti left Steve Cummings at home. Geraint Thomas fractured his pelvis and broke his nose in a nasty crash during the time trial at Tirreno–Adriatico and had only just returned to racing at the Giro del Trentino at the end of April. Froome's chief duty would be to work for the Colombian climber Soler in the mountains.

The hot gossip swirling around Venetian cafés concerned the controversial return to professional cycling of one Lance Armstrong. It had been reported the previous September that the seven-time Tour de France winner had been planning to hook up with former team manager Johan Bruyneel at Astana for a tilt at an eighth Tour title. Big Tex was back, and at the centenary Giro, his first ever appearance at the race. It was typical of the brash American to roll into town, gatecrash someone else's birthday celebrations and steal all the headlines.

On the simple out-and-back course along the huge 11km-long sandbar that shields Venice from the Adriatic Sea, Barloworld finished eleventh in the TTT although they did well to limit their loss to under a minute considering Diego Caccia and Paolo Longo Borghini came untethered from the back of their train. Columbia put Cavendish in pink, by pipping Garmin-Slipstream by six seconds.

On Stage 3, after 198km winding around the vineyards of Treviso, Alessandro Petacchi sprinted to his second stage win in two days on the undulating finish into Valdobbiadene to steal the pink jersey from Cavendish who had become caught up behind a crash with just 10km to go. The British rider was one of a large number forced to stop and step through the wreckage as a group of around 50 riders raced clear. Riding smartly at the head of the race, Froome was the only British rider to make the 57-strong front group and found himself 31st overall at the end of the day.

With Froome's able support, Soler came agonisingly close to winning Stage 4, the first summit finish of the race at San Martino di Castrozza, a mountain resort in the lap of the Dolomites. He attacked in the last 1.5km of the climb and seemed to have victory in the bag, but Danilo Di Luca, a serious contender for the overall title, timed his jump perfectly with 500m to go, streaking past Soler to take victory on the line. Froome performed sterling work in positioning Soler for his attack and came in a highly respectable 48th, 1:31 down on Di Luca.

Froome again performed manfully to put Soler in a potential stage-winning position on the brutal 25km of climbing, from Prato all'Isarco to the finish at Alpe di Siusi, which concluded Stage 5's journey through the Dolomites. The Colombian lost out again, this time to Rabobank's Denis Menchov who broke clear from a leading group of seven with 3km to go. Froome passed and dropped Damiano Cunego and Lance Armstrong to finish in 28th place. Bradley Wiggins refuted accusations that he couldn't climb with a brilliant ride up Alpe di Siusi to finish 21st. Wiggo, the British track star turned road racer, riding in his third Giro, found himself shoulder-to-shoulder again with Froome the next day on Stage 6's spring Classic-style route into Austria, a 248km trek over hilly terrain from Bressanone to Mayrhofen.

The 2009 Giro was threatening to turn into a race where formerly suspended riders (such as Basso and Petacchi) returned to recapture former glory, hopefully this time without the aid of banned substances. Michele Scarponi, who had been implicated in the *Operación Puerto* doping case, embarked on a 200km getaway with a quintet of riders in the break of the day. They were eventually reeled in by a slow-burning charge led by LPR Brakes and Team Columbia, but Scarponi managed to stay away, leaping clear of Caisse d'Epargne's Vasili Kiryienka 10km from the line and pedalling like the clappers to Mayrhofen as the peloton bore down on him. Froome and Wiggins, who was experiencing his best ever Grand Tour form to date, came in together in the second group on the road, 1:15 behind Scarponi.

Stage 7 entailed a long, steady climb from Innsbruck to the summit of the Passo Maloja, back across the border into Italy via Switzerland. In dismal weather conditions through the swish resort of St Moritz, the rain-soaked road was treacherous on the high-speed, winding descent to Chiavenna. However, the peloton, including Froome, negotiated its way safely to the finish. Robbie Hunter came close to bagging Barloworld its first stage win, but

Norwegian young gun Edvald Boasson Hagen relegated him to second place with a perfectly timed final kilometre burst of speed.

The racing continued into the second weekend with a medium-mountain day on Stage 8 from Morbegno to Bergamo, 209km in length. Team Columbia pulled another rabbit out of the hat in Kanstantsin Siutsou, who was first over the cobbled climb to Bergamo Alta and descended like a madman to the finish. Froome rode well – 41st on the stage, 31 seconds behind Siutsou – to maintain his 34th place overall, six minutes adrift of race leader Danilo Di Luca.

Spain's Pedro Horrillo suffered a horrific, career-ending crash on the descent of the Culmine di San Pietro. The 34-year-old Rabobank rider plunged 60m down a ravine, suffering fractures to his thighbones and neck, and a punctured lung. He was airlifted off the mountain. Horrillo's crash cast a dark shadow over the race and would have immediate repercussions on proceedings the following day in Milan, a criterium-style circuit taking in ten laps of the city centre.

Because Rome was stealing Milan's thunder as host to the Giro finale on 31 May, it was only fair that the business and fashion capital be accommodated – although with hindsight it might have wished the race had swung past its city limits and continued on to the first rest day in Cuneo.

The fast, awkward circuit along narrow roads and round tight corners, with cars parked along many sections, was a recipe for disaster. And so it proved with early crashes leading to a riders' protest and the stage being neutralised – even though Mark Cavendish won a spectacular bunch sprint from Australia's Allan Davis to make it three stage victories in a row for his Columbia team, the result would not count towards the GC.

Froome paid little heed to the brouhaha and rode steadily into the second week of the race. The queen stage (10) of the race was a mammoth 262km excursion over the huge Alpine mountain passes of Colle del Moncenisio and Sestrière, from Cuneo to Pinerolo. The course initially mirrored the exact route of Fausto Coppi's magnificent Stage 17 win in the 1949 Giro, a romantic homage, but landslides, closed roads and a strange conflict between French and Italian radio frequencies meant the stage had to be reshuffled. Froome again worked gallantly to put team captain Soler at the business end of the race – the Colombian eventually finished sixth as Di Luca cemented his lead with a commanding stage win. Importantly for Froome, he was finding his climbing legs as the race wore on.

Two days later it was time to test that prowess in combination with his growing time-trial skills in the long, rolling 'race of truth' from Sestri Levante to Riomaggiore. It was the stage Froome and Soler had so assiduously reconnoitred. Advance knowledge helped Froome to 34th, again Barloworld's top placed rider and two minutes faster than his team leader. Stage winner Denis Menchov tamed the intimidating route with a display of raw power, overturned a deficit of 1:20 on overnight leader Danilo Di Luca and seized the race lead.

Corti's team were still searching for their first stage win. Hunter had got close again on Stage 11's flat stage to Florence, but he was outsprinted once more by the irresistible Cavendish, who raced to his third win ahead of Alessandro Petacchi. Froome celebrated 20 May, his 24th birthday, by coasting home with the main bunch to maintain his place in the top 30 overall.

★

Dave Brailsford watched intently as Cavendish raced to victory in Tuscany's capital, birthplace of the Renaissance. He was plotting a different kind of renaissance altogether – a reawakening of British road racing in the form of Team Sky, set to debut in the 2010 season. The 45-year-old performance director at British Cycling, the man who had masterminded Olympic and World Championship track success for a host of Brits including Chris Hoy, Bradley Wiggins, Victoria Pendleton, Geraint Thomas and Mark Cavendish, was poised to make a bold attempt to transfer his unprecedented domination in the velodrome to the major road races of Europe.

Brailsford was in Florence with several of his staff to scout the British talent on show and talk to race organisers about securing a place for Team Sky in the following year's Giro. They were spotted strolling about carefully observing the operations of other teams. But any wooing of Cavendish would have to wait; the sprinter was under contract with Team Columbia. He would top Brailsford's wish list for 2011. In Bologna the next day he was surely impressed by the performance of another British rider: Chris Froome.

★

The serpentine route of the 172km fourteenth stage, starting in Campi Bisenzio, just outside Florence, with its five categorised climbs – including a nasty hilltop finish to Bologna's San Luca, the traditional finish of the autumn one-day race Giro dell'Emilia – offered perfect terrain for a break. On a sweltering Saturday afternoon Froome and Italian teammate Giampaolo Cheula found themselves in a fourteen-man move that had wriggled loose of the field after just 12km. It was a spontaneous decision by Froome and Cheula; there had been no discussion beforehand with Corti or the other Barloworld sports directors to go for a stage win. 'I felt good and I liked the route, so I decided to go with the break and try for the win,' Froome said.

At its peak the escape had built up a lead of four minutes over the chasing bunch. On the fourth climb of the day, the Category 3 Mongardino, Froome crested the summit in first place to take the King of the Mountains points ahead of Rubens Bertogliati and Evgeni Petrov. With 20km to go, the break could sense the peloton hovering closer behind, although the pink-jersey group of Menchov would never have felt threatened by the breakaway – Froome was the highest placed rider among them at over fourteen minutes down in 29th place on the GC.

As the lead group hit downtown Bologna, passing under the sandstone arch of the Pontecchio Marconi with 2.7km left to race, ISD's Andriy Grivko took flight and powered to the foot of the final climb up to the Basilica Santuario della Madonna di San Luca. The Ukrainian flew onto the bottom slopes, a lung-busting 500m section averaging 13.6%, but rapidly wilted and was soon pegged back and dropped by Froome and Australian Simon Gerrans who set an even faster tempo as the road became less steep. But in the next 500m with a devilish 16% pitch, the road kicked up again.

'I hadn't ridden this climb before, but my teammates who have ridden the Giro dell'Emilia told me about it; they said it was like the Mur de Huy,' Froome said afterwards.

Froome looked strong as he led Gerrans up the unforgiving slope – a first Grand Tour stage win was within his grasp. But as the road ramped up again, the man in Barloworld red began to toil. Past a gallery of colourfully dressed *tifosi*,[14] urging their heroes on, Froome lifted himself from his saddle and stood up on the pedals, pushing his entire bodyweight into every stroke, weaving all over the road and almost grinding to a complete halt. It was excruciating to watch.

Froome had told the Barloworld mechanics he would need extra gears for the San Luca ramps but he'd been over-ruled. He must have been cursing them roundly as Gerrans ploughed on under the *flamme rouge*, not once looking back, oblivious to the fact that Froome had blown, his head buried in his handlebars as he strained to turn each pedal. Gerrans had barely travelled 50m past the 1km banner when Froome disappeared from view, a dot in the distance. He was passed by four more riders and ended up sixth, losing a massive 36 seconds to the Australian victor in that last, grim kilometre.

'I'm happy that I was up there, but I'm disappointed that I wasn't able to finish it off,' Froome told *Cycling Weekly*. 'In the finale I really thought I could get the stage win, but the second kick up on the climb finished me off, and I didn't have the legs to get up it. I needed an extra gear, maybe a 27 cog, to spin more. It felt like my legs just seized up. I actually felt great before

14 An Italian word, literally 'typhus sufferer', for the fanatical spectators at sports events, such as football, motor racing and bike races.

that moment and was planning to go again to try and get away from Simon. Instead I just stopped and started going backwards. At least that's what it felt like.'

His only consolation was that he was hitting top form as the race entered the final week, and with more stages in the Apennines to come in the next few days he knew there were other chances to land a stage win. 'I always seem to ride into an event and get my legs going,' he said. 'Breakaways don't often make it, but the way the Giro is playing out overall means there's a chance for breaks to get away. When I've recovered from this effort I'll have another go.'

Unfortunately he spoke too soon. Stage 15, a strength-sapping, undulating course from Forli to Faenza, was a day to forget for all the British riders left in the race. Froome's legs gave out. Leonardo Bertagnolli mimicked Gerrans's win as the strongest man in a long breakaway. Froome and six fellow Brits finished in a group over 22 minutes behind Bertagnolli. Scotsman David Millar, still recovering from a broken collarbone sustained at Paris–Nice, abandoned halfway through the stage.

But Froome recovered admirably, proving again he had the legs for the high-mountain stages. In roasting temperatures and with a tortuous final climb up the slopes of Monte Petrano, Stage 16 proved to be the toughest of the centenary Giro and turned into a real battle for survival among the majority of the 172 remaining riders. To his enormous credit Froome stayed the distance and lost touch with the leaders only in the latter stages, finishing 25th, top dog for Barloworld – Soler retired with recurring tendonitis – on a day when the thermometer hit 38 degrees with a road temperature ten degrees hotter.

Froome got to cool his burning tootsies on the rest day in Chieti. He'd certainly earned it. From there on, it became an exercise in damage limitation – he shed more time on the post-rest day ascent of Blockhaus, in the beautiful Majella massif, and on the slopes of Mount Vesuvius – as the race wound its way to the finale in Rome. He even summoned a second wind to finish with the sprinters in twentieth place on the penultimate stage in Anagni. Denis Menchov survived a dramatic late fall on a rain-drenched final stage time trial to win the 100th anniversary edition of the Giro from Di Luca. As rain lashed the streets of Rome, Froome finished in 32nd place, exactly a minute behind surprise stage winner Ignatas Konovalovas to wrap up a highly satisfying debut Giro. He was 36th overall.

★

Froome and Wiggins rode alongside each other again in South Wales at the end of June as the best of British gathered for the annual national road race championships. It was a high-quality field with ten ProTour riders vying for the red, white and blue British champion's jersey. The weather conditions in Abergavenny on 28 June were hot and humid with temperatures reaching 28 degrees at the top of the dreaded Iron Mountain, better known in the cycling world as the Tumble, waiting at the exact halfway point of the 180km course.

A nervy start brought several crashes and a number of early dropouts from the large field of 190 riders. The peloton broke into pieces on the 5km ascent of the Tumble. From the town of Llanfoist the climb starts gently and ascends on a long, steady uphill drag through bleak moorland to over 400m above sea level.

In Llanfoist, Wiggins launched a fierce attack that splintered the field behind him. Froome immediately locked on to the wheel of the Olympic pursuit champion, and the pair led the race over the steep slopes to the Tumble's summit. They worked hard together on the descent to Abergavenny to build a one-minute lead over a group containing Mark Cavendish, Peter Kennaugh, Daniel Lloyd, Kristian House, Ian Stannard, Evan Oliphant, Roger Hammond, Alex Dowsett and Andy Fenn. One lap into the ten-lap finishing circuit, the lead was cut to less than 40 seconds and falling rapidly. Froome grabbed his chance and took off on a solo break, as Wiggins was absorbed into the chase group.

Thousands of fans lined the route of the Welsh town roaring Froome on as Dowsett and Fenn led the charge to reel him in.

Encouraged by the support, it looked like Froome might stay away for a famous win on his national championships debut, but Kennaugh, Lloyd and House were not finished yet and bridged the gap. The Kenyan-Brit made one last effort to shake the trio, but they streaked past him on the finishing straight, House beating Lloyd and Kennaugh into second and third place.

After his heroic efforts in the 'Rumble on the Tumble' Froome had to settle for fourth. It was a sweet victory for the plucky underdogs over the ProTour riders. But being denied a podium place was a sore one for Froome to take. 'It doesn't feel nice to miss out after being in front all day and having it taken away in the last 150 metres,' he said after the race. One consolation was the fantastic support he'd received from the roadside fans in Abergavenny. If any British fans had reservations about Froome's claim to competing for the national champion's jersey, they evaporated that day. 'It was amazing. I was so touched by the support. People were shouting my name; it was incredible. I wanted to thank them all personally and I wanted that jersey so badly,' he said. 'It was great to be very active in the race. Because of that, a lot of Brits see that I am now a Brit and I am racing there.'

★

Since there was no Tour de France to go to, Froome filled his time after the nationals with the odd small race. On 18 July, back in South Africa, he won the 150km Anatomic Jock Race, and started talks with teams about a new contract for 2010. With Team Barloworld's future uncertain and no guarantee of a new sponsor for 2010, Froome had already set his sights on changing teams for the next season.

Brailsford's Team Sky had already emerged as favourites to secure his signature. Froome's prominent showing at the nationals would only have served to enhance his chances of being invited to join the exciting new British team.

While it was hugely disappointing for Froome to miss out on riding the Tour, he took advantage of his July downtime to do something he'd never done before – watch the race in its entirety on television. And, as always with Froome, he turned it into a learning experience.

'This year was the first time I've really watched the Tour de France every day. It was frustrating not to be there, but it was also inspiring watching Bradley Wiggins in the mountains. I watched him and thought, That's what I want to do.

'I was really interested in how he lost weight and climbed so well. I've been training without eating breakfast and I feel really light and really lively. But you can't race on an empty stomach, so I never feel as light and responsive in a race.'

Diet had always been an important aspect of Froome's preparation and something he had taken seriously since back in Kenya when he was picking root vegetables to eat with David Kinjah.

'Chris has always been very into nutrition,' says John-Lee Augustyn. 'He showed me a lot of new things, all the natural products, organic food.' Augustyn tells me that since the sport had been tainted by doping scandals, diet had become an extremely important tool for riders like himself and Froome to maintain their status as, what he calls, 'natural cyclists'.

'We support each other in being clean, to race clean,' Augustyn says. 'For us I feel the key is the food, so if you look after yourself and have enough talent then you'll definitely get to the top. It just takes time. Chris is very attentive to detail in everything he does.'

Froome refuted the notion that his eating habits were quirky but admitted he liked to keep everything as natural as possible and eschewed the pasta on which Italians loved to load up on pre-race. 'I find it really heavy and difficult to digest,' he said. 'You end up feeling sleepy afterwards.'

At times it was difficult for the independent-minded Froome to adjust to the traditional food at the Italian-based team. 'Claudio Corti is old school,' he said. 'He believes in eating meat and pasta before a race.'

In an early stage of the Giro that year he recalls stocking up on fruit for the day's racing while his teammates opted for sandwiches. 'It's impossible to finish the Giro d'Italia without eating my bread rolls,' Corti told Froome. 'I find fruit easier to digest than bread,' Froome said. 'So when Corti said that, I thought, Right, well, I'm going to reach Rome without a single one of your rolls!'

★

On 9 September Froome confirmed via Twitter the news that he had, as expected, signed for Team Sky on a two-year contract. His name was among six British riders (Cummings, Thomas, Russell Downing, Peter Kennaugh and Ian Stannard were the others) to be unveiled as the first members of the new British ProTour outfit. Exciting times lay ahead. He could now officially look forward to being part of a new British cycling revolution. 'I've known for a while I'd be joining the team but I didn't actually sign the contract until 1 September,' Froome told *Cycling Weekly*.

It was an easy decision for Froome to opt for Team Sky. He had reached the end of his two-year deal with Barloworld, who were in the process of winding down anyway after boss Claudio Corti was unable to attract new sponsors for the 2010 season to replace the outgoing South African corporation. So, contract or no contract, Froome had no choice but to move on. It was fortuitous timing for him that a new British team was starting up just as he was about to enter an uncertain period in his career.

Sky was already watching his Barloworld teammates Cummings and Thomas, so it was natural, with his British passport-holder status, that they would keep an eye on Froome. His ally at British Cycling, Doug Dailey, made sure of that. Another attraction was the fact that he had already ridden in British colours at the 2008 worlds in Varese. Sky had most of the same staff – Dave Brailsford, Rod Ellingworth, Shane Sutton and company – as British Cycling. It was a familiar set-up, with coaches and riders he knew and respected, and with whom he felt comfortable. Finally, unlike at the Italian-based Barloworld, there would be no troublesome language barrier – although he had become near fluent during his time living in Lombardy and Tuscany. All Froome knew was that it felt like the right move at the right time.

'I don't think many Pro teams out there will be able to match the level of detail and the depth of back-up they are putting into place. From my point of view, as a younger rider, I want to get to the bottom of what I can achieve. I don't want to be just "going to races". I want to get the maximum out of myself and I think this team will help me do it.'

But the season wasn't over yet. He still had a few races left with Barloworld, including the upcoming Tour of Britain, and was hoping to make the British squad for the World Championships in Mendrisio in the last week in September. He would have to contain his excitement at signing for Sky for a few months more until the new team's first official get-together, set to take place in Manchester in November.

★

Three days after the Sky-signing news, he travelled to Scunthorpe with Barloworld for the start of the Tour of Britain. The highlight of the week-long race came on the showpiece final stage in London when Froome and Geraint Thomas led out the 25-year-old Italian Michele Merlo to his first ever win as a professional. Edvald Boasson Hagen took the overall title after an incredible four successive stage wins. Froome finished 50th. It had been a low-key outing for him. He'd rarely been at the sharp end of the race, content to finish with the bunch most days. But it was satisfying to return full-circle to the same tour in which he had impressed Claudio Corti and Robbie Hunter enough to earn his first fully professional contract two years before.

★

In the town of Mendrisio, on the Swiss–Italian border, on 23 September, the eve of the World Championships time trial, Froome wrote on Twitter: 'Seriously impressed with the whole British Cycling set-up at the worlds – covering every tiny detail,' before adding, with a tongue-in-cheek dig, 'The Kenyan Cycling Federation have got a "little" catching up to do.'

Local hero Fabian Cancellara of Switzerland, the reigning Olympic champion in the discipline, steamrollered to victory in front of a rapturous home support on the 49.5km circuit for his third time-trial title in four years. Froome finished a highly commendable eighteenth – 'Happy with that, but I know there are lots of things I can work on to better it,' he said. Bradley Wiggins was three places further back having been caught and passed by Cancellara after suffering mechanical problems on the final lap.

Two days after the time trial, Froome failed to finish the 262.2km road race as Australia's Cadel Evans raced to a surprise first world title with an opportunistic attack at the foot of the final climb, 5km from the finish line.

★

Froome had been due to ride his last ever race for Barloworld at the Giro dell'Emilia on 10 October. In the end he didn't compete but travelled to the start at Sassuolo to act as team cheerleader and enjoy a farewell knees-up with his Barloworld buddies at the race finish in Bologna before they went their separate ways. There would have been huge relief on Froome's part that, on his return to Bologna, he hadn't been forced to cycle up the ramps of San Luca, the scene of his Giro calamity in May. However, he would surely have been forgiven for jokingly reminding the mechanics of the nightmare of 'gear-gate' over a farewell glass of wine.

★

In his first season at Barloworld Froome had been tossed headlong into the deep end of European pro racing. The second season in Claudio Corti's team was used to bridge the gap from riding at an amateur level to keeping up with the big boys. Every aspiring pro rider who has ever pushed a pedal says that the gap between best amateur and professional is huge. Even former British stalwart Sean Yates, the great strong man, finished his first season as a pro in a state of collapse.

Each year had seen an upward shift, albeit a slightly uneven one, for Froome, from showing up at Konica-Minolta looking like a happy-go-lucky 'fun rider' to learning how to be a professional at Barloworld. Corti's coaching methods had taken him so far. At Barloworld, in terms of training and diet, they were given a free rein whereas Sky would adopt a rider–centric philosophy. Each team member would set their goals, and everything would be constructed to enable them to achieve them. Dave Brailsford couldn't believe how other Tour teams operated. 'Between races they don't even see their riders,' he said. 'They don't know where they are, never mind what they're doing. It's bonkers.'

Froome told *Cycling Weekly*: 'Racing with Barloworld was a great introduction to professional racing, but it was a lot more basic. They were on a shoestring budget. They got us to races, we rode them and then went home afterwards, but there wasn't too much interaction in-between.'

Froome was looking forward to Team Sky's attention to detail, the open, creative ethos – which would be adapted from Brailsford's own radical British Cycling model – that had trans-formed track cycling's fortunes in the UK from under-achievers to indomitable world leaders. They were poised to take this holistic, lateral-thinking, fanatically precise, sports-science approach to problem solving and the pursuit of excellence, from the velodrome on to the road. For better *and* worse, Froome felt Barloworld had been mired in the old ways, simply following the traditions laid down by generations of cycling teams before them. It was time for something new, modern, different.

Froome had shrugged off the friendly teases of Barloworld teammates that his diet was eccentric. Now it didn't matter. He was going to the right place to be unconventional. At Team Sky, idiosyncratic behaviour, an obsessive attention to minutiae, was considered normal, even requisite.

'At British Cycling you get a feeling that everyone is treated like an individual,' he said. 'They understand that people respond differently. It amazes me now, in 2009, that there are so many people who do things because that's how they've always been done.'

If the now defunct Barloworld represented cycling's past, Team Sky, with Chris Froome ready and willing to embrace their cycling revolution, was its future.

CHAPTER 9

The Thin Blue Line

The venue for Team Sky's glitzy official launch party on 4 January 2010 was the 26th floor of London's Millbank Tower, overlooking the River Thames and the Houses of Parliament. New Labour ran its successful election campaign from the same building in 1997. Since the tower was no stranger to spin, it provided an apposite setting for Dave Brailsford, the mastermind behind the foundation of the new British team and a man with a penchant for new age homilies.

As the launch got underway the words 'Inspiring a generation. Winning. Clean.' flashed up on a giant screen. *Sky News* presenter Dermot Murnaghan played host as the slick launch was broadcast live on Rupert Murdoch's rolling news channel.

The squad of riders were introduced on stage clad in their minimalist black-and-sky-blue kit. The sleek outfits were far removed from the garish collages of sponsors' names and logos sported by other teams in the peloton. Stunning-looking Pinarello bikes and plush Jaguar team cars provided expensive props for the lavishly choreographed show. Taking the mic on stage, Brailsford reiterated his ambition to win the Tour de France with a British rider within five years.

The name of Bradley Wiggins was in perpetual rotation on the news ticker running across a billboard-sized television. The undisputed team leader had finally joined in December after a protracted wrangle to buy him out of his Garmin-Slipstream contract. 'It's like coming home,' he said. The former track star had come fourth at the 2009 Tour de France with the American outfit – equalling Robert Millar's best ever performance by a

British rider, in 1984. Brailsford had ardently pursued Wiggins because he knew the team lacked someone capable of aiming for the podium at the Tour, a genuine British contender. Wiggins was the essential final piece in Sky's jigsaw.

Compared to the big bucks splashed on securing the services of Wiggins, Froome, without the British rider's stellar credentials, was definitely a bargain acquisition. In his first two seasons in Europe Froome's progress as a neo pro had been steady but unspectacular. In two whole seasons at Barloworld he had just one victory to his name – a stage of the Giro del Capo. And that was in South Africa. Third place at the Giro dell'Appennino was his best result on European soil. Indeed his only consistency had been his *in*consistency.

Froome's appeal for Brailsford lay perhaps in his untapped potential. The 24-year-old had shown flashes of talent in his two years at Barloworld. But only flashes. When the Sky supremo created a giant database of hundreds of riders and analysed their statistics with the help of the English Institute of Sport, Froome's results wouldn't have leaped off the page. He had a Europe Tour ranking of 533. Coming from a second-tier team like Barloworld meant that he didn't qualify for World Calendar race points. Not that he'd scored many on his appearances in any big races. Of the various riders Brailsford coveted for his dream team Froome wasn't an obvious pick; he was one of the 'hidden talents . . . riders on the cusp of breaking through', as Brailsford put it.

Brailsford, in his other guise as performance director at British Cycling, had been in Melbourne at the 2006 Commonwealth Games when Doug Dailey alerted him of Froome's nascent talent and British credentials. 'Doug played a pivotal role in those first impressions,' says Brailsford. 'From that moment on we took a keen interest in his development and watched him closely, especially when he was at Barloworld with Steve Cummings and Geraint Thomas.'

But unlike Cummings, Thomas, Wiggins, Cavendish and a list of others, Froome wasn't the product of anything resembling the British Cycling system. 'The first time I met Chris he didn't come across as your usual bike rider,' Brailsford says. 'Partly because of his expat upbringing but also because he learned the sport as he was going along, unlike, say, the guys who have been absolutely immersed in it and it's been their lives since they were kids.'

Brailsford's initial take on Froome as a rider was that he lacked a cycling education. 'To start with I think it'd be fair to say that he was quite impulsive, eager to be at the front all the time. He'd grind himself into the ground on some stages and pay for it days later,' he says. 'There were glimpses of obvious talent – he was a good time trialler and had shown he could climb fantastically well – but it was relatively inconsistent.'

While Wiggins, Cavendish, Thomas and crew were graduating with honours from the British Cycling system, collecting Olympic and world track gongs along the way, 'I was probably out riding a mountain bike somewhere in the Kenyan bush,' Froome said. Now he had landed in the best possible place to catch up on those lost school years.

Over the past six years Brailsford had assembled a crack team of backroom staff. Froome and Sky race coach Rod Ellingworth had crossed paths at the 2007 Giro delle Regioni when the pair had chatted about Froome's nationality. Ellingworth had been responsible for spotting young talent for British Cycling's Italy-based Under-23 road race academy. One of his most successful alumni in recent years had been Mark Cavendish. Former Australian professional, head coach and a rugged no-nonsense trouble-shooter, Shane Sutton, was in charge of dealing day to day with the riders and coaches. Sutton, who had also been Brailsford's right-hand man with the British track squad, had ridden with ANC-Halford's in the 1980s.

Also on the staff was legendary ex-British pro Sean Yates.[15]

15 During his fifteen-year professional career the popular Englishman, nicknamed 'The Animal', rode for Peugeot, Fagor, 7-Eleven and Motorola and was a teammate of Robert Millar and Lance Armstrong. He became the third Briton to wear the yellow jersey at the Tour de France, in 1994, and rode twelve Tours, completing nine and winning a time-trial stage in 1988 with a record time for the Tour against the clock. Before joining Sky he was sports director for Astana, after stints in a similar role at Team Discovery Channel. Yates worked with Armstrong during his final Tour de France victory in 2005 (since voided following an admission of doping), and Team CSC under Bjarne Riis.

From his home in Uckfield, Yates tells me that he knew very little about Froome until he appeared at Sky. 'But then again I don't pay much attention to any guys outwith my immediate team – unless you see some guy performing spectacularly or crashing every race, then you make a note of it.' Contrary to Brailsford's claim that nationality had no bearing on his original signing policy, part of the reason Sky had signed him 'was because he had a British passport. And he'd obviously shown not only a good bit of talent but also a great deal of willpower, guts and determination to come over to Europe and join a team run by Italians.'

★

Since taking over from pioneering track coach Peter Keen at the helm of British Cycling in 2004, Brailsford had continued Keen's obsession with seeking perfection in every area of cycling performance. Brailsford has a fanatical belief in micro-management and good practice encapsulated in his philosophy 'the aggregation of marginal gains'. He set in place a system whereby every area of performance was explored. The idea was that if small percentage improvements were made in numerous areas – diet, psychology, aerodynamics, ergonomics – the cumulative improvement would be substantial. In a nutshell, if you did every little thing right then almost without noticing you could achieve something big. An intriguing mix of pragmatist, idealist and dreamer, Brailsford had the radical view that if every area was exploited to the maximum, cyclists could compete drug-free at the highest level.

Brailsford had turned the fortunes of Britain's track cycling team around from a single Olympic gold medal in 72 years – Chris Boardman's track pursuit victory at Barcelona in 1992, masterminded by Brailsford's predecessor, Keen – to bagging seven gold medals from nine events at the 2008 Beijing Olympics. This was made possible by a combination of lottery funding and an obsessive approach to technical excellence.

Now he would attempt to transfer the same world-beating

'marginal gains' ethos from the track to the road and take it to its absolute limit. He demanded from his new road team the same high ethical standards he had instilled in his track riders and that meant a zero-doping policy facilitated by the 'marginal gains' mantra.

The track is the nearest thing cycling has to a controlled environment. You can feasibly target a medal if you know what time is necessary to win a race over 4,000m or 1km. But surely road racing was too big and too unpredictable? It was like comparing a sprint to a marathon. Another of Brailsford's favourite Confucius-style mottos was 'controlling the controllables'. Possible on the track where the unpredictable factors are no more than 1 or 2%; on the road it must be closer to 25%. How can you possibly control a *single* 200km mountain stage at the Tour de France let alone a total of 21 stages?

Sky's support mechanism and attention to detail bordered on the avant-garde, the *recherché*. At the team's first official get-together in Manchester in November a goodie bag was handed out to Froome and the rest of the squad that wouldn't have been out of place at the Oscars. Among the gifts were an iPhone – with a Team Sky branded cover – and Macbook Pro laptop. There were even packets of Team Sky M&Ms. A thin, sky-blue line ran down the back of the team jerseys to serve as a constant reminder of the narrow margin between winning and losing, failure and success, between being good and becoming great. 'It [the line] challenges everything we do and we ride it every day' was printed on the top tube of the sleek black Pinarello bikes. There were sky-blue stripes in the team toothpaste to match those on their shirts, bikes, official vehicles and the waistband of their regulation underpants. OK, that last one is made up, although, who knows?

A chef would travel with the team to races, installing himself in the kitchen of each hotel, sourcing local produce and cooking bespoke meals for the riders, modified to match the type of race or stage. Froome's days of Claudio Corti's bread rolls and plain spaghetti for breakfast were over. Taste, nutritional sustenance and presentation were the key to chef Søren Kristiansen's cooking.

Even the chef's 'whites' were black with a thin blue line running down the back. During a big stage race – like the Tour de France – staff would travel ahead to the next hotel and install anallergic bed sheets to inhibit the risk of any stray infection, and a thermogel mattress in the bedroom of each rider. Hotel rooms would be scrupulously cleaned and dusted before their arrival. Marginal gains.

Froome was entering a world of pampering, in cycling team terms, on a par with the Beckhams. Little wonder he proclaimed that he was 'absolutely blown away' by Team Sky. 'The way I look at it, if it's in there, they'll help me find it,' he said. 'If it's not in there, they'll turn over every stone looking for it.' And the stones would probably have thin, sky-blue lines painted on them.

★

One of the many advantages of being at Sky that excited Froome was that they had been awarded a four-year ProTour licence, which guaranteed entry to all the biggest races – including the three Grand Tours. A constant air of uncertainty had always hovered over Barloworld's annual calendar with invitations to races offered or withdrawn at short notice.

And so, for the first time in three years he would start with proper structure and a training schedule that would be precisely tailored for each race. 'I'm looking forward to being able to plan a whole season,' Froome said. 'I've never had that luxury because Barloworld has always been a wildcard team, relying on invites to the Giro or the Tour. To be able to start a year knowing what my targets are will be great.'

A carefully selected racing programme – Tour Down Under, Tour du Haut Var, GP dell'Insubria, Tour de Murcia, Volta a Catalunya, Amstel Gold, Flèche Wallonne, Liège–Bastogne–Liège, Tour de Romandie – would take Froome up to May and his second Giro d'Italia.

★

Weather conditions in South Australia in late January range from scorching to tar-meltingly hot. It was like riding a bike in a sauna. At the Tour Down Under, with his light build and classic, slim climber's frame, Froome was ill suited to the role of jobbing *domestique* on flat stages and lead-out man for Sky sprinter Greg Henderson. At the end of a sizzling week in the saddle, on his first proper outing for Sky, he ended up 76th.

★

In his first European race of the new season, the Tour du Haut Var, a two-day race on the Côte d'Azur, Froome performed well on the hilly second stage from Draguignan to Montauroux, to finish ninth overall behind the winner Christophe Le Mével of Française des Jeux.

A week later he tumbled over railings on the descent of the Formarco climb on the last two laps of the finishing circuit at the Gran Premio dell'Insubria-Lugano in Switzerland. He was incredibly lucky to walk away from the crash with only a few cuts and bruises. Among the five other riders involved in the spill was the unfortunate Rinaldo Nocentini who ended up in hospital with a broken leg.

At the Tour de Murcia, in the first week of March, Froome found himself in a high-quality field that included his Team Sky leader Wiggins, Murcia defending champion Denis Menchov and other Grand Tour contenders such as Team Radioshack's Lance Armstrong and Andreas Klöden. The *parcours* of the five-day race, with Category 1 climbs on both the second and third stages, but no mountaintop finishes, coupled with a completely flat, 22km ITT on Stage 4, played more to Wiggins's strengths. The Londoner finished third overall behind HTC-Columbia's Frantisek Rabon as Froome sunk to 55th.

It was an inauspicious start to Froome's Team Sky career and he fared little better on his next outing, the Volta a Catalunya. For years the Spanish stage race took place in June and was one of the prime races for preparation for the Tour de France. Its past winners included star Tour acts like Miguel Indurain, Claudio Chiappucci, Joseba Beloki and Roberto Heras. Since the inception of the ProTour in 2005 it had been relegated to a May slot, overlapped by the Giro d'Italia, attracting only B teams and Tour riders well off their peak form.

For 2010 the Catalonian tour was staged nearly two months earlier than previous editions thanks to the move of the popular Tour of California to May. New life had been breathed into a stale format, and now riders such as Mark Cavendish and Andy Schleck, who aimed to use it as a build-up to the Ardennes Classics, were on the start list. Like Schleck, Froome's schedule featured the triple whammy of hill classics in late April.

A decent opening time trial and a comfortable showing on Stage 2's flat run from Salt to Banyoles was as good as it got for Froome as he came undone on Stage 3 in the hills behind Barcelona, losing fourteen minutes to stage winner and local boy Xavier Tondo. He consistently gave away more minutes on each subsequent stage, reaching the finish at the Montmeló motor-racing circuit near Barcelona in 72nd place overall – specialist climber Joaquim Rodríguez seized the title. It was a disappointing return for Froome and Team Sky, whose highest placed rider, Steve Cummings, finished in 54th place.

April, the traditional month of sudden showers, turned into one of giant ash clouds and calamitous events for Froome. 'Flights cancelled, trains full, this is going to be a long drive up to Belgium!!' he tweeted on 17 April, the eve of the Amstel Gold Race (which is in the Netherlands. Didn't he know?!) He was caught up in the biggest disruption of air traffic since the Second World War. Hundreds of planes were grounded in the travel chaos caused by the eruption of Icelandic volcano Eyjafjallajökull. From 14 to 20 April ash covered large areas of northern Europe forcing twenty countries to close their airspace. Italy was among the twenty countries put on hold, and Froome was one of the 100,000 travellers affected. After a mad dash north from his new base in Prato, near Florence, Froome made it to the start line in Maastricht. Big-name Spanish-based riders like Wiggins, Carlos

Sastre, Alejandro Valverde and Luis León Sánchez were all victims of Eyjafjallajökull's wrath and failed to make the trip to the Low Countries. Caisse d'Epargne could field a team of only three riders.

Froome might well have wished that he'd stayed at home or else felt that the week of racing in the Dutch Limburg and the Ardennes were some kind of belated April Fool's hoax. The long drive north, in cramped conditions, didn't help matters. After a hellishly tough slog over 257.8km and 31 vicious climbs, he finished Amstel in 76th place, over ten minutes back on the Belgian winner Philippe Gilbert. '20km too long for these legs,' Froome tweeted. 'It's been a while since I've seen an average of over 300w for 260km.'

The next in a succession of mishaps for Froome had nothing to do with racing and arrived in the form of a news story in the *Vers l'Avenir* newspaper. The Team Sky rider had been targeted by members of an environmental group called La Coalition Nature who spotted Froome, Belgian Benjamin Gourgue and Frenchman Blel Kadri on television coverage of Flèche Wallonne on 21 April participating in 'acts of pollution'. The trio's crime: discarding empty water bottles and food wrappers at the side of the road; a common practice in riders usually tolerated by regions hosting races, with the bottles often picked up by fans and cherished as souvenirs. The group argued that Froome and his partners in crime had violated Walloon law and lodged a complaint against them at a court in Namur. During the course of a race, cyclists can get into trouble for all kinds of offences – holding on to team cars for instance – but Froome must have been one of the first in cycling history to get nailed for littering.

'It's funny that they've singled out three riders and not the whole peloton. I can see their point and can only apologise,' said Froome. 'I respect the environment, and we're starting to use biodegradable bottles at Team Sky, but perhaps the race organisers should come up with some kind of solution such as drop points for rubbish.'

His public outing as a litterbug wasn't the only notable event of Flèche Wallonne. Early in the race Froome did extremely well to latch on to a move of seven riders who surged out of the peloton over the Côte de Haut-Bois, a counter-attack aimed at chasing down a five-man escape group. Froome's group quickly ate into the breakaway's five-minute lead but their efforts only served as a spur to the peloton to up its game. A big crash 70km from the finish wrecked their chances of at least staying clear before the dreaded finishing circuit.

Froome's race slowly unravelled by the third trip up the savage incline of the Mur de Huy and, as World Champion Cadel Evans went past Alberto Contador with a final burst to take his first ever Flèche victory at the summit, Froome lost eleven minutes to finish 119th. Three days after the race Froome made light allusion to his recent bust in a tongue-in-cheek tweet: 'Got to watch my back for a while – apparently Greenpeace are after me for ditching a race bottle in Wednesday's Flèche.'

★

Liège–Bastogne–Liège completed a triple bill of Ardennes flops. Before the start of *La Doyenne* Froome appeared in confident mood, talking up his and Team Sky's chances despite team leaders Simon Gerrans and Thomas Löfkvist being affected by illness and injury in the build-up to the Classics. He thought that the change to the race route, because of road renewal works in the Côte de la Haute-Levée, would mean a bigger group of riders would come together in the final part of the race. 'Riding 260km in itself is never easy, and then racing in the Ardennes on narrow country roads makes it an even harder test,' Froome said. 'I think it will put more tension on the second part of the race towards the end.' Sadly he didn't get a chance to test his theory and arrived in Ans 138th, third from last, almost eighteen minutes behind the winner Alexandre Vinokourov.

★

Glad to see the back of Belgium and Holland, Froome headed to Switzerland for the Tour de Romandie, starting in Porrentruy on 27 April with a short, flat time trial. What could possibly go wrong? Alas, his reputation for unintentional mishaps, had preceded him. Colliding with race commissaires, riding with the wrong size of bike, wrong gears, lost out training in the hills of Lombardy . . .

'Who gets chased up a tree by a hippo?' Sean Yates says with a laugh. 'Crazy things happened to Chris that didn't happen to anyone else. Initially at Team Sky he had a bit of a reputation for stuff happening to him, like crashing at silly moments or losing his bike or his shoes at silly moments. He sort of had his head in the clouds.'

One incident in particular sticks in Yates's mind from the 2010 Tour de Romandie. 'Chris was feeling a little bit sick before the prologue so we told him to just take it easy, not to push it.'

Like the Tour de Suisse and Dauphiné Libéré, Switzerland's Tour de Romandie is a vignette of Grand Tour-style racing – time trials, sprints and mountains – crammed into a single week. For Froome and Team Sky it was perfect preparation for the upcoming Giro d'Italia. In a gentle introduction to the race, all Froome had to do was negotiate a dead flat run over 4.3km in Porrentruy.

Yates takes up the story. 'Coming into the final straight there was a tricky right-hander swooping down to the finish, and Froomey flew into the turn way too fast and ended up in a flowerbed. He wrecked himself and his bike and couldn't start the next day.'

However, injured or not, Froome had picked himself up to finish second last on the stage, 1:24 behind winner Marco Pinotti. Fortunately he escaped without any serious injuries, just scrapes and bruises, but it was enough to end his race – more a *Jour* de Romandie than a Tour. Crucially he now faced a battle to regain full fitness in time for the start of the Giro d'Italia on 8 May.

It had been a reckless piece of riding from Froome, a moment of madness. In fairness, he wasn't the only rider to have a problem on the difficult corner. Six riders took it badly and either crashed or had to unclip their foot to get round safely. Cervélo's Joaquin Novoa Menedez came a cropper and went flying into a hedge. But Froome had ignored team orders to take it easy, and they weren't happy with him.

'Chris is a bit knocked up by the crash,' Sky race coach Rod Ellingworth said, 'but he really wants to ride the Giro. He'll be gutted to miss it, so we'll do what we can to help him get fit for it. The thing with Froomey is that he's so keen that he compromises himself at times.'

It also turned out he had ridden Liège–Bastogne–Liège while ill, having woken up on the eve of the race feeling rough. But he hadn't informed Yates or Ellingworth. Another *faux pas*. It was at least, however, an explanation for his poor form in the race. But Ellingworth was disappointed that Froome had kept his illness to himself. 'I guarantee any rider who's come through the [British Cycling] academy will be up front about things like that. They're encouraged to be honest, not just grin and bear it and make things worse. With some of the riders we are fighting little bit of a barrier because of the culture they are used to. But you can't change these things overnight.'

The problem was that Froome was set in his ways. Before he joined Sky he'd spent eight years doing everything for himself, making his own way in the sport. At first he found it difficult to do as he was told. He either trained too much or in the wrong way. He raced on the rivet when he was being asked to take it easy and burned himself out chasing crazy breaks when he was needed to work for the team. Ellingworth's frustration with Froome was that 'sometimes you can tell him something but he thinks he knows the best way'. The Sky coach continued: 'Chris has got quite some talent, but he's a rough diamond and he needs a lot of polishing. I've said to him, we all make mistakes, but if you don't learn quickly enough, you'll not survive in this sport.'

Suitably admonished, Froome travelled home to Italy to recuperate from his various ailments, but not before being teased by his Sky teammates for his spectacular tumble into the flowerbed. It bore a certain resemblance, they joked, with another famous

Froome crash – at the worlds in Salzburg in 2006. 'But as Swifty [Ben Swift] said, "Chris has got some guts." He'd gone there as a Kenyan, on his own, and has done everything himself,' said Ellingworth.

Although his grazes and bruises still smarted from the crash he showed that his sense of humour had survived intact on his Twitter feed that same evening: 'Nothing broken but left a good chunk of skin on that final bend – wonder if that also counts as littering . . . ?'

CHAPTER 10

Identity Crisis

Froome's sole purpose at the 2010 Giro d'Italia was to support Team Sky leader Bradley Wiggins, who was using the second biggest race on the calendar purely as preparation for the Tour de France in July. They could never admit it publicly – the Italians would have gone loopy – but privately Team Sky was saying that the Giro was a recce for the Tour.

The race started in Amsterdam on 8 May, the first time in nine years it had visited the Netherlands, with a prologue in Groningen in the north of the country. Wiggins hit the ground running in the Dutch capital and, resplendent in his all-white British TT champion's outfit, roared around the 8.4km time-trial course, over bridges and along canals and dodging tram lines, to win by two seconds from the American rider Brent Bookwalter. It was a landmark moment for the 30-year-old in a road race: his first individual win in a Grand Tour stage and his first leader's jersey – also the first for a British professional team.

Froome completed the circuit 59 seconds slower to come 138th, but Wiggins's victory meant Sky put their disappointing Classics campaign behind them in spectacular fashion.

The next day Wiggins was brought down in a mass pile-up with 40km remaining and then got stuck behind another crash 7.2km from the finish in Utrecht, which split the field. In the mayhem Wiggins lost touch with the leading group. Froome led the charge to save the *maglia rosa* but to no avail and Cadel Evans stole his leader's jersey after an eminently forgettable single day in pink for Wiggins. 'That was absolute carnage!! Literally bodies EVERYWHERE,' Froome wrote on Twitter.

The havoc continued on Stage 3 when virtually the whole of Team Sky was involved in a crash with 10km to go and limped to the finish in Middelburg in pieces. Thanks to the nasty spill on a 90-degree turn and a stubborn chain problem, Wiggins lost four minutes. Isolated from his team and further back in the main field Froome lost double that amount.

The race left the Netherlands and restarted back in Italy, after a transitional rest day in Savigliano, and Froome was in trouble again on the 33km TTT to Cuneo. Sky's woes had continued earlier when Chris Sutton punctured shortly after the squad left the start house and had to change bikes. Then, in the closing stages, as rain teemed down on the Piedmont roads, Froome, Mathew Hayman and Morris Possoni got detached from the rear of the train after pulling big shifts at the front of the group. Despite crossing the line with only five riders coupled together, Sky still finished a close second to Liquigas-Doimo.

A day later, while ensconced in the hermetically sealed cocoon of the travelling Giro circus, Froome took time to send a message of support to his old friend David Kinjah via Twitter on the occasion of the launch of the Safari Simbaz website: 'What a legend!! Keep up the good work David Kinjah. Inspirational to say the least. This is the man who got me into cycling back in Kenya. So down to earth and full of enthusiasm – perfect for the youngsters he's helping . . .'

On Stage 7, as Tuscany's famed *strade bianche* (white dirt roads) were turned a muddy sludge brown in heavy rain, Froome arrived in Montalcino 24 minutes adrift of stage winner Cadel Evans, muck-splattered and physically broken. Evans won the mud fight, but Alexandre Vinokourov regained the race lead he'd relinquished to the incumbent *maglia rosa* Vincenzo Nibali on Stage 3.

When the first real mountains of the race loomed into view in the shape of the Abruzzese Apennines on Stage 8, Sky sports director Sean Yates dispatched Froome and Steve Cummings up the road in a seventeen-man escape group. Eventual stage winner Chris Anker Sørensen attacked from the group with 10km to race as Froome and Cummings drifted back in support of Wiggins.

The former Barloworld duo pulled their team leader through the fog to the summit finish at Monte Terminillo in sixteenth position, to lift Wiggins to 23rd on the GC. It was perfect teamwork from Froome and Cummings. After his selfless endeavour Froome lost another twelve minutes, but it had been a more solid outing from the 24-year-old after a tough opening week in which he'd failed to finish a single stage in the main peloton.

He was even looking forward to helping Wiggins again in the upcoming high mountains, and his mood was upbeat despite the development of a worrying twinge. 'I have a little issue with my right knee, there is something pulling one of the tendons, but apart from that, I am on the up,' he said. 'I hope I will be there on the climbs to support the likes of Brad and Dario [Cioni].'

The experienced Canadian rider Michael Barry had performed an outstanding job at the race as the *domestique* who shadowed Wiggins most days. Barry shared a room with Froome throughout the 2010 Giro and recalls his teammate being a restless, distracted individual, unsure of his place in the team and struggling to adapt to the expectations. 'I don't think Chris realised how he should have been taking care of himself or what he should have been doing in training,' Barry tells me. 'He was quite scatty and didn't seem fully focused on his job, but that changed.'

Inevitably the tag that Froome couldn't shake – that of being the perennial greenhorn – crops up in our conversation. Barry says that not only was Froome charmingly naïve in his first season with Team Sky but that 'he still is'.

Froome was also extremely inexperienced in the arcane ways of the European peloton, Barry says, and his lack of sophistication stood out like a sore thumb, particularly in the big races. 'It was apparent he didn't know how to ride in the peloton,' Barry explains.

'When the team taught him what he should eat and how he should train, sleep and so on he was able to begin to perform well,' Barry adds. The genial Canadian says that a combination of Froome's African background and his late introduction into the sport meant he had a completely different perspective on cycling to his European, American and Australian teammates. 'Chris is certainly an anomaly. He is just not like any other cyclist. He came from nowhere and he had no history behind him. He wasn't seen as a time triallist or a *domestique* or as a climber so he had a blank canvas to work with.'

Froome was suffering from an identity crisis. He had no defined role as a rider. In certain ways, says Barry, his innocence worked in his favour. 'Sometimes it pays to be a bit more naïve. I don't think Chris realised what his capabilities were, which was perhaps a slight disadvantage at the start but ultimately began to pay off. He also doesn't know a lot about the history of cycling or about the big riders, and so they don't intimidate him. In pressured situations not being aware of the history or who won what means that he treats every race the same. To Chris and also Edvald [Boasson Hagen] it's just another bike race. On one level that's a big advantage.'

Froome's free-spirited approach to cycling, refreshingly unburdened by the weight of history and expectation, was a trait he shared with the precociously talented young Norwegian, Boasson Hagen. It was a blessing and a curse. While it was hard for Froome to fit in he had certain advantages in his favour: he was a blank slate whose enthusiasm still informed his ambition and spirit, the fire in his belly not quashed by too much discipline.

As another teammate, Steve Cummings, said about the odd couple, 'People like them [Froome and Boasson Hagen] are lacking awareness. But sometimes it's good, because they don't realise. If you've grown up living the dream, it can be a bit daunting. When you don't know how big a race is, you just light up the road.'

Unfortunately for Froome he was in no fit state to light up any roads at the 2010 Giro. He was still suffering the debilitating effects of his nosedive into the flowerbed at the Tour de Romandie. Not to mention the illness that he'd kept quiet about at the Ardennes Classics.

'To be honest, I had a tough time coming into the Giro,' Froome told *Cycling Weekly*. 'I got sick just before the Classics and then I got sick again after them. The crash also compromised my training quite a bit. But no matter what form I had coming into this Giro, I came here to do a job. I can definitely feel my form is improving.'

In reality Froome's form fluctuated from decent one day to dreadful the next. On Stage 10, as the race traversed Italy from Avellino to Bitonto, Froome and Morris Possoni rode at the front of the peloton for 200km and were instrumental in hauling back a three-man breakaway only for teammate Greg Henderson to crash at the very point the Team Sky train were leading the New Zealander into position for the sprint finish.

Bedlam ensued on a remarkable eleventh stage to L'Aquila, over 262km, run off in monsoon conditions. Bradley Wiggins was a major benefactor of the rain-soaked madness, finding himself in a group that gained over twelve minutes on most of the overall contenders to catapult him back into the top ten on the overall standings. By contrast, Froome was in the mother of all *gruppetti* and lost a massive 46 minutes at the finish.

After Stage 12, as he celebrated his 25th birthday, Froome tweeted cheerily, 'Great day in the sun with the guys today actually the best so far this Giro . . . Overwhelmed by all the happy messages!!,' as if nothing untoward had happened the day before.

But his wildly oscillating form was confusing for him and his Team Sky superiors. 'You're only as good as your last race,' Sean Yates says of Froome's first season, 'and Chris had never really performed beyond certain flashes of brilliance, or not brilliance but he had something. One day he'd be terrible and the next he'd be back to normal. But that went hand in hand with everything else that happened with Chris. You never really knew what to expect.'

Neither Yates, nor Froome for that matter, could have predicted the headlines that would greet his eventual exit from the race on Stage 19, a day of relentless climbing. The day before, he'd finished 151st, in last place, on the stage to Brescia – coming home alone on the road over two minutes behind the entire field. The niggling knee injury Froome had complained of after Stage 8 had gradually worsened, and he finally succumbed to it on the climb of the brutally hard Mortirolo, stepping off his bike at the summit. To Froome's surprise the UCI issued a *communiqué* after the stage, referring to article 12.1.040.18 [against taking motorised assistance] and stating that he had been disqualified and fined 200 Swiss francs. 'One of our commissaires saw him holding on to a motorbike on the Mortirolo climb,' said UCI jury president Vincente Tortajada.

Riders regularly take long pulls from their sports directors when grabbing a water bottle out the window of the team car. The UCI jury typically ignores this sort of assistance and only focuses on the more serious violations.

The following day, 29 May, *Cycling Weekly*'s headline read: 'Froome disqualified from Giro d'Italia.' The truth was more prosaic as Froome explained: 'I just felt shattered, and the knee really wouldn't go any further. As a result I ended up quite far behind the team and I was even behind the *gruppetto*, so I then tried to ride up to the feed zone [at the summit of the Mortirolo] to call it a day. In order to get up there I held on to a police motorbike and I think the commissaire thought I was still racing, so he wanted me to get off the bike and officially pull out of the race as opposed to just riding up there to the feed zone. I was so close to the end of the Giro d'Italia, but I am still happy with my work.'

Froome had been lying in 104th position overall, nearly two-and-a-half hours behind the race leader, Spain's David Arroyo Durán. As his knee injury put paid to his hopes of making it to the time-trial finale in Verona, Wiggins too had cracked badly on the Mortirolo and uphill finish to Aprica. He lost 35:17 to Stage 19 winner Michele Scarponi and slipped from 26th to 35th on GC on an action-packed day when the lead overall changed hands from Durán to Ivan Basso. Next day, the Team Sky leader suffered horribly again on the hallowed slopes of the Passo Tonale – another 35 minutes gone – before salvaging some pride on the final day in Verona. Wiggins placed seventh in the 15km ITT to finish 40th overall. Basso sealed his second Giro crown on his comeback after being implicated in the *Operación Puerto* blood doping investigation.

★

'Heading over to the UK for the national champs on Sunday. It's a shame Steve and Brad won't be joining us. Bigger fish to fry,' Froome wrote on his Twitter page on 24 June. He was, of course, referring to the Tour de France. Wiggins and Cummings (and Michael Barry) were on a week-long training recce of the Alps and Pyrenees. Froome didn't make Team Sky's nine-man line-up for the Tour through a combination of illness, injury and poor form. There was no lasting damage from the knee tendon complaint and surely only bruised pride from the Giro disqualification, but it was a major blow. He needed the experience in his legs. What use was it to do something once if you never got the chance to do it again? He would have been eager to use the knowledge from his 2008 debut on a second Tour outing. And he was missing out on a recce of the high mountain passes.

Familiarity with the famous climbs of the Tour de France was key to his development. It was important to see what he had to tackle. Knowing the run-ins to the climbs and the descents helped with gear choices. It also allowed the rider to know when to conserve energy and when to leap off on an attack. Knowing what lay ahead on the road could be the difference between perfectly judging a tricky corner on a descent and performing a spectacular John-Lee Augustyn-style dismount (on the Col de la Bonette) into the deep blue yonder. It was frustrating that he wouldn't be on the start ramp in Rotterdam on 3 July, but he would just have to be patient.

On Sunday, 27 June, the hottest day of the year, and on an undulating circuit that wound through the picturesque Lancashire countryside Team Sky recorded a remarkable road race 1-2-3 at the British National Road Race Championships. Unfortunately Froome wasn't one of the winning trio. Geraint Thomas later described the route as 'harder than any World Championships course I have ridden on'. Thomas claimed his first individual professional road race victory by outsprinting teammate Peter Kennaugh. Froome failed to join his Sky teammates in an early break that built an unassailable lead and came in eleventh, a colossal 17:45 down on Thomas, who would now don the British champions jersey on Team Sky's Tour de France debut.

Sky's lofty pre-Tour ambitions for Bradley Wiggins of improving on his fourth place with Garmin in 2009 foundered in the high mountains of France. Out of sorts, knackered from his exertions at the Giro, he was never in contention and in Paris had faded to an anonymous 24th, 39 minutes behind the overall winner, Alberto Contador.[16]

It would have been stretching credulity to expect to achieve Dave Brailsford's bold projection – that Sky would win the Tour with a British rider within five years – in their rookie season. But, as Brailsford recalled later, having launched the team with a loud fanfare in January, their induction into the hothouse world of the Tour that July turned into a traumatic experience. Brailsford's podium-or-bust objective went bust. From the first mountaintop finish at Morzine-Avoriaz on, Wiggins was unable to stay with the leaders when the road tilted upwards. Sky failed to place a rider in the top ten or win a stage. By Paris Wiggins wasn't even the team's top man on GC, after young Swedish rider Thomas Löfkvist leapfrogged him in the Pyrenees to finish seventeenth overall.

'For Brad as an individual, and for us a team, certainly for myself, the suffering was agonising,' Brailsford said. 'It was a horrendous experience.'

As debut Grand Tours go it wasn't, as Wiggins called it, 'a disaster', but it wasn't far off. The crushing disappointment arose from the disparity between pre-race expectation and the realisation that it just wasn't happening. The French media slammed them for their perceived geeky preoccupation with sports science and 'numbers'. Arriving in a vast, customised, state-of-the-art, £750,000 bus with blacked-out windows – jokingly nicknamed 'The Death Star' by David Millar – driving Jaguar cars, and

16 On 30 September 2010 it was revealed that a urine sample Contador had given on 21 July, a rest day in the 2010 Tour de France, had contained traces of a banned substance, the steroid Clenbuterol. The Spaniard was subsequently disqualified and stripped of his Tour title elevating the second placed rider Andy Schleck to first on the general classification.

erecting a Perspex wall to hide their riders from public view as they warmed up on rollers before stages, endeared them to no one.

'If I could wind the clock back we would have a much more humble arrival into professional road cycling,' Brailsford said. 'There was a real element of hype, and I'll hold my hands up and say I got caught up in that. We would tone that down if we could start all over again.'

★

Froome had to make do with a less glamorous July double-header, the Tour of Austria and the Brixia Tour in Italy. Austria's national tour – run over eight stages, traversing the country from Dornbirn in the far west to Vienna in the east – was dominated from start to finish by the disgraced Italian Riccardo Riccò of Flaminia Ceramica, who returned from a two-year doping suspension to take the overall win. Meanwhile, Froome's form blew hot and cold. On his hottest day, the fifth stage from Bleiburg to Deutschlandsberg, he excelled on a gently undulating 150.3km route that resembled a Flemish spring classic. Froome joined a twelve-man break on the descent of the first classified climb after 50km and stayed with the main contenders as they battled it out in the closing stages to finish in fourth place.

On the penultimate stage Froome flew round the 26.9km time-trial circuit in Podersdorf am See to finish fourteenth behind stage winner Joost Posthuma of Rabobank. Morris Possoni reached the finish in Vienna as Sky's best-placed rider in fourth overall; Froome was 60 places further back.

In the glorious Italian Alpine location of Livogno, Froome spent a week training at altitude with teammate Davide Viganò, the picture-postcard-pretty mountain setting prompting the Twitter post, 'It's a cyclist's Mecca up here. Going to have to drag myself down to do Brixia in six days time. Shortly followed by San Sebastián and Burgos.'

It was Possoni again – racing in his native Lombardy – and another teammate, the Australian Chris Sutton, who outshone

Froome at the Brixia Tour – starting in Palazzolo on 21 July – in an all-round show of strength from the British team. On Stage 2, from Buffalora to Lumezzane, Froome matched Possoni all the way, lagging behind only when the tiny climber forged ahead up the steep slope to the finish at the summit of Cima Poffe, coming in an impressive ninth to Possoni's third. Sutton claimed Stage 3 and came mighty close to doubling up on the final Stage 5 in Orzinuovi, while Froome finished in the main peloton. On this occasion Froome shared Possoni's local knowledge of the narrow country roads of Romano di Lombardia. The stage had rolled off in Chiari, giving him a chance to revisit his familiar stomping ground and perhaps reflect on how far he'd come in the two years since he moved to the little Italian village after turning pro with Barloworld. A seemingly revitalised Froome could be satisfied with the sterling service he provided to catapult Possoni to a podium finish in second place overall, behind race winner Domenico Pozzovivo, with his own twelfth place signalling a return to some semblance of consistent form.

But Froome didn't make it to Spain for the San Sebastián Classic, a one-day climbers' race on 31 July, or the Vuelta a Burgos in the first week of August. He was struck down once more by the mystery illness that had blighted his debut season at Sky. It would take a winter visit to his birthplace of Kenya to get to the bottom of his health problems.

★

'That's the last time I get sick this year!! Back with a vengeance now . . .' he wrote on Twitter on 6 August as he prepared for the upcoming Eneco Tour, a week-long stage race crossing the border between Belgium and the Netherlands.

Froome had been drafted in as a replacement for Bradley Wiggins who would then take Froome's place at the GP Ouest-France. An average showing in the opening prologue time trial in Steenwijk was followed by two steady days of racing before he caved in on the hilly third stage around Ronse. The stage, with a multiple ascent of the Oude Kwaremont, the traditional fearsome finale to the Tour of Flanders, was a Hieronymus Bosch nightmare for Froome who lost twenty minutes. On Stages 5 and 6 he shed a combined total of 35 minutes, struggling to the line in Heers, after an interminably tough sixth stage, in last place.

On a 16.9km circuit of Genk, Froome lost over two minutes to Tony Martin, who sealed overall victory to confirm his status as a true rising talent in the sport. Short time trials didn't play to Froome's strengths, but it was an uncharacteristically slow ride against the clock. Something was seriously wrong.

Again his teammates superior efforts merely highlighted Froome's own poor showing; Edvald Boasson Hagen was in the thick of the action on every stage finish, claiming the points jersey for best sprinter and ending up third overall while Greg Henderson stormed to victory in Roermond on Stage 4.

★

'Last couple of hours before this afternoon's British National TT Champs in Wales. It's getting darker by the minute. Skin's waterproof, apparently . . .' Froome tweeted on 5 September as ominous clouds gathered over Llandeilo for the 52.7km time trial. It was another Team Sky 1-2-3 and joyously this time Froome was in among the triumphant trio. Bradley Wiggins scorched round the course to retain his title, over a minute faster than Froome who held off Geraint Thomas's challenge by thirteen seconds. Second place was a notable result for Froome; a rare beam of light that illuminated what had been months of decidedly mixed fortunes on the bike.

While Sky sent a strong team to the Tour of Britain, starting in Rochdale on 11 September, Froome left for his first ever trip to North America with a B team to compete in two inaugural ProTour races held in the Canadian cities of Québec on 10 September and Montréal two days later. French road champion Thomas Voeckler and Dutch climber Robert Gesink claimed victories in North America's first ever ProTour races, but Froome failed to finish either. He wasn't alone – the field was decimated on both occasions. Obviously the long hard season was weighing heavily on everyone's legs.

★

Season almost over – he could be forgiven for muttering 'good riddance' – Froome returned to South Africa for two weeks to unwind before he was due to fly to Delhi in October for the Commonwealth Games. Turning back the clock to his amateur days in late September he wrote on Twitter: 'Got my arse kicked this morning in a local race here in South Africa. Great to see so much young talent over here.' He even managed to get lost on one of his famous solo training rides. This time he didn't have John-Lee Augustyn on speed dial to give him directions home. 'Lost out training in the middle of nowhere, and a local to direct me who only speaks using clicking sounds . . .'

★

In Delhi on 10 October, riding in England colours for the first time, he finished 44th in the Commonwealth Games road race, won by Allan Davis of Australia with David Millar third. Three days later he was out of the medals again but a respectable fifth behind Millar who turned his road bronze into time-trial gold for Scotland.

From India he travelled to Kenya to visit his older brother Jeremy and family. Back in the land of his birth the UCI did a blood test on him in a routine check of Froome's biological passport.[17]

'I kept getting sick so something wasn't right. I'd gone to Kenya to see family and did the normal UCI blood passport tests. At the same time I said to the doctor, "Can't you scan for anything that's not right in my blood?" He came back straight away and said you're riddled with bilharzia.'

---

17 Under pressure from the World Anti-Doping Agency (founded in response to the doping scandals surrounding the 1998 Festina affair) the UCI established a 'biological passport' in time for the start of the 2008 season to monitor a rider's blood and hormone levels over a long period.

Also known as schistosomiasis, bilharzia is a tropical disease that infects millions of people worldwide, mainly in developing countries in Africa, South America and the Far East. It is the second most common parasitic disease in the world after malaria – with 90% of cases in Africa. It kills more than 200,000 people a year, according to UN figures.

Since childhood, Froome has had a fondness for swimming in the wild. Going on fishing trips and taking a dip in the lakes and rivers of Kenya were part and parcel of his outdoor lifestyle. Unfortunately bilharzia is a water-borne parasite. Microscopic larvae are released into bodies of water by a certain type of freshwater snail, thus contaminating the water.

'It [the larvae] goes through the pores in your skin,' Froome said. 'Back home in Kenya, if I even touched a river or a lake, I could have got it that way.' Once inside the skin the larvae grow into tiny flatworms that slowly start attacking the carrier in the most insidious way: they feed on the blood. The parasites could have been active in Froome's system for a year or longer before they were identified by the UCI blood test. It is a common infection in Kenya – affecting 40% of the population – but, because it can take many years for the detrimental effects of infection to be felt, most cases go undetected.

Froome had no idea he was even ill.

CHAPTER II

Solving the Riddle

Unfamiliar with bilharzia, Team Sky's doctors had failed to recognise it from Froome's symptoms and kept prescribing him medication for other less serious ailments. The effects of the disease are to some extent fairly generic, such as rashes, lethargy, fever and headaches, and intestinal and urinary discomfort. For the past year or more Froome had gone through periods of feeling tired and run down and vulnerable to illness. But his symptoms were common to other infections, so, despite his African background, the European doctors wouldn't necessarily have considered bilharzia in their diagnosis.

The parasitic infection behaves like a vampire, with a voracious appetite for red blood cells, the oxygen-carrying blood cells that are so critical to the performance of an endurance athlete. The effect can be devastating. Loss of oxygen in the blood induces lethargy in the sufferer. For a normal person, extreme tiredness impairs the ability to work. For a professional athlete like Froome it was a disaster. The bilharzia explained the conundrum which had been bugging Sky coaches since 2009: they knew what Froome was capable of – his 'numbers' were good – but they were puzzled as to why it was not happening for him on the road. Fresh as a daisy at the head of the race, pulling his teammates up a mountain one day and then the next, legs like cement, breathing as if through a straw, riding to the finish, at, aptly, snail's pace.

'It was the reason why I sometimes was abnormally tired and was just average with Team Barloworld and my first year at Sky. It drained my immune system. I was always getting little colds and coughs, nothing serious, but it always kept me from being at 100% fitness,' Froome said.

Froome's confidence was completely undermined by not knowing why his form was so haphazard, so impossible to predict. Ditto Sky and their obsession with numbers and statistics. Given the nature of the illness, it is extraordinary that Froome managed to race at all in his first season with Sky, never mind almost complete the Giro d'Italia.

Sean Yates posits the theory that the presence of bilharzia in Froome's system might even have been responsible for his lack of focus and scatty behaviour. 'It could explain why he was always crashing or always forgetting stuff. It might not just affect you physically but mentally too.'

Yates says it was certainly odd that Froome would show bursts of scintillating form, followed by weeks of nothing. Not for the first time in his cycling career he was turning into the invisible man. The effects of the bilharzia meant he wasn't performing at a level that would get him noticed or put him in the frame to be considered for the Grand Tours and were jeopardising Froome's chances of succeeding at Sky. He was slipping out of the picture, on the fringes of the squad.

'We were probably more focused on our other riders in bigger races, and a guy like him is slightly forgotten about until he shows himself to be consistently good,' Yates says. 'You tend to concentrate on your best guys.'

It was a relief to know what was wrong. Now all Froome had to do was get better. Happily, there is a readily available and fairly effective treatment for bilharzia, a drug called Praziquantel (Biltricide). It paralyses and kills the flatworm. Then the body's natural immune system kicks in and finishes the worm off. Or at least that's the theory.

In January 2011 Froome underwent the first of three bouts of treatment. As effective as it was, biltricide wasn't without its side-effects. He said the medication was 'basically like taking rat poison . . . It hits everything in your system in the hope that it kills off the infection. My readings [from blood tests] have dropped from 500-something to around 100. They have to go to zero.' He would get another test in six months time to assess if the bug was still active in his system. It would be timed to coincide with the end of the Tour de Suisse, the final preparation race on his schedule before the Tour de France in July. Obviously he was hoping to make up for the disappointment of missing *La Grande Boucle* in 2010.

★

After a good few months of training in South Africa, Froome returned to Europe and headed straight for Mallorca in late January for Team Sky's first training camp of the new season. Fresh from the warmth of Johannesburg he arrived to see snow on the peaks of the Serra de Tramuntana during stints of climbing training.

The drugs seemed to have worked. Froome was cautiously optimistic. But he'd been burned by the bilharzia too many times before to relax completely. The medication kept the parasites at bay, enough at least for him to get on with his first race of the season, the Tour of Murcia in the first week of March.

After three years in Italy Froome moved to Monaco, the week before his much-delayed race debut in Spain. 'It can be a strange place, but you get from it what you want,' he said. 'There are some people who spend their time in the casinos, but for a bike rider Monaco's perfect. I swim most days in the sea, and it's ideal cycling territory.' The ostentatious wealth of the principality hadn't curbed his love for African bush culture. In his spare time he enjoyed going spear fishing in the Mediterranean, getting 'some odd looks walking up the beach past tourists'.

Russell Downing was his roommate at the three-day stage race in south-eastern Spain, and tweeted in jest on the eve of the start in the small fishing town of San Pedro del Pinatar, 'Loving being back in a room with Froomey my roomie in Murcia. He forgot his Kenyan skirt though.' Froome replied jovially, 'It's called a kikoy[18] . . . I moved house/country last week, hence the missing "skirt".'

After his protracted recuperation, Froome eased himself back into competitive action at the Murcia race, finishing 62nd overall. He was well off the pace set by eventual race winner Alberto Contador on Stage 2's finishing climb to the summit of the Category 1 Alto del Collado Bermejo, losing over eight minutes to the Spaniard, but managed a top twenty finish in the final ITT in the city of Murcia.

Initially the course of bilharzia treatment seemed to have done the trick, and he mined a rare seam of good form at a trio of races in March and April. On the opening stage of the Volta a Catalunya, Spain's second biggest bike race, a rusty Froome 'felt like the motor bikes were setting the pace uphill' going up the Category 1 Alt de Sant Grau on the road to Lloret de Mar, and he did well to finish with the peloton. Throughout the week in Catalonia, Contador was once again the form man, stamping his authority on the race with victory on day three, the mountainous queen stage (3) from La Vall d'En Bas to Andorra-Vallnord. Froome lost nine minutes, but his Colombian teammate Rigoberto Urán soared to sixth place on the overall standings.

However, on Stage 5, a 213.5km slog south hugging the hemline of the Murcian coastline from El Vendrell to Tarragona, Froome joined a four-man break on the ascent of the stage's first categorised climb, the Category 2 Alt de Fatxes. The quartet – comprising Jelle Vanendert, Rémi Cusin, Francesco Masciarelli and Froome – built up a maximum advantage of 5:20 with 65km to go, but the presence of Masciarelli, 1:57 down on Contador and thus the race leader on the road, plus the sprinters' teams collective desire for a bunch gallop ensured the break's demise. But the escapees put up a valiant effort – Froome's trademark dogged resistance to the fore – and were overhauled close to the finish in Tarragona.

18 Froome is fond of wearing his *kikoy* – an East African version of a wrap or sarong – after a stage race or Grand Tour.

Disappointment was tempered by the thrill of being in a meaningful piece of action, and Froome took huge encouragement from his outing in Catalonia, finishing comfortably with the main bunch over the final two stages to end up 62nd overall, behind race winner Contador, by the finish in Barcelona.

There were further encouraging signs at the Vuelta Castilla y León, in north-western Spain, that the worst of the bilharzia was behind him. On Stage 3's key mountain stage he took advantage of Contador's mechanical problems in the last 3km to out-climb the Spaniard up to the mountaintop finish at Lagune de los Peces and finish a strong twentieth, only 41 seconds behind the stage winner Filippo Savini.

Froome finished tenth in the time trial the next day, completing the 11.2km course in Zamora in a blistering time just 38 seconds slower than Contador. After five days racing at full gas Froome wound up an impressive fourteenth overall, Sky's second-best finisher and only 1:32 adrift of race winner Xavier Tondo.

Froome's streak of fine form continued at the Tour de Romandie at the end of April. Drafted in as a late addition to the team in place of the ill Michael Rogers, on the evening of the opening day he tweeted that he was 'happy to report I stayed upright and didn't demolish a flowerbed in this year's Tour de Romandie prologue!!' While the landscape gardeners of Martigny may have breathed a sigh of relief, 88th place was an average opening salvo by Froome although he made up for it in some style over the next two stages.

On a cold, rainy day in Switzerland, he went over the top of the first of two Category 1 climbs, the Col du Pillon, in fifth place to finish eighth on Stage 1, just behind Cadel Evans, at the summit finish in Leysin. A delighted Team Sky race coach, Rod Ellingworth said: 'Froomey's happy with his performance and we're pleased with him as well. He'll be our main GC contender from now on, because we're expecting him to put in a good show in the time trial on Saturday and he seems to be in great condition.'

Froome was prominent again on the next day's punchy, rolling course to the hilltop town of Romont, and led Team Sky home in eleventh place, two seconds behind stage winner Damiano Cunego. It didn't quite work out as Ellingworth had hoped for Froome in the penultimate stage time trial. Well positioned in sixteenth overall, less than a minute behind race leader Pavel Brutt, Froome laboured on the undulating 20.1km course from Aubonne to Signal-de-Bougy to finish in 50th place, 1:49 adrift of winner David Zabriskie and 1:31 off the pace of teammate Bradley Wiggins. But fifteenth place overall, top Sky man again, by the race finish in Geneva was a highly commendable return. It showed he was a growing force in stage races. A final stage victory for Ben Swift rounded off a satisfying week for Sky as Cadel Evans took his second stage race win of the season.

It seemed that Froome was approaching something like his best form when the bilharzia, slowly but surely, began to rear its ugly little head again, undermining his performances at the Tour of California in mid-May, where he finished 66th overall and then the Tour of Luxembourg at the start of June, placing 71st. Once again his confidence was shattered by his yo-yoing form.

The pattern continued at the Tour de Suisse. With the Tour de France looming larger and larger on the cycling horizon, the nine-day race represented the last major stage race for the overall Tour contenders and sprinters to get an important block of racing in their legs. Froome put in a solid opening prologue TT around the 7.1km course in Lugano to finish eleventh, climbed to twelfth the next day in the mountains to Crans-Montana, lifting him to ninth on the GC, but then it all went haywire again. 'I was just feeling great, and then the next mountain stage came and I couldn't even stay on the wheels, let alone think of attacking.'

And the suffering wasn't over yet. Over eighteen minutes were leaked on Stages 3 and 4 and nearly 22 minutes atop the *hors catégorie* Triesenberg/Malbun ascent. He salvaged some pride with ninth position in the final ITT test, but by then the damage had been done and he slipped down the overall rankings to 47th as Levi Leipheimer pipped Damiano Cunego to win by four seconds overall.

After the Tour de Suisse, and feasibly still in contention for a Tour de France place with Sky, Froome started a second course of Biltricide. This time it appeared to have finally rid him of the parasite, but it was too late. The extended period of treatment and recovery had effectively ruled him out of consideration for the Tour de France.

In the last week of June he travelled to the north-east of England for the British National Road Championships. 'Kikoy is packed. Hope they let me start,' he tweeted. They did, but unfortunately he didn't finish the race. As Bradley Wiggins soloed his way to victory in the village of Stamfordham, Northumberland, to add the national road race title to his time-trial one, Froome abandoned. Three long loops taking in the punishing double-ramped climb of the Ryals proved too much for his tired legs. It was another clean sweep for Sky: defending champion Geraint Thomas and Peter Kennaugh claimed second and third respectively.

In a stroke of catastrophic bad luck for Team Sky, Bradley Wiggins only lasted a week at the Tour de France in his British champion's jersey. On Stage 7, from Le Mans to Châteauroux, he was forced to quit the race with a broken collarbone after being caught up in a big crash in the peloton with 40km remaining. Wiggins's injury woes coincided with an easing of Froome's health worries.

★

'Finally 100% healthy again and raring to go!' Froome tweeted cheerily on 12 July. With, fingers crossed, the tropical disease finally behind him, he could look forward to the Brixia Tour, a five-day Italian stage race at the end of July, and then a possible first appearance at the Vuelta a España, starting in Benidorm on 20 August.

Health restored, Froome could concentrate fully on training and racing for the first time since he had joined Sky. When his form wasn't being devastated by the grim infection Froome had felt a huge benefit from the influence of former top-class pro Bobby

Julich, brought into the Team Sky coaching set-up for the start of the 2011 season. Through the American's wisdom and gentle coaxing, the team were, as Julich put it, 'about to discover a butterfly that had once been a caterpillar'. When Julich was assigned to Froome for the 2011 season his task was to round off the rough edges and bolster Froome's fragile confidence. One thing that wasn't in doubt was Froome's dedication to improvement.

'From day one, his attitude and work ethic were phenomenal,' said Julich. What baffled the Sky coach were the results from Froome's early season lab tests. Julich was so stunned he thought the machinery must be faulty. 'When we started getting some consistent data on him between January and March, some really impressive numbers popped up,' Julich said. They were so striking that he asked Team Sky race coach Rod Ellingworth if the machine had been calibrated correctly because 'these were the numbers of a guy who would finish on the Tour de France podium'. Ellingworth checked Froome's SRM PowerMeter[19] and, to Julich's astonishment, said the results were accurate.

On first hooking up with Froome, Julich sussed straight away he was rather chaotic (not an unusual trait among novice riders). 'He was a real tinkerer – always changing his shoes, his training, his diet or whatever. As soon as I met him, I could see that he was switched on professionally, but maybe he was a bit over his head in the day-to-day life stuff.'

Julich also noticed Froome had continued to train too much even when his body was weakened by the parasite, 'which had knocked his confidence as well as his energy levels'. And when he was fit to race, Julich said Froome was prone to making mistakes and was being hampered by his tactical naïvety.

Beyond teaching Froome life-management skills, the American says somewhat modestly that his input was very basic; he helped develop Froome's training plans and, perhaps most importantly, imparted the wealth of his experience as a top-class rider who had finished third at the 1998 Tour de France.

---

19 The SRM PowerMeter is a training system mounted on the bike. It measures the power output in watts produced by the rider, which is displayed on a screen attached to the handlebars.

At the Brixia Tour in July, Julich recognised all the good and bad traits that made Froome such a challenge. He was a Jekyll and Hyde character on a bike. And this had nothing to do with any lingering physical ailments. As far as the doctors were concerned that was behind him. This was a mental issue.

'You could see those glimpses of greatness,' said Julich, 'but again he was still making those mistakes in racing – going too early and blowing himself up, going too deep.' In short, 'Chris didn't know how to race.'

★

The Brixia Tour kicked off in Ponte di Legno in the north of Lombardy on 20 July. That same day Froome might have cast an envious glance south-west to Pinerolo, near Turin, as teammate Edvald Boasson Hagen rode to his second stage win as the Tour de France crossed the border into Italy. While Boasson Hagen took the plaudits in Pinerolo, Froome had to make do with another mixed-bag performance at the Brixia, finishing 45th by the race finish in Verona.

'I needed to teach him how to get the watts out at the right time,' Julich said. 'To do that we tried to hold him back in the first few days of big stage races, get him to race steadily. We started focusing much more on the way that he raced – his calmness, his confidence, his technique, the way that he moved in the peloton, the ways he saved energy.'

A massive advantage for the pair's working relationship was that Froome's Monaco base was a short hop along the Côte d'Azur from where Julich lived in Nice.

'Bobby's played a huge part in keeping me on the right track,' Froome told *Procycling* magazine. 'We meet quite often to talk about training and plans going forward, and obviously Bobby's done his time in the peloton, and there's an abundance of knowledge that comes with that. I would say Bobby's played a really big part in getting me ready for the Vuelta and in moving me forward this season.'

Sean Yates is unequivocal: Julich was dead set on solving the riddle of Chris Froome. 'Bobby was the perfect guy for Chris because he gave him a lot of attention and spent a lot of time nurturing him, coaxing him. He really wanted to find out why this guy was not performing. Can we get more out of him? Why is he so inconsistent? He wanted to get to the bottom of it and sort it out. Then suddenly you get the finished product and you get Froomey flying.'

Julich was hired to mentor a number of Team Sky's younger riders but with his main focus on Froome, a role that is unique among the ProTour teams. 'The directors are busy – driving to and from races and so on – so looking after a rider's training becomes very difficult,' he said. 'How can they really follow them, analyse them, organise them?'

'You can only take a person on face value to a certain extent and when you're trying to win races or you're under pressure to put the best team out you don't have so much time to wonder why this guy isn't performing – that's more a job for the coaches,' confirms Yates.

From one of Julich's coaching reports, Yates noticed Froome had shed a significant amount of weight, one indication that Julich's methods were working. 'In April or May 2011 his weight was 73kg, and come September it was 68kg. With that 5kg loss everything started to fall into place. It was the catalyst for his form going into the Vuelta.'

While Froome was blowing hot and cold at the Brixia Tour, Team Sky leader Bradley Wiggins was at home with his feet up, watching the rest of the Tour de France on TV and waiting for his collarbone to knit. Before the crash, Sky coach Shane Sutton had said, 'Wiggins is in the form of his life.' So Wiggins had to set a new target: the Vuelta a España. It would be his first time at Spain's biggest race and it would help top up his form for the world championships in Copenhagen thereafter.

The Tour of Poland at the end of July provided Froome with the perfect week-long workout to hone his race sharpness – he coasted to 85th overall – and he enjoyed a quick trip to the UK to take part in the 2012 London Olympics road race test event, the London-Surrey Cycle Classic, on 14 August.

Froome soaked up Julich's advice and approached the Vuelta ready and primed to perform his role as Wiggin's mountain *domestique*. 'I'm really looking forward to the mountain stages and doing everything I can for Bradley to help him in the GC,' he said. 'Obviously if an opportunity presents itself to get a stage result then I'm all for it.'

Under Julich's watchful eye, Froome trained hard in the hills around Monaco, as Wiggins prepared for the Spanish heat on a turbo trainer in his shed with the heaters on full blast. The likely sweltering temperatures in Spain wouldn't be a problem for Froome, accustomed as he was to African summers.

At the back of Froome's mind lurked the realisation that his two-year contract with Sky was coming to an end and there had been no talk of an extension. He badly needed to come up with the goods – any goods. His last win, his only professional victory, in any race had been with Team Barloworld at the Giro del Capo in South Africa on 5 March 2009 – 29 months ago.

If he didn't make an impression at the Vuelta then it looked probable that he could be invisible for good in 2012. He was on his way out. The Vuelta was less a bike race, more a last-chance saloon. 'If there were any nerves, it was around being selected for the Vuelta because I wanted to have a really big goal for the season,' he told *Procycling*.

Sky teammate Steve Cummings, who had ridden with Froome in Poland, says there were still no guarantees that Froome would make Sky's final Vuelta selection, even by the end of the Polish stage race on 6 August. 'They were still mulling over whether to put him in the team for the Vuelta. He was on the way out of Sky,' says Cummings. The British team eventually confirmed their nine-man line-up four days before the start of the Vuelta, with Froome on board. 'Froomey was going so well, his numbers were great, and I was really happy because he was a guy who worked so hard to improve and he finally got what he deserved,' adds Cummings, who was leaving Sky for BMC Racing at the end of the season and therefore wasn't selected.

Above: Chris Froome on the winner's podium at the 2006 Tour de Maurice in Mauritius. The 21-year-old sealed his first ever stage race victory after climbing to the Stage 2 win up the volcano in Curepipe.

Below: Froome finished fourth overall at the GP Tell in Switzerland, the second last round of the 2007 UCI Nations Cup, in the colours of the UCI development squad.

Above: A smiling Froome receives a massage at the Tour of Japan in May 2007, where he finished 6th overall after a terrific solo victory on Stage 6. *John Robertson*

Below: Froome rode in the Under-23 individual time trial at the 2006 UCI World Championships in Salzburg where he collided spectacularly with a race official in the first 150m. *Roberto Bettini*

Left: Froome races to sixteenth place in the 53km time trial from Cérilly to Saint Amand Montrond on Stage 20 of his debut Tour de France in 2008. He finished 84th overall. *Roberto Bettini*

Below: Froome (right) was back in South Africa in March 2009 to race with Team Barloworld at the Giro del Capo where he won Race 2 to claim his first win as a professional. *Raymond Cox*

Above: Froome points to Sky teammate Bradley Wiggins, in the race leader's red jersey, as they cross the line together at the summit of La Farrapona Lagos de Somiedo on Stage 14 of the 2011 Vuelta a España.

Left: Froome celebrates as he crosses the finish line to win Stage 7 of the 2012 Tour de France from Tomblaine to La Planche des Belles Filles. *Getty Images.*

Above: Froome stands just below his teammate, Bradley Wiggins, at the end of the 2012 Tour de France, determined to win the following year. *Getty Images*

Left: Froome prepares for the men's individual time trial at the London 2012 Olympic Games, where he would win a bronze medal. *Getty Images*

Above: The podium of the Tour de Romandie (left to right) second-placed Slovenian Simon Spilak, overall winner Chris Froome and third-placed Rui Costa of Portugal. *Getty Images*

Below: Froome at the 2013 Critérium du Dauphiné: seen in action during the queen Stage 7 between Le Pont-de-Claix and Superdévoluy. Winning the Dauphiné was a crucial part of his preparations for the Tour de France. *Getty Images*

Left: Froome approaches the summit of Mont Ventoux on Stage 15 of the 2013 Tour de France, breaking away from Colombia's Nairo Quintana in thrilling style in the final kilometre to secure the stage. *Getty Images*

Right: Froome wears the King of the Mountains jersey on the podium after Stage 19 of the 2013 Tour de France from Bourg-d'Oisans to Le Grand-Bornand. He held the famous polka dot jersey, awarded to the best climber, for five days of the race. *Getty Images.*

Above: Winner of the 2013 Tour de France, Froome, in the *maillot jaune*, celebrates with Team Sky teammates as they cross the finish line together on the Champs-Elysées in Paris. *Getty Images*

Below: Froome atop the podium in Paris, surrounded by former five-time Tour winners Miguel Indurain, Eddy Mercx and Bernard Hinault. *Getty Images*

But Froome didn't feel driven to perform in order to secure a new contract or through a need to prove himself. He simply wanted to get himself to the start of Spain's national tour in Benidorm on 20 August and get on with the race. 'It just feels that every race I'm going to, the form is getting better and better,' he said. 'I'm just really looking forward to getting stuck in to the Vuelta.'

Froome being Froome, even getting from his home in Monaco to Spain's Alicante coast in time for the start of the most important race of his career to date was not as straightforward as it should have been. After his morning flight from Nice was cancelled on 18 August he was forced to take a circuitous route via the party island of Ibiza, finally arriving at the Team Sky hotel in the wee hours of the morning, sixteen hours after his teammates. Most people would have been a nervous wreck after such a long, tiring, stressful journey. Not Froome: 'In those situations, you aren't going to get anywhere faster by getting uptight,' he told *Cycling Weekly*. 'That's the life of a cyclist – airports and waiting around.'

When quizzed about his Team Sky contract, or lack of one, for 2012, he said, 'I haven't sorted anything out for next year but, all being well, I'd like to stay.' In his book, *Sky's the Limit*, Richard Moore says that Sky had offered Froome a new deal for 2012, at a rumoured £100,000 a year – a modest sum. Moore quotes a Sky insider who said the offer 'was effectively "goodbye"'.

CHAPTER 12

Froomey is Shining

Team Sky was in fine fettle going into the Vuelta a España. Wiggins's broken collarbone had almost fully healed, and there was, according to Froome, 'a huge buzz around the team'. Sky's nine-man line-up was looking forward to throwing their substantial weight behind undisputed leader Wiggins's GC aspirations.

The 2011 Vuelta turned out to be one of the most eventful and thrilling in the race's history. Designed for climbers, it was the most mountainous route in years and had only one ITT, over 47km. It produced the third closest finish ever. Nine different riders donned the red leader's jersey and a totally unexpected winner claimed it when the race rode into the finale in Madrid on 11 September. And because the route returned to Spain's cycling heartland, the Basque Country, for the first time in 33 years, there was a huge swell in the number of rabid roadside fans.

On the last visit to the fractious region, in 1978, during a period of huge political turmoil in Spain, stages had to be shortened, there were barricades on the streets and the final time trial was cancelled after political demonstrators knocked riders off their bikes. The Vuelta left the Basque Country under a huge cloud. On its return in 2011 no extra security was put into place. Political tension and threats of violence had eased since the Basque separatist group ETA[20] had declared a partial ceasefire. The only warning on the pre-stage press briefing was about the possibility of another heatwave. Passionate Basque cycling fans, who display a quasi-religious fervour for the sport,

---

20 *Eukadi Ta Askatasuna* ('Basque Homeland and Freedom') is an armed Basque nationalist and separatist organisation.

springing from their obsession with autonomy, would be out in droves.

An especially strong Vuelta field was headed by defending champion Vincenzo Nibali, the Spaniards regarded as the Italian's most likely rivals, Carlos Sastre, Luis León Sánchez, Joaquim Rodríguez and Igor Antón, plus Russia's two-time Vuelta champion Denis Menchov. All of these riders featured prominently, but in a wild twist to the tale, none of them ended up in contention for overall victory. Instead, after eight riders had swapped the race lead, the battle for the red jersey was fought out between two riders expected to act as key lieutenants to more experienced riders on their respective teams.

'Sky got off to a bad start in the short 13.5km TTT, on a tricky technical course with complex cornering at Benidorm's colourful beachfront. Kurt Asle Arvesen crashed early, splitting the team and putting them immediately on the back foot.' Then four riders, including Froome, went off the front, detaching Xabier Zandio who was forced into a desperate chase to bridge the gap (the finishing time is taken on the fifth rider). To make matters worse Steven de Jongh, Sky's sports director in the team car, was trying to relay instructions to the front four to ease up in the closing kilometres to allow Zandio to rejoin them, but the noise from the crowd drowned him out. In the end Zandio tagged on to the back of the decimated train as fifth man, but Sky finished third from last, losing 42 seconds to Leopard Trek. Given the presence of British Cycling pedigree time-trial specialists it was an embarrassment. Australian Chris Sutton restored some pride the next day, with a perfectly timed move on the uphill sprint finish into Playas de Orihuela, for his maiden Grand Tour stage win and Sky's first Vuelta victory.

In torrid heat and on roads familiar to him from his March outing at the Tour of Murcia, Froome ushered Wiggins safely to the Stage 3 finish in Totana as the race prepared to enter the high mountains in earnest on the next day's summit finish at Sierra Nevada.

Froome led Wiggins through the mountains like a devoted St Bernard. It was on the exposed slopes of the ascent of Sierra

Nevada on Stage 4 that he translated those impressive numbers which had amazed Julich into performance for the first time in his Sky career. In sweltering conditions Froome followed orders from Wiggins to crank up the pressure with around 5km to go on the final 23km haul to the Andalucían peak's summit. (Heat exhaustion had forced Mark Cavendish to step off his bike and abandon the race on the Category 3 Puerto de los Blancares climb, possibly with one eye on the upcoming World Championships.) The stage route resembled what 'sierra' means in Spanish – the serrated cutting edge of a saw. As Wiggins sat comfortably in his slipstream, Froome's steady increase in tempo into a strong head-wind blew Euskaltel's main hope, Igor Antón, away and whittled the select front group down from 40 to 30 riders, with Daniel Moreno surging past Chris Anker Sørensen for the stage win.

On his Twitter page that evening Froome posted a link to his Training Peaks data for his selfless ride up the Sierra Nevada. It gave a fascinating insight into the intense effort required to compete at a Grand Tour. According to the statistics, Froome averaged 358 watts and a 153 heart rate on the final climb. The last twenty minutes of the stage he averaged 361 watts and maxed out at 165 on the heart-rate monitor. He had ridden himself into the ground for Wiggins. Incredibly he had felt uncomfortable all day and found it hard to up the pace, only starting to feel good when the accelerations from Sørensen and Moreno started with 7km to go, nevertheless he could rely on an innate ability to go deep into the hurt locker. What kept him going when he was riding on the limit? 'I go into survival mode and tell myself that the other riders have to be feeling the same as I am,' Froome said.

What no one could have predicted – not Froome, not Wiggins, not anyone at Team Sky – was that he would become totally reliable as the Londoner's loyal right-hand man every time the road hit a steep incline. Sky's instructions were for Froome to put in a solid ride in the sole service of Wiggins and then hang on for dear life. He was exceeding that expectation by a street. And he was about to dispel all accusations of an erratic nature with a string of stunning rides.

On Stage 5, at the Andalucían hilltop town of Valdepeñas de Jaén, as diminutive Spanish climber Joaquim Rodríguez opened the turbo chargers in the final kilometre up the 23% ramp to the finish, Froome and Wiggins crossed the line together just twenty seconds back. Again on the cruelly steep uphill conclusion to Stage 8 in San Lorenzo de El Escorial, 45km north-west of Madrid, the British duo was shoulder to shoulder as they approached the line in the shadow of the castle and monastery of El Escorial, the historic residence of the kings of Spain since the sixteenth century. Rodríguez proved himself again untouchable on the acute climb up to the royal site to soar into the race lead. But the Siamese twins, Froome and Wiggins, limited their losses once more to just twenty seconds at the line with each moving up two spots in the GC, Froome in nineteenth and Wiggins a place behind. Sky's new lead partnership, with Froome as able lieutenant to Wiggins, was proving to be highly effective.

The race reached its first 'real' summit finish on Stage 9's 179.5km leg from Villacastín to La Covatilla, a 2,000m peak located above the ski resort of Sierra de Béjar in the high mountains of southern Salamanca. 'Had my bike scanned for a motor at the finish today. I wish it were that easy. No shortcuts in this sport!!' Froome said at the end of an exhilarating stage.

Two Irishmen, Dan Martin and his cousin Nicolas Roche, attacked with 5km to the summit. As one half of the Irish tandem, Roche, foundered in the closing stages, Martin set off alone, joined by Vincenzo Nibali, but the pair was soon caught by the irrepressible Froome, driving the red jersey group of Rodríguez up the mountain, with Wiggins locked to his wheel. Froome's unrefined riding style – all bobbing head and angular arms, flapping like a wounded gull – while a trifle unpleasing to the eye was proving extremely effective in action. If David Kinjah was watching he might have declared, 'Look, *murungaru* is starting to fly!'

After Froome was done burying himself in the strong crosswinds, in the process putting race leader Rodríguez in all sorts of trouble, Wiggins took over in the final 2km and forced a relentless pace as the small elite group of seven riders passed under the *flamme rouge* marking the final kilometre. Just as it looked as if Wiggins might ride everyone off his back wheel and on to victory, Martin jumped clear with 200m to go to take a fine win ahead of Dutchman Bauke Mollema, whose second place lifted him into the leader's red jersey. Rodríguez's hopes melted into the baking hot asphalt as he crept home 50 seconds adrift. 'Froomey is shining' as Wiggins put it afterwards.

It was another sensational performance from the British duo. They had performed like a tag wrestling team. Froome put in an awesome turn on the front to first reel in the day's earlier escape duo – Sebastian Lang and Pim Ligthart – and then left the rest scattered across the mountain in his wake before Wiggins provided the final knockout blow in a blistering finish. The GC shake-up saw Wiggins move into thirteenth, exactly a minute behind Mollema, with Froome a place and three seconds further back. The two of them were perfectly poised to excel further in the long time trial in Salamanca the following day where it was assumed Wiggins, a specialist against the clock, would exert his authority over the younger, less experienced Froome. As Sky sports director Steven de Jongh commented: 'Tomorrow we are in Bradley's playground.'

There was speculation before Stage 10's 'race of truth' show-down that Froome might be ordered to take it easy and save himself for the coming mountain stages in servitude to Wiggins. But de Jongh quashed the rumours, saying, 'Froomey also has some good time-trialling skills and will be going full gas as well.'

On the rolling 47km course around Salamanca, Froome was up against arguably the three best time triallists in the world in the shape of three-times Olympic track pursuit champion Wiggins, Switzerland's quadruple World Time Trial Champion Fabian Cancellara and the young German pretender to his throne, Tony Martin. The stage was set for Wiggins to become only the fifth Briton to lead the Vuelta a España and gain some serious time over his rivals. The distance and course suited him perfectly – the route climbed from Salamanca towards the village of Morille before looping back down into the city's Plaza Mayor.

Wiggins flew off the ramp like a greyhound out of the trap and set the fastest time after 13km, the first intermediate split, passing it a second quicker than Martin. Froome was also going well, though he trailed his team captain by 24 seconds. But Wiggins had miscalculated his effort. He'd gone too hard too soon. By the next time check, at 30km, he was now nineteen seconds slower than Martin. More surprisingly, his lead over Froome had collapsed; it was now just one second. What began as a challenge for the overall race lead had turned into an exercise in damage limitation.

By contrast Froome had paced his effort to perfection. As Wiggins wilted he grew stronger. Sports director Marcus Ljungqvist was egging Froome on with time updates and words of encouragement through his radio earpiece: 'You've got a really good time . . . Just keep going!' Froome said later he'd felt rough after his Herculean efforts for Wiggins the day before at La Covatilla. He was hurting badly and didn't feel he was going particularly fast. 'It was fantastic to have that information and encouragement – at least I knew I wasn't doing too badly.'

He wasn't doing too badly at all; in fact he had pulled off the performance of his life to take over the race lead from Mollema. At the stage finish he was second behind Martin, but 23 seconds ahead of Wiggins, who moved up to third overall. Incredibly, without a European professional victory to his name, it was Froome, not Wiggins, who became only the fifth Briton to take the leader's jersey at the Vuelta a España. His two previous best time-trial rides were a second at the 2010 British Championships and ninth at the Tour de Suisse in June. Now he'd just beaten the reigning world champion, Cancellara, by almost half a minute.

As a teenager in Kenya, Froome discovered that the cycling champions of each country get to wear a special jersey adorned with their national colours. Keen to find out how he could compete for such a prize he called the Kenyan cycling federation and asked them when the national championships were. We don't have any, they replied. Well, how do I get to wear the national champion's jersey then? They laughed and told him if he designed his own jersey and sewed it together himself then he could be the national champion. So the precocious youngster did just that.

Now, on the podium in Salamanca, as the sun set over the beautiful, baroque Plaza Mayor, a blushing, shell-shocked, bewildered-looking Froome was presented with a special champion's jersey, a real one, not of his own design – the jersey *roja*, as leader of Spain's national tour.

'When I realised where I was standing as Bradley Wiggins crossed the line I said, "I'm in trouble", but now the trouble will be to hold the jersey and ride hard for two more weeks,' Froome said shortly after the stage finish. 'This situation was never the plan. I got the green light from the team to go for the time trial as hard as I could. I'm over the moon.'

Visibly trembling at the post-stage press conference, Froome looked stunned by the scale of his achievement and perhaps a trifle sheepish too that he'd outshone his team leader. One journalist observed: 'He seemed to be thinking, What the fuck am I doing here?' Where was Bradley Wiggins? Wasn't this supposed to be his big moment? It was like Robin had stolen the keys to the Batmobile and sped off on a joyride.

A sporting Wiggins tweeted: 'Not my best TT of the year but after the events of the last seven weeks got to be happy. Chris Froome was amazing and deserves all he gets.'

Fortunately, the next day, 30 August, was the first rest day. It couldn't have come at a better time. It was a welcome opportunity for Froome to recuperate, understandably 'shattered after the last few days'. His older brother Jonathan and father Clive were due to arrive in Spain that day to follow the race.

On the huge career milestone of leading a Grand Tour for the first time, Froome told *Cycling Weekly*: 'It's been overwhelming but definitely worth all the hard work. Before, I was too impulsive but now I've learned how to control my strength, and my health is better.'

Typical of Froome he also took time to share kind thoughts for Txema González, Sky's *soigneur* who had tragically died after falling ill at the previous year's Vuelta. As a mark of respect, Team

Sky withdrew from the race before the start of Stage 8. 'It's an honour to be in the red jersey, with Txema in mind,' he said. 'If he was there then he would be smiling from ear to ear.'

Everyone was in a tizzy about this tall, reserved British rider who spoke with dulcet tones. Or was he Kenyan? To many pundits Froome wasn't the twelfth Briton to lead a Grand Tour but the first African. The man in red was in no doubt as to where his allegiance lay. 'I've given away my Kenyan passport. I don't regret it. I'm racing under a British flag.'

And what about his contract for 2012? Surely Sky would want to renew it now? He'd been in talks with Dave Brailsford since July, but Sky had been dragging their heels with rumours of Mark Cavendish's imminent arrival for 2012. But Grand Tour contenders didn't grow on trees; they got chased up them by hippos. Suddenly Froome had gone from being invisible to invaluable. 'I'm really happy for Chris, his career has been transformed overnight. He's also tripled his contract value,' his agent Alex Carera told *Cycling News*, adding that although his client would love to stay at Team Sky, four other big-name ProTour teams had now expressed their interest in signing him. Brailsford kept schtum, saying Froome would be in the team in 2012 but refusing to elaborate on when a deal would be reached.

Contract hoo-ha aside, Team Sky had more immediate concerns. The rest day gave them a chance to take stock and consider what to do next. Should Froome, in his leader's red jersey, return to riding in support of Wiggins when the race resumed in the Cantabrian mountains? Or should the roles be reversed and Wiggins become Froome's *domestique*? Suddenly Froome and the team were in uncharted territory. There was no guarantee the young rider could hold it together for the full three weeks. The shadow of bilharzia still loomed large. He said there were a few days where he felt 'pretty sketchy'.

Despite his young lieutenant usurping him as the team's top dog in the race, Wiggins was relaxed that he remained the unopposed leader. To have his teammate leading the race was almost a luxury. Froome in red deflected the pressure away from Wiggins.

It was a nice little problem for the team to have. And, Wiggins said ominously, he would be 'there in the wings, ready to take over when necessary'.

'Nothing has really changed in the team,' Froome said, echoing senior coach Shane Sutton who reiterated Sky's party line that 'it's all about Bradley' when he flew in on the rest day to support de Jongh and Ljungqvist. 'I'm going to try every day,' Froome added. 'The Angliru will obviously be a crucial moment, but we need to get there first. But with Bradley there as well we've got two cards to play.'

Froome led Jakob Fuglsang of Leopard Trek by twelve seconds, with Wiggins third at twenty seconds. Italian *grimpeur* Vincenzo Nibali hovered a further eleven seconds back in fourth, not about to give up his title easily. Sky could feasibly launch a twin assault on the overall classification.

But Wiggins was clearly still the ace in the pack and Froome the joker as the race resumed on Stage 11 with a mountainous 171km-route from Verín to Estación de Montaña Manzaneda. The joke would certainly not have been lost on Froome as he drove the lead group up the laborious final 19km ascent to the exposed summit finish at Manzaneda. It was an arresting spectacle to see Froome, clad in bright red, Wiggins comfortably on his wheel, getting an armchair ride up the narrow, poorly surfaced road. As Froome ground out a steady tempo, Wiggins spun a small gear, saving his legs for when the climb ramped up. When the inevitable attacks came on the upper slopes Froome chased them down, absorbing the blows for his team leader, before his legs eventually gave out and he was distanced with 3km to go. Rodríguez launched a stinging attack 1.3km from the finish, but Wiggins, with fresher legs, helped run down the Spaniard and finished in a dozen-strong group of favourites. Veteran French rider David Moncoutié rode alone to the finish to take his fourth Vuelta stage in four years and close in on a fourth King of the Mountains crown. Froome lost 27 seconds, allowing Wiggins to leapfrog him into the race lead. Froome had sacrificed his red jersey for Wiggins. It was the Team Sky game plan all along

– perfectly understandable given the callowness of Froome, but nevertheless bamboozling for many to witness, especially those close to Froome.

Watching on TV back in South Africa, John Robertson couldn't believe his eyes. In the summation of Froome's former sports director at Konica-Minolta, 'instead of defending the jersey when Chris had it, he lost the jersey back to Wiggins and then Wiggins lost the jersey again . . .' Robertson understood that Froome had come from nowhere to win in Salamanca, so Sky couldn't depend on him, but, 'I think if a guy is as good as that to beat the best in the world in a time trial then you damn well know he's going to go just as fast or beyond the next day. So roll the dice!'

Standing alone at the finish on the scrubby mountaintop in Galicia, Froome surely felt the same. He had turned himself inside out for the purpose of losing his own lead. It was altruism gone insane, but it was professional cycling.

Wiggins was effusive in his praise, knowing all too well the self-sacrifice involved, from which he had so handsomely bene-fited: 'Froomey rode tremendously well, as he seems to be doing every stage at the moment, and it was a really nice touch that he rode straight over to me and congratulated me at the end there.' Wiggins was in red, so it seemed to matter little that Froome had dropped to second overall, a scant seven seconds down. But how Froome and Sky would later rue those lost 27 seconds at Manzaneda.

The next two mountain stages, 13 and 14, to Ponferrada and then La Farrapona, were an *amuse-bouche* for the main course, the dreaded Angliru. From Sarria to Ponferrada over the Category 1 climb of the breathtaking Puerto de Ancares, Wiggins stuck to Froome like a limpet as the pair fended off a series of dangerous attacks from rivals. Nibali scooped an early six-second time bonus at an intermediate sprint to move above Froome into second place, four seconds adrift of Wiggins as the Sky pair finished together in a depleted peloton.

On the second of three increasingly tough mountain stages, 173km from Astorga to La Farrapona the unstoppable tandem was back. Froome and Wiggins worked together to shred the field and only eight riders – including stage winner Rein Taaramae of Estonia – were able to grab hold of the Sky duo's elusive wheels before they disappeared up the road. Rodríguez was long gone. Nibali had blown a gasket, his Vuelta crown rolling away down the slopes of the spectacularly beautiful Asturian peak. Wiggins had strengthened his hold on the red jersey. Only the Spanish dark horse, Juan José Cobo, at 55 seconds, posed a serious threat. Froome pointed to Wiggins as he crossed the line one place behind him in sixth. A show of unity between Sky's two best climbers? You're the man Wiggo? Or watch out, I'm going to get you?

And so on to the Alto de L'Angliru, Spain's most feared climb and the scene of many race-defining battles in the Vuelta. It was crunch time for Froome and Wiggins. The fearsome climb is 12km long, with an average gradient slightly above 10% but dotted with even steeper sections in the last 7km, the worst at Cueña les Cabres, 2.5km from the finish at 23.5%.

Wiggins started the day seven seconds in front of Froome and 36 seconds ahead of Bauke Mollema, so the mission for Team Sky was simple: minimise the Brit's losses and if possible try to bolster, if not increase, his overall lead. The tactic went pretty much to plan. An innocuous breakaway of three riders escaped with 80km to go. The main field came back together at the foot of the Angliru. Wiggins's cause was immediately compromised when he dropped his chain after coming off the high-speed descent of the Alto del Cordal, forcing him to stop and chase back on to the leading group, expending vital energy before the climb had even begun.

As they hit the Angliru, Carlos Sastre attacked first and was joined by Igor Antón who quickly left him behind, disappearing amid the gauntlet of shrieking, flag-waving fans lining the road. Then Cobo launched himself up the climb and overhauled Antón. Froome patiently paced Wiggins through the roadside throng, dropped Antón and then went off in pursuit of Cobo. But the Spaniard tore away from the British tandem with 5km to go and rode stealthily up the thin ribbon of road between two delirious walls of spectators. With 3km to go, Wiggins, weakening, was in danger of losing his red jersey. Wouter Poels and Denis Menchov – the only riders able to stay with the pace set by Froome in the chasing group – started applying the pressure and Wiggins slipped further back. With 1km to go Cobo led by 1:10. In the scramble, at least two motorbikes hit the deck on the hill, one of them a television camera moto. As the sole surviving TV camera followed Cobo, images from Wiggins's red jersey group were lost, and the outside world missed the moment the Sky leadership changed hands. As Cobo raced relentlessly to victory and the crucial twenty-second time bonus for the stage winner – exactly enough to propel him into the overall lead – it was Froome, not Wiggins, who emerged, thrillingly, courageously, through the mist atop the smouldering, emerald beauty of the Angliru. The caterpillar had shed his *domestique* pupa and was now riding for his own position. As Bobby Julich had predicted, Froome was now emerging from his chrysalis to become a butterfly.

'Bradley is the team leader. Today was about who had the legs,' said Froome. 'There really wasn't a decision about you go, I stay. I've got no regrets. I went simply as hard as I could.' He conceded that neither of them could match Cobo's surging attack. 'On a climb like that, there's not really much pacing that you could do. I knew Cobo was the big threat and he was up the road, we had to try to get as close to him as possible. I kept waiting on him to blow, that didn't happen. Hats off to him. He was stronger than us today.'

No regrets perhaps, but Froome was more than a little peeved by the time bonuses available for those finishing in the top three on a stage or winning intermediate sprints. By virtue of first, second and third place finishes, Cobo had amassed 40 seconds in finish-line time bonuses. Froome and Wiggins had none. Menchov had pipped Froome to third place on the line at the top of the Angliru, denying him eight seconds. The time difference on GC between Froome and Cobo was exactly what the Spaniard earned back with his stage win. Time bonuses were proving damaging to Sky's hopes.

'Time bonuses on mountaintop finishes – I am not for that,' Froome said. 'It's a pity that only because of the time bonus, we're not leading any more, but there's still a week to go and we haven't said our last word yet.'

Time bonuses and the wrong choice of gears. Why were Froome and, in particular, Wiggins churning their pedals as if through butter while Cobo was gaily spinning his, tra-la-la, like Pee-Wee Herman on a child's tricycle? Because they didn't have the option of a low enough gear. It was (again) a schoolboy error on Sky's part and committed because neither Froome nor Wiggins had recce'd the climb beforehand. They were going into the unknown on what they knew would be the decisive stage of the Vuelta. What had happened to Sky's mantra of 'controlling the controllables'? The Angliru climb was so unremittingly steep, Froome revealed, that they used 38x32 'because it was asymmetric gearing, and they could have been a bit smaller for me. But even when you hit those gradients, over 23%, it didn't feel that easy. We made the most of what we had, but a little more gearing and energy in the legs would have been good.'

Wiggins was again generous in his post-stage Twitter comments: 'The revelation of this race is Chris Froome.'

On the second rest day Sky would have to reassess their leadership stance . . . again. This was getting more and more complicated. Was it still 'all about Bradley'? There were no more time trials to come, and Froome was clearly the better climber, which surely made him better placed to try to become the first Briton to win a Grand Tour. The Spanish press agreed, questioning the wisdom of making Froome support Wiggins while in red, the daily newspaper *As* declaring the young apprentice 'the real strong man of Sky'. A decision was made. They would have two protected leaders but with Wiggins riding in support of Froome if the latter kept his nose ahead of his erstwhile leader.

As if the Sky pair didn't have enough to contend with in possibly their last chance to overturn their deficit to Cobo, the final mountaintop finish of the 2011 Vuelta a España was set to provide further obstacles by playing host to herds of stampeding bison. Yes, bison. Not real ox-like ruminants, just humans dressed up as the beasts, running up and down the slopes of the 6km climb to Peña Cabarga cheering on race leader Juan José Cobo. Cobo's nickname is 'The Bison of La Pesa' – a reference to his bullish stocky build and the suburb of his Cantabrian hometown, Cabezon de la Sal. The summit finish overlooked the bay of Santander, the capital of Cantabria. Cobo was a local hero. Busloads of supporters dressed up in bison suits and headgear were set to descend on the upper slopes of the mountain *en masse*. Froome and Wiggins would have their work cut out keeping one eye on Cobo and the other on the rampaging bison. 'It's going to look like a safari park,' one excited fan said. The British pair was about to enter a hostile savannah.

On the morning of Stage 17, 7 September, Froome confessed that he and his Team Sky buddies were so addled by their efforts over two weeks of brutal racing in Spain that, as they gathered 'at breakfast it took us a while to work out what day of the week it was – it's been a hard Vuelta so far!' He then added with a cheeky wink in Cobo's direction: 'I wouldn't want to be trying to defend the red jersey on a finish like today's.'

Positioned just 22 seconds adrift of race leader Cobo before Stage 17, Froome launched an audacious last-ditch, do-or-die bid for the red jersey on the short, brutal ascent to Peña Cabarga. As the longest stage of the race, at 212.5km, entered its final few kilometres, Froome and Wiggins continued to track Cobo. Then with just over 1km to go, on the steepest part of the climb, which rears up at one-in-five, Froome lit the blue touch paper and fired himself off the front of the red jersey group in a dramatic attempt to dislodge Cobo. *Soigneurs* and team mechanics watching the action unfold from inside the Team Sky bus at the base of Peña Cabarga erupted in cheers of 'Go Froomey! Drop him!'

The Spaniard initially matched the Sky man's pace but then Froome opened a gap of about fifteen bike lengths as they passed under the *flamme rouge*. It looked as if the local man might lose his race lead in front of his home crowd. The relatively passive roadside bison caught a whiff that one of their herd, Cobo, was in trouble and turned on the perpetrator with a terrible vengeance. 'Obviously the spectators were quite passionate,' Froome said afterwards, with classic understatement. 'I had one guy run up to me and say, "You win, I kill you." It was in broken English, but I got the message. I thought, This guy's a fruitcake, so I forgot about it. Then after a few hundred metres I had two or three other guys say the same thing.'

Unperturbed by deranged death threats Froome rode on, head hunched, bobbing from side to side and gripping the handlebars like he was trying to wring the last drops of water out of a rolled-up towel. But Cobo stayed calm, at his own pace, pegged Froome back and led coming round the final bend. But with one immense, last-ditch effort, Froome, showing incredible split-second presence of mind, sneaked past Cobo on the inside to cross the line first and take the finest win of his career. It was a sensational finale to a spectacular duel.

Not enough to topple Cobo from the race lead, but with the stage winner's time bonus Froome had reduced the deficit to a tantalising thirteen seconds, with four stages remaining. TV shots showed Froome, elated and exhausted, slumped against the barriers at the finish. The Kenyan-born Brit had won the day and undoubtedly the hearts of many fans with his superlative double attack. Wiggins sloped in 39 seconds adrift of both men, his challenge for the overall title effectively over, although he hung on to his third place on the GC. In a wild reversal of fortunes his top mountain *domestique* had just cemented second place at the Vuelta. 'It's a day I will never forget,' Froome said later. With his boyish appearance, button nose and tuft of blonde hair, Froome's nickname at Sky was 'Tintin'. Even Hergé would have been hard pushed to conjure an adventure story as stirring as this one.

He had come to Spain to help Wiggins but had overshadowed his team leader, out-gunning him in the race's only ITT and out-climbing him in the mountains to emerge as the revelation of the 2011 Vuelta. He'd proved without doubt that he was a legitimate Grand Tour contender with the all-round ability in the mountains and against the clock to battle for the GC over three weeks. He was hot property. The increasing transfer speculation, while flattering, became an unwanted distraction for Froome. He had enough on his plate trying to win the race without having to make life-changing decisions about his future.

During the Vuelta, RadioShack had apparently made a tentative offer worth €750,000 a year. That was dwarfed by the €1.4m allegedly offered by French team Ag2r, a figure Astana said they would match. Sky's offer of £100,000 now looked derisory. Team Sky chief Dave Brailsford flew into Spain on the eve of what could be the critical Stage 19 in the Basque Country. Whispers on the grapevine had it that Brailsford had chartered a private jet to fly in especially to secure Froome's services against a scrum of others clamouring for his signature. But Brailsford, inscrutable as ever, refused to bow to outside pressure to finalise a new contract with Froome, saying that negotiations might affect his performances with the race outcome still hanging in the balance.

'You wouldn't go to the Olympic Games and start talking to Sir Chris Hoy about his contract the night before he races. I flatly refuse to do it,' he told *Cycling News*. 'What I've said to Chris is that he will be staying at this team, we will find a solution, but he should concentrate on what is a breakthrough performance. I've told him to put all his efforts into his race and moving his career forward in that sense, without having to worry about his contract. I don't think there could be anything more adverse to do in such a critical period.'

Froome's breakthrough prompted questions about Sky's decision to use him to set the pace for Wiggins, even while wearing the race leader's red jersey. For some aficionados of cycling's famous etiquette it was an insult to the red jersey to watch the leader of the race, who would ordinarily be protected by his team, sacrifice his own chances for his team leader. Froome was sanguine about the fact that the 27 seconds he'd lost at Manzaneda in ceding his red jersey to Wiggins was about to cost him the overall victory. Not to mention the energy he'd expended flogging himself on the lower slopes of the Angliru to help Wiggins regain touch with the leaders after his chain slipped, allowing Cobo to make the race-winning move.

Robert Millar, the last Briton to contend for overall honours in the Vuelta wrote in the *Guardian* that he was puzzled by Sky's tactics. (In 1985, in a grubby episode from the annals of the sport, which became known as 'The Stolen Vuelta', Spanish teams formed an ad hoc coalition and ganged up on the Scottish climbing specialist, who led the race on the penultimate stage, to ensure victory for home rider Pedro Delgado.) 'They've stuck with Brad as team leader because he has the pedigree and the proven successes, but there is the question Froome's performance raises of what if the tactics had been different. What if they had used him differently; for example, the day Bradley took over the red jersey [Stage 11] and Froome did a massive amount of work despite being race leader, because that's been the only occasion where he lost any time to his team leader.'

Thirteen seconds was all that separated Froome from a miraculous victory in Madrid on 11 September. The race was all set to go down to the wire. But he was rapidly running out of meaningful stages to claw back the precious seconds. Time bonuses of twenty, twelve and eight seconds were awarded to the first three riders over the line in each stage, with six, four and two available at intermediate sprints. Cobo's team Geox-TMC would be happy to see breakaways ride clear over the final four stages to chew up the critical intermediate and finish-line bonuses that Team Sky would try to snag. The odds favoured Cobo. It was far easier to defend the red jersey than chase it.

As predicted Froome and Cobo declared an informal truce the next day, permitting a large escape to dominate Stage 18 and win the available time bonuses. The escapees were given ten minutes leeway by Cobo's Geox team so that Froome would have no chance of sprinting for the time bonuses, and the strongest at the finish in Noja proved to be the Italian Francesco Gavazzi, ahead of the Belgian Jurgen Van der Walle, the peloton almost eight minutes behind.

With two days to go, the race entered the Basque Country for the first time since violent demonstrations provided the backdrop to its last visit in 1978. On the 157.9km Stage 19 from Noja to Bilbao, Froome had two final chances to wrest the jersey from Cobo in the shape of the Category 2 ascent of the Alto El Vivero – to be tackled twice in the final 60km to the finish. The climbs were difficult, but they were arguably too far from the finish. It was a long shot. But so long as the Vuelta was still there for the taking, Froome vowed to go down swinging. Sky did their best to set him up to win the six seconds on offer at the first sprint of the stage but were thwarted, after which the day's escape went clear, meaning the only remaining bonuses were for the stage finish. With Wiggins now assuming *domestique* duties, Sky's top pair, led by their young Swedish teammate Thomas Löfkvist, rode hard at the front in an attempt to soften up the field on the first turn over the Vivero. Wiggins then tried valiantly to set up Froome to launch another Peña Cabarga-style 'furious offensive' 1km from the summit of the second ascent, but the climb wasn't quite steep enough and the implacable Cobo had little difficulty gluing himself to Froome's rear wheel. The victory went to Igor Antón of the Basque squad Euskaltel, whose lone escape was the script the organisers must have been hoping for after their brave decision to bring the race back to the politically tense region.

On the penultimate stage, 20, a comical moment punctured the climactic tension when Froome mistook the 20km banner for the last intermediate sprint – controversially, race organisers had announced a last-minute switch of the hot sprint to 16km from the line in Vitoria. When Froome heard over the race radio that the sprint was coming up he suddenly jumped away to try and grab the available four-second time bonus – Carlos Barredo of Rabobank was already up the road on a lone breakaway – but he only realised he'd made a mistake as he went under the banner. 'I took off thinking it was the bonus, but Cobo was ready for it too. I had a red shadow today and he never left me alone.'

Still, Cobo refused to declare himself the victor, even at the Vuelta's usual winner's press conference, held on the evening of the second to last stage. There was no traditional round of applause from the gathered media throng, but surely it was in the bag for the Spaniard?

In the end 'The Bison of La Pesa' successfully shadowed Froome all the way to Madrid, the small gap of thirteen seconds proving unbridgeable. Wiggins held on to third, 1:39 behind Cobo. Froome, full of admiration for Cobo's tactics as a leader in the final week, joked on the morning of the last stage promenade to Madrid that Cobo 'didn't even let me stop for a pee without stopping too. We were even joking in the bus [on the way to the start of Stage 21 at the Jarama motor-racing circuit] about how I should get in the lead-out train [for sprinter Chris Sutton] this afternoon, and we'd be sure to get Cobo there too, as an extra man for the sprint!'

It was an incredible achievement by Froome and Wiggins. It was the first time two British riders had finished on the podium of a Grand Tour. Indeed it was the first podium finish for any Brit since Robert Millar's second at the Giro d'Italia in 1987. Wiggins highest finish yet at a Grand Tour – although he couldn't hide his disappointment at the finish in Madrid that he missed out on winning the race – was eclipsed by a simply astounding performance from his junior teammate Froome, the first African-born professional cyclist to set foot on one of the top three steps of a Grand Tour podium.

'Three weeks ago I couldn't envisage such a result and I believe it's the beginning of great stuff,' Froome said at the finale in Madrid. 'For the first time I got the opportunity to ride a Grand Tour in the best conditions and I took my chance. Over the last week, when it became clear that my early form and time-trial performance were not one-off results, I really began to enjoy myself and came to the realisation that I can now compete with some of the best GC riders in the world.

'It's all been so quick. There have been a lot of things I've had to overcome that I've never had to deal with before, like the stress of having the leader's jersey [after the time trial at Salamanca]. That took me completely apart. I just went out there in the time trial and had a good ride. I was totally shocked.

I could barely sleep at night just for thinking I was leading a Grand Tour.'

He hinted later that his elation at second place was tinged with a little regret at what might have been had he been allowed to relinquish his *domestique* duties earlier and given a free rein by Sky. 'I've definitely thought about where I could have made up that time, but it's too easy to look back like that. At the end of the day, this is how it happened and that's bike racing.'

By the end of the three weeks Bobby Julich said, 'Froome was so stable and so confident and riding so much better that we saw him transformed into a Grand Tour contender.' The question that remained was whether the diffident Froome had the temperament to lead a team. In the Vuelta he had the advantage of being an unknown quantity and had inherited the leadership by dint of his own remarkable display, rather than having to wrestle it from Wiggins.

'In terms of becoming the guy who calls the shots he definitely needs more experience, but after the Vuelta he got a lot of respect from his teammates, the coaches, the directeurs and his competitors. He's not done yet, he's got more work to do, but with this new confidence in himself and with the system we've got, the sky's the limit for this kid.'

Speaking of Sky: on 16 September Froome put an end to any doubts surrounding his future when he tweeted: 'I'm very happy to officially announce that I will be continuing with Team Sky for the next 3 years.'

After his win at Peña Cabarga eight teams had been in contention for his services. But the 26-year-old elected to stick with Sky. A five-year deal was tabled. In the end he signed for three years, for a rumoured £1.2m a year, twelve times the salary he had been offered just a few weeks earlier. If they'd only trusted the numbers on Froome's SRM power meter a month before they could have got him a lot cheaper.

CHAPTER 13

Strength in Numbers

A week after securing his future with Sky, Froome travelled to Copenhagen for the 2011 UCI World Road Race Championships on 25 September. In the perfect end to a fairy tale season, in the city of Hans Christian Andersen, Froome played an instrumental part in an incredible Great Britain team that propelled Mark Cavendish to Britain's first world title in 46 years, since the late, great Tom Simpson in 1965. Froome and Steve Cummings were the two riders assigned to sit at the front of the peloton in the early segment of the race and help maintain the high tempo that would keep any breakaways in check. The pair rode at a ferocious pace with the aim of setting up Cavendish for a sprint finish on the final straight up to the city's ultra-modern Opera House.

It was an astonishing show of collective strength and spirit by the seven-man British squad. British Cycling coach Rod Ellingworth's meticulously planned – famously 'no stone was left unturned' – Project Rainbow Jersey, three years in the making, delivered Cavendish to a historic victory.

But even with Ellingworth's obsessive-compulsive preparation, Cavendish's winning margin was just three-hundredths of a second. In the final straight, as the Australian lead-out train prepared to launch Matt Goss to the line, Cavendish was by now alone. His exhausted teammates were out of the game. Froome and Cummings had buried themselves in self-abnegation to the Manx sprinter's ambition and didn't finish. Cavendish saw the smallest glimmer of daylight to his right against the barriers and slid through the gap in a fluid explosion of pace. It was an electrifying *denouement* to a thrilling race.

Fifteen days after his world title win Cavendish's signing for Team Sky was confirmed.

★

Froome finished the season in style in China with another high-profile podium place at the inaugural Tour of Beijing. In the Chinese capital he may have reflected ruefully on the disappointment of being denied a place in the 2008 Great Britain Olympic team on a course that was perfect for his talents. He relished his two weeks in China and topped it off with fourth place in the opening ITT, eventually riding to third overall behind Tony Martin and David Millar.

★

During the holiday low season in Mallorca, the Vanity Hotel Golf was deserted except for a rotating posse of cyclists clad in distinctive black-and-sky-blue kit. From December 2011 to the end of January 2012 Team Sky had set up base at the luxury beachfront hotel in the resort of Puerto Alcúdia. The sea lapped gently on the golden sands of the yawning Cala Mesquida bay. There was a laid-back, drop-in arrangement; riders came and went according to their winter schedules. As usual, Froome's annual hiatus was spent enjoying summertime in South Africa.

Froome was listed in Sky's squad for the Mallorcan Challenge through 5 to 8 February. The four-day event, run as a series of individual road races, gives riders a chance to feel their way into the new season. He was down to ride in the Trofeo Palma, on the flat circuit, and then the hillier terrain of the Trofeo Serra de Tramuntara but illness forced him to pull out of both races. The latter had to be cancelled due to the unusually inclement weather on the Spanish island. Snow and ice covered the roads on the climbs of the Puerto de Soller and Puig Major.

'It's been a turbulent start to the season to say the least. I arrived at the Mallorca training camp in January in good shape but feeling like something wasn't quite right on the bike,' Froome wrote on his website at the start of 2012.

Something wasn't quite right off the bike too. Back on mainland Europe he lasted only three stages of his first proper race outing of the season at the Volta ao Algarve. He started the Portuguese race well, finishing with the peloton on the first two days of racing, helping teammate Edvald Boasson Hagen take his first win of the 2012 season on Stage 2's flat run from Faro to Lagoa.

The next day, on the 194.6km queen stage from Castro Marim to the summit finish on the Category 2 climb to Alto do Malhão, Froome was prominent at the front of the Team Sky train. He even claimed King of the Mountains points over the final two climbs before the finish, cresting the Category 3 Alte in first place. As the race splintered under Sky's relentless hammering on the final ascent, new season signing Richie Porte capped a stellar team effort to take the stage victory and the leader's jersey. Froome, though, struggled up the climb to Malhão over six minutes down, paced to the finish by teammate Thomas Löfkvist. He didn't start the next day. He'd picked up a nasty chest infection, which completely wiped him out. 'It kept me bedridden for almost two weeks and then lingered on for another two,' he said.

At the end of February he was removed from Sky's eight-man roster for Paris–Nice, the first UCI World Tour calendar event of the season on European soil, due to start in Dampierre-en-Yvelines on 4 March. The Spanish veteran Xabier Zandio took his place.

Team Sky doctor Richard Freeman announced that 'it's nothing serious' and that 'skipping Paris–Nice gives him ample time to recover'; however, the truth was that it could have been very serious. Froome's girlfriend Michelle Cound told *Procycling* magazine that the chest infection turned out to be flu 'which nearly developed into pneumonia'.

By the end of the first week in March he was able to leave his sick bed in Monaco and resume training. While the Paris–Nice peloton worked their way down to the Mediterranean – Froome even managed to visit the Sky team in Antibes after the penultimate stage with Bradley Wiggins in yellow and poised to seal overall victory – he headed to Italy and to Sky's operational base in Quarrata, Tuscany, to train.

Within days of his arrival blood tests confirmed that the accursed bilharzia had returned. The horrible little parasitic worms were active again in Froome's system, feasting on his red blood cells, draining him of energy. It explained why the chest infection had affected him so severely and why he had taken so long to recover.

'Bilharzia is a nightmare to get rid of,' he said. 'Even if there's a trace of it left in your system it starts multiplying again and it can build up. That's why every six months you need to check it. I've taken about four treatments now for it, but hopefully the most recent will be the last.'

★

Medication would have to wait until after his brief return to racing at the Critérium International, starting in Corsica on 24 March. Considering his extended lay-off, Froome performed creditably in the two-day event, coming twentieth in the time trial, but the lack of race conditioning was apparent on the mountaintop finish when his legs gave out on the tough ascent up to Col de l'Ospedale and he lost ten minutes to Sky trio Lars Petter Nordhaug, Michael Rogers and Thomas Löfkvist, and overall winner Cadel Evans, to place 65th.

Home in Monaco he began a course of Prazitel (Praziquantel), a strong anti-parasitic medication, in another attempt to rid his body of the insidious disease. 'The treatment is pretty rough,' Froome said. 'There was more than a week when I could not even touch the bike.'

It was a depressing feeling of *déjà vu* for Froome. The spectre of bilharzia had plagued him throughout the 2011 season, causing his form to peak and trough wildly and cost him a potential starting place at the Tour de France. He took some consolation in knowing what to expect this time round. He'd conquered the illness twelve months before and gone on to finish second at the Vuelta. That podium place gave him the belief he could overcome it again.

Team Sky's strategy for the Tour de France was to deploy Froome and Richie Porte as Wiggins's loyal mountain men in the Alps and Pyrenees. The trio were supposed to be inseparable throughout 2012 – even down to mirroring each other's post-stage warm-downs at races – but Froome's illness had scuppered that plan, and they hadn't raced or trained together since Froome abandoned the Volta ao Algarve. While Wiggins and Porte flew south to Tenerife for Sky's altitude training camp at the beginning of April, Froome stayed home, took his medicine and got some decent kilometres in his legs.

★

'All the signs are looking good,' he wrote online on 23 April, on the way to Sky's hotel in Geneva for the start of the Tour de Romandie. 'It will probably take me a bit of time to get used to the race rhythm again, but physically and mentally I'm ready to race again. At last!'

On his return to major stage racing at the Tour de Romandie, it was business as usual for Froome as Bradley Wiggins's mountain *domestique*. Despite so little racing going into the six-stage event, Froome looked lean and focused. Looks, however, proved to be deceiving. As Wiggins soared to top form in Switzerland and overall victory, Froome was out of sorts from the prologue in Lausanne to the time trial finale in Crans-Montana.'

Richie Porte was an impressive fourth overall, with another key Wiggins support man, Michael Rogers in fifth, whereas Froome was content just to make it through a tough week of racing in 123rd place. He'd ridden nearly 700km over thirteen ranked climbs in western Switzerland. And while Sky actively discouraged the idea of using races for training, Froome, given his unusual health problems, would have been allowed a little leeway in order to jump-start his legs into a race tempo impossible to replicate in training. 'This race has been completely spot on for what I needed to do in terms of getting that race rhythm back and finding a bit of extra form,' he told *Cycling Weekly*. 'Every day we've been on the front, we've not sat back. That's a lot of hard work, but you know it's for the bigger cause.'

That bigger cause was the Tour de France. Sky and Wiggins had already laid down markers at Paris–Nice and now the Tour de Romandie. In July, they would be aiming to make a bold bid for glory and give Wiggins, in the road race form of his life, the best possible chance to become Britain's first ever winner of *La Grande Boucle*, indeed any Grand Tour.

In an interview with *Cycling Weekly* in May, Froome was upbeat about his own, more frustrating, illness and injury-blighted start to the season. 'I know what's potentially in front of me and how things can go if all is well. I'm not panicking. It's still very early days in the season – there's still the Tour, the Olympics and Vuelta. It's not too late. What's happened so far this year could turn out to be a real blessing in disguise.' Perhaps, Froome's logic went, his enforced break would have worked as salutary time, leaving him fresher than others for the challenges ahead. By the time the Tour rolled around he would have managed only twenty days of racing, a figure that would put even Lance Armstrong's traditionally light pre-Tour schedules to shame.

Not many elite athletes would describe dealing with the scourge of a tropical disease as a blessing. But then Chris Froome isn't like most other athletes. It typified his positive outlook on life, a trait inherited perhaps from his unconventional background. Growing up in Kenya helped him keep things in perspective. 'It made me realise that nothing comes easy; nothing is given to you. In Africa I realised you have to make things happen for yourself.'

His close friend, Namibian cyclist Dan Craven, the pro rider who has most in common with Froome, told *Procycling* magazine: 'He has a relaxed, happy-go-lucky side to him which is very African, but he also has more mental strength when it comes to applying himself to training than anyone I've ever met.'

For almost two decades the Hotel Parador in the Teide National Park in the centre of Tenerife has been a favoured destination for professional cycling teams to come for high-altitude training camps. After their deeply disappointing first appearance at the Tour de France in 2010, Team Sky sought out a new training environment – one that allowed Wiggins and company to concentrate on producing big efforts at high altitude and improve on the shorter, steeper climbs that had previously been their undoing. They settled on a location even more eerily quiet and remote than the Overlook Hotel in Stephen King's horror classic *The Shining*.

The surreally isolated hotel is the only building in the vast expanse of the nature reserve – 25km from the nearest village – and is dominated by the giant extinct Mount Teide volcano, sitting at 3,718m above sea level. The vast volcanic cone rising high above the hotel as it sits in a desert of solidified igneous rock lends the dramatic landscape a prehistoric aura.

While breathing doesn't come easy in the thin, dry air, the benefit for athletes is that it enhances the body's ability to utilise oxygen. Froome, born at altitude in Nairobi, and bred on the Highveld plains of South Africa, was one of the few riders in the team comfortable with the rarefied atmosphere.

On the drive from the airport up to Teide to begin Sky's two-week boot camp in May, Froome felt less like he was travelling back in time and more landing on another planet. It was like nothing he'd seen before in his life. 'Kilometre after kilometre of twisty uphill, the road snaked up into the clouds taking us to what I would imagine travelling to Mars would be like. Black volcanic rock and undulating heaps of sand and shrubs surrounded us. There were very few signs of human life at all, except for the Parador Hotel that became our sanctuary after each day of training.'

And the high altitude training was certainly tough. In 2010 Dave Brailsford had brought in Tim Kerrison, an Australian sports scientist who had trained Olympic swimmers and rowers but knew nothing about cycling, with a completely open brief to think outside the box and rewrite the team's training schedules. Not a stretch for the radical Kerrison. He spent the first season following the team at races in a campervan, observing and monitoring how they performed their practices.

After Team Sky's underwhelming first season and disastrous 2010 Tour, Kerrison identified three significant obstacles to Brailsford's founding ambition of winning the Tour within five years: the ability of the riders to cope with heat, mountains and altitude. In January 2011 he scouted locations in Tenerife and settled on Teide. He gathered data from the riders' performances at the 2010 and 2011 Tours and devised a training schedule, which he believed demonstrated the power outputs in watts – the all-important 'numbers' – a cyclist needs to win the Tour de France.

The unassuming boffin also introduced a method called 'reverse periodisation', which, in a nutshell, meant starting training earlier than usual, introducing power and speed work from the off and intermingling long training camps – in Mallorca and Tenerife – with races which had to be tackled flat out, to win. The old-school cycling concept of using races for training was ditched. Froome adopted Kerrison's system, fed through his coach Bobby Julich, on his way to his breakthrough second place at the 2011 Vuelta. Wiggins had already scored two major stage victories in 2012 – Paris–Nice and the Tour de Romandie. The new philosophy and training model had worked. Brailsford confessed to being 'blown away' by Kerrison's results and called him 'the best man in cycling'.

There is no flat on Teide beneath the upper reaches of the volcano. The single road is either a climb or a descent. And the only way back to the hotel was up, often beyond the clouds, which circled the high crater like a smoke halo. Kerrison's training programme involved six-hour stints, with 4,000m of vertical climbing per day. The aim was to put a colossal 100,000m of climbing in Froome, Wiggins and the select group's legs leading into the Tour (Michael Rogers, Richie Porte, Christian Knees and Kanstantsin Siutsou were also there). Among the delights on the menu were 25-minute intervals in 35C heat to be ridden at the kind of maximal intensity Froome would expect to adopt in a prologue time trial. This would be followed immediately by big gear efforts at low-pedal revolutions, with Froome close to breaking point, nose and throat burning in the oxygen-deprived high altitude.

One morning, descending round a tight bend at high speed, Froome's front tyre blew and he hit the deck, skidding down the asphalt on his right flank. There is a photo on his website of him sitting on a rock at the side of the road, jersey off, cycling shorts rolled up, angry abrasions all the way down his right leg. His face set in a puzzlement of pain, the image brings to mind David Millar's acerbic quip that if any mere mortal wants to know what it's like when a professional cyclist crashes at high speed, next time they are in a car travelling at 65kph think about jumping out the door on to the road – naked.

Froome was fortunate to escape more serious injury, but the resulting road rash hampered his enjoyment of the boot camp. 'The crash took a lot out of me, and I didn't feel too great on the bike to say the least,' he wrote on his website. 'Only in the last few days did I feel like I was able to complete the planned workouts.'

★

Froome's final competitive action before the Tour de France would be at the prestigious Critérium du Dauphiné. He opted out of the British National Road Race Championships on 24 June along with defending champion Wiggins and Geraint Thomas to conserve energy and fine-tune his preparations for *La Grande Boucle*. Even without their top three riders Sky displayed the depth of their talented squad with a 1–2 finish in North Yorkshire, Ian Stannard soloing to victory ahead of Alex Dowsett (with team-mates Ben Swift and Jeremy Hunt fourth and fifth).

At the week-long Dauphiné, comprising a 5.7km prologue and seven stages, Team Sky imposed their will firmly on the race.

Located in the mountains of south-eastern France, the Dauphiné is traditionally referred to as a mini-Tour de France because of its varied challenges – two ITTs, one short, one long, flat stages for sprinters, undulating slogs for the *rouleurs* and tough mountaintop finishes. Wiggins arrived in Grenoble on 3 June as the defending champion. The Dauphiné has a rich history going back to 1947 and a roll of honour that includes Eddy Merckx, Bernard Hinault and Miguel Indurain. Two British riders, Brian Robinson in 1961 and Robert Millar in 1990, had taken the overall title before Wiggins.

On Stage 4 Wiggins trounced his rivals, including World Time Trial champion Tony Martin and reigning Tour champion Cadel Evans, with a blistering performance in the long 53km time trial from Villié-Morgon to Bourg-en-Bresse. Froome finished an excellent sixth, ahead of Evans, 1:33 down on the meteoric Wiggins.

In a terrifying show of power and confidence – for their Tour rivals, at least – Team Sky obliterated the field on the sixth stage from Saint-Alban-Leysse to Morzine. The 116.5km stage included six ranked climbs, including the *hors catégorie* Col de Joux Plane. On the latter, a wickedly deceptive 11.6km climb – ask Lance Armstrong who cracked horribly here on Stage 16 of the 2000 Tour – Sky effectively rode a mountain TTT, leaving a mess of floundering riders in the vapour of their slipstream. The expected fireworks in the tussle for the GC never happened. Sky imposed a comprehensive lockdown on the mountain. Of the first ten riders over the top, four were from Sky, Froome cresting the summit in fourth right on Porte's wheel. Only eventual stage winner, Movistar's Colombian climber Nairo Quintana, and Australian favourite Cadel Evans could match Sky's relentless average 1,700 VAM[21] and were first to catch the stunning view of the Mont Blanc massif.

---

21 *Velocità ascensionale media* – a term coined by the controversial Italian physician and coach Michele Ferrari, meaning average ascent speed in English and used to measure the speed of elevation gain, usually stated in units of metres per hour. It is a parameter used in cycling as a measure of fitness and speed. Team Sky have adopted this system of performance analysis to calculate the stamina and sustained effort of their riders when training for climbing.

Wiggins had thrown down the gauntlet to his Tour challengers. He was the man they had to beat in July's big showdown. Froome negotiated the hair-raising descent to Morzine in sixth and jumped to fourth overall. Australian Porte said much later that the Joux Plane climbing clinic was the moment the team knew their preparation was on course to win the Tour de France.

'The Dauphiné was a great opportunity for us to test our line-up under race conditions and it couldn't have gone any better,' Froome agreed. 'We have strength in numbers without a doubt.'

Sky controlled a tricky final stage into Châtel the next day, 10 June, to ensure Wiggins retained his Dauphiné crown. For Froome, who remained fourth, it was far and away his best result of a rudely interrupted, stop-start season.

★

Such a sparkling return to top form was hugely satisfying, and the timing, with the Tour start in Liège less than three weeks away, was perfect. The Sky squad stayed on for a further week in the Portes du Soleil. They took up residence in the Maison Blanche et Verte, a luxury chalet, for a final training camp to hone their race condition and also recce three key Alpine stages of the Tour. Even though Sky's Tour squad was still to be finalised it wasn't just about training. A laidback vibe permeated the chic retreat overlooking the charming village of Châtel.

★

The reconnaissance rides took in Stages 7, 8 and 9 of the 2012 Tour de France route. Froome, Wiggins and a select few headed north from Châtel to climb the final stretch of what would be the first summit finish of the race at La Planche des Belles Filles. The 5.9km climb, with an average gradient of 8% and maximum in excess of 13%, had never previously featured on the Tour. From there they went into the Jura Mountains to ride the last 60km of Stage 8, over two ranked climbs, with the summit of the Category 2 ascent of the Col de la Croix just 16km from the finishing descent to Porrentruy. Visions of a certain floral crash pad were still burned into his retina as Froome joked on Twitter back in Châtel that evening, 'Rode past the scene of my 2010 Tour de Romandie crash today . . . painful memories!'

Finally, Sky's elite mountain posse rode the full 41.5km of Stage 9, the first long time trial of the race, from Arc-et-Senans to Besançon – for Wiggins, Froome and Team Sky it could be the decisive stage for the final GC. On fire against the clock all season, Wiggins would be trying to put as much time as possible into his rivals on a rolling course that was ideal for him in both length and style. Ditto Froome. Could the young pretender cause another Salamanca-style sensation and outrun his number one to Besançon?

Recces completed, the training was adapted to each rider's specific needs. Those lucky enough to make the nine-man line-up would be away from their families and partners for a full month. Sky allowed riders to spend down-time with wives and girl-friends at the base. Froome fitted in some solid blocks of training in-between chilling out with his girlfriend, Michelle, amid the glorious high peaks of the Haute-Savoie. Meanwhile Wiggins left Châtel and flew to Mallorca with his family for relaxation and gentle training.

Back in Monaco, in the week before the *Grand Départ*, with his place in Sky's line-up confirmed, Froome balanced some light training with a few tougher workouts, motor pacing behind coach Bobby Julich on a scooter on the roads around the Côte d'Azur – 'perfect for getting the race rhythm into the legs,' he said. Julich's motorbike was the ultimate training partner for Froome. The practice of riding behind a motorbike – very much *à la* Eddy Merckx – is the closest possible way to recreate the sensation of racing in the slipstream of a professional cyclist.

He also took to his website diary to muse on possible Sky team tactics for the Tour. In light of the high drama that was about to unfold, one that would feature him evolving from a support player into a starring role, it made for an intriguing read.

'We will undoubtedly be riding to give Brad the best shot at winning the Tour, but we potentially have another three guys in the squad who could be up there on the GC.'

The assumption was that he was including himself in the other three contenders for a tilt at the top prize. Whatever his true feelings, on the eve of the big start in Liège Froome diplomatically talked up Wiggins's chances while playing down his own. His Vuelta ride had given him clearer ambitions for the future, he said, but for the next few weeks his mind would be focused on one goal: winning the Tour de France for Bradley Wiggins. 'I've shown I can ride a Grand Tour consistently for three weeks and I'm sure when the time is right I'll get the chance to go for it myself with everyone behind me 100%. This Tour is all about the team. We have huge goals, and it will take everyone pulling all their weight to achieve that. You can't talk about personal ambitions. I have to do the best job I can for Brad, or Mark [Cavendish], when he needs it on a flat stage.'

After their dominating displays in Romandie and at the Dauphiné, Froome sensed that Sky had developed a mental edge over their rivals, with the peloton looking at them to take control of a race. 'It's not a bad position to be in,' he told the *Guardian*. 'We've got strength in depth that other teams don't have. We've got other guys besides me who can get up there in a big tour – Richie Porte, Mick Rogers, Kanstantsin Siutsou.' All could be team leaders in other squads. Froome was just one of a number of riders in Sky who made up what Dave Brailsford termed 'a group of world-class riders fighting to be in the team within the team'. It would force the opposition on to the back foot in the mountains, Froome said, because they would be unable to second-guess what card Sky would play next.

CHAPTER 14

Out of a Clear Blue Sky

2012 Tour de France (99th edition)

30 June 2012
Prologue: Liège, ITT, 6.4km

All the pre-Tour talking was just that: talk. Tactics sounded simple, but they were just words on paper. All the hype and propaganda, the skirmishing in early season races was over. Now for the action. Froome needed to pump himself up, get in the zone for high-octane speed while at the same time preserving an inner calm. Time-trial days are always long days. With 198 riders going off at one-minute intervals, for the last men off there's a lot of hanging around before the day's seven-odd minutes of all-out sprint effort. A lot of time to get 'quietly nervous' as Froome admitted afterwards.

He had a pre-race massage to loosen up his body and then warmed up on a turbo trainer to a tempo set by Sky numbers guru Tim Kerrison. Heart-rate monitors measured his exertion. Like his fellow Sky teammates, Froome watched and absorbed a precise video presentation of the route of the short ITT on the screen at the front of the team bus. He had studied the prologue map in the race book. He knew from personal recces that the course through the streets of the Belgian city was quite 'technical', because of the abrupt changes in direction, sharp corners, tight bends, a constricted width in some stretches and niggly cobbled sections. In addition, there were tramlines and awkward roundabouts to negotiate. If you didn't have good bike-handling skills you could easily lose vital seconds. There were the two long straights where Froome could hit warp speed and power along the banks of the Meuse river.

A team carer – Sky had renamed their *soigneurs* – handed Froome two small pieces of cotton wool dipped in Olbas Oil (a menthol decongestant) to plug into each nostril. They clear the airways and help feed oxygen to the muscles. Marginal gains. Retained while pedalling away on the turbo, they were to be removed before rolling off the start ramp.

Froome was due out at 4.45 p.m. on the dot, in 166th place. Plenty of time for jangling nerves to build to a crescendo. In his excitement Froome burst down the start-house ramp with the nose plugs still in and rode the entire time trial with them stuck up his hooter. It was a silly schoolboy error. Yet, he still finished eleventh, only sixteen seconds behind a rampant Fabian Cancellara, the Swiss 'motorbike of prologues', taking his fifth Tour prologue.

'If he did that time just breathing through his mouth, how fast can he go breathing through his mouth *and* nose?' said Dave Brailsford with a laugh afterwards.

Wiggins, sci-fi cool behind his mirrored time-trial shades, rode a composed, consistent race to finish second, at seven seconds.

'I guess I had this one coming . . .' Froome wrote on Twitter, nerves long ago punctured by the incessant teasing of his team-mates about the nose plugs, with a link to a photograph of Bernie Eisel clowning around at the dinner table with paper napkins stuffed up both nostrils.

1 July 2012
Stage 1: Liège–Seraing, 198km
The first stage proper of the Tour de France is always a twitchy affair. A large peloton, jam-packed with the best riders in the world, in peak physical condition, champing at the bit, eager to impress, to shine, to be set loose *en masse* on closed roads, is a highly charged organism. Compact one minute, fragmented by a burst of attacking the next, shattered by a crash, boiling into an unruly mob in the closing kilometres, it is a seething mass of energy, excitement, aggression and danger.

'The last time I did the Tour was in 2008 as a neo-pro with Team Barloworld,' said Froome. 'I remember being shocked at how sketchy and nervous the first week was before we hit the high mountains.' Riders constantly overlap wheels, fearful of losing their good position in the peloton. The pace is fast from the gun. Every team director is on the race radios telling their team to stay safe at the front, a logical impossibility – there is simply not enough space for almost 200 riders to all be at the front. Pile-ups, punctures, tumbles and spills are pretty near unavoidable.

To Froome and everyone else's relief the start was fairly relaxed. A six-man group attacked almost immediately and became the break of the day as the race began its loop around Liège–Bastogne–Liège country. 'I began to write off my trepidation about the start of the Tour and put 2008's experience down to being a neo-pro,' Froome said, before adding, 'Boy, was I wrong . . .'

With 100km to go, the peloton cruised through the feed zone at Baraque de Fraiture. As riders rifled through the contents of their *musettes*, small cotton shoulder bags containing food and drink, a temporary truce was called and the break's lead stretched to four minutes. The skies darkened over the unremarkable Ardennes countryside and a steady drizzle fell. Slick roads would make the run-in to Seraing even more treacherous than usual. If the rain continued there could be carnage in the finale.

Suitably refuelled, the rampaging Tour beast awoke from its slumber, ratcheted up the pace and, as Froome recalled, 'more and more teams pushed their way to the front, and it wasn't long until we started hearing that dreaded squeal of brakes followed by the sound of bike parts sliding along the tarmac. From then on it felt as if it was every man for themselves, no holds barred!'

Michael Rogers, Sky's trusty road captain for the mountains, hit the deck with 23km to go after a crash in the centre of the peloton but remounted unhurt and chased back alone to rejoin the back of the peloton. Then Luis León Sánchez of Rabobank went down, swiftly followed by Julien Simon, the latter taken out by a spectator, an idiot who stepped onto the road to take a photograph. The crashes only served to jolt the peloton to life, heighten the pace again. Wiggins, meanwhile, replicating the smart strategy on flatter stages he'd adopted, with great success, in Paris–Nice, spent the entire stage within sight of the vanguard of the peloton, glued to the wheel of Christian Knees.

Froome too had somehow survived the mayhem unscathed . . . 'Until 10km to go, when I had the misfortune of puncturing as the peloton entered a fast, cross-tailwind section. There couldn't have been a worse time!' It was horribly close to the finish, as the peloton charged along the banks of the Meuse river into Seraing at full pelt. The early break continued to rage against the dying of the light but was about to be given its quietus by the Lotto-Belisol train, the needle on the speedometer now gliding past 70kph. Porte and Knees stopped to pull Froome back to the front, but it was impossible to catch up, with riders peeling off the back of the peloton at an alarming rate, like fragments of rock tumbling off the tail of a blazing comet. Froome crossed the line 1:25 down on stage winner Peter Sagan. It was a sickening amount of time to lose so early in the race – and through brutal bad luck. For a dejected Froome it was a day best forgotten.

On a buoyant note for Sky, Edvald Boasson Hagen finished third behind Sagan and Cancellara, with Wiggins still sitting pretty in second on the GC.

Froome didn't escape the havoc on Stage 3's agitated 197km run from Orchies in Belgium to Boulogne-sur-Mer in north-eastern France, finding himself on the ground twice, thankfully without any real damage. His teammate Kanstantsin Siutsou wasn't so fortunate. All-rounder Siutsou, a vital cog in the Sky machine, broke his leg in a crash and was the first to abandon the 2012 Tour, a huge blow for the team, although the loss probably had the effect of stiffening the Sky resolve.

Despite his own brace of tumbles, as the peloton, like a giant churning washing-machine, hit spin cycle, Froome said he was in tip-top condition – 'my legs are feeling great' – and he was eager to simply get through the next three stages without mishap, then 'get into the mountains and away from these flat, nervous roads'.

The crash carnage on Stage 6 (the riders called it the Metz

Massacre) eventually ended the participation of twelve riders in the Tour, but Froome stayed clear and readied himself for the first significant mountain finish of the race to La Planche des Belles Filles. The climb, making its debut in the Tour, has the steepest final 350m of any stage the race had ever tackled.

This Saturday, 7 July, had already been earmarked as a particularly important day for Team Sky. A few weeks before, Wiggins's key support riders – Froome, Porte and Rogers – had recce'd the final ascent from their base in Châtel. It was time to see if their preparation would pay off. The team were nervous. It was all very well dominating mountain stages in smaller races like the Dauphiné; this was the Tour, the true testing ground of whether Sky could perform on the biggest stage in cycling.

7 July 2012
Stage 7: Tomblaine–La Planche des Belles Filles, 199km
'The strategy?' Sean Yates said. 'Turn the screw. Just keep turning the screw, and then one by one, they will pop.'

Froome's role at the Tour de France was that of the classic mountain *domestique*: to set a high pace on the climbs in order to discourage attacks by keeping every rider at his limit, or else to respond if a dangerous rival to Wiggins went clear. The pre-arranged order in which the Team Sky train would work in the mountains was this: Bernhard Eisel and Christian Knees pulled at the front on the flat, then Edvald Boasson Hagen would put in his turn, before the climbers took over, led by Michael Rogers, Richie Porte, Froome and Wiggins as they progressed towards the final ascent. Their stint of toil done, each would peel off and conserve energy to the finish, ready to do the same the next day. This was Team Sky's invariable tactic: full team cooperation and collaboration, day after day.

As the seventh stage approached its climax, and the gradient of the climb to La Planche des Belles Filles ramped up to a nasty 14%, then a horrifying 22% wall climb to the finish line, Yates's strategy was working a treat. One by one the peloton *did* pop, like blown bubbles in the wind, unable to cope with Sky's infernal tempo.

As Porte drifted off the front, his labour over, Froome signalled the start of his own stint to coast ahead of Wiggins in the driver's seat by pushing away an over-enthusiastic fan running alongside him. Only a tiny elite group of strong men – defending champion Cadel Evans, Italian climber Vincenzo Nibali and Cofidis's young Estonian hope Rein Taaramäe – now remained with Sky's British tandem. Yellow jersey Cancellara was riding through treacle further down the mountain. Only seven seconds had separated him from Wiggins at the start of the day. The famous *maillot jaune* was slipping from the race leader's shoulders. Froome cranked up the pace. When Evans leaped away with 1km to go – in a last-gasp attempt to steal some seconds from Wiggins – he couldn't shake Froome, Wiggins or Nibali. In the final brutal 100m Froome had the legs and guile to dart round Evans and take his first Tour stage win. Wiggins raised a fist in delight as he crossed the line two seconds later, glued to Evans's rear wheel.

Vivid television images of the final moments of the stage show Froome's yellow racing helmet emerging above the brow of the last hill, like a miniature helicopter taking off, followed by his lean frame and bike rising into the cerulean sky. He glides up the mountain on an invisible escalator before rolling over the crest to the flat, sitting down on his saddle and pedalling to the line, looking back at Evans once before lifting his arms to the heavens in victory, a huge grin lighting up his face.

'It's a dream come true. I'm chuffed to bits,' said Froome afterwards. The bonus points for the stage win also gave him the King of the Mountains jersey. 'It wasn't the plan to go for the stage win. My only concern was keeping Bradley up there. We'd come to see this climb previously, and I knew what the finish was like. When it came to it I thought, I'm there, I've got the legs, so why not give it a kick and see what happens. I gave it a nudge and I just couldn't believe it when Cadel couldn't follow my wheel. I thought, Wow!, this could actually come off, and it did.'

Team Sky now led the Tour de France for the first time, with Wiggins in yellow, Froome in the polka-dot climber's jersey *and* stage winner. Sky had also soared to the top of the team standings with three riders in the top ten on the GC: Wiggins, Froome in ninth, Rogers in tenth. All the hard work and sacrifice, the intense training at the team camps in Mallorca and Tenerife, the recce of the route, had paid off big time.

'It's fantastic – Froomey's taken the stage and is King of the Mountains, and I'm sat here at the top of the mountain in yellow, so it was an incredible day,' Wiggins said. He had sympathised with Froome after his bad fortune with the puncture on Stage 1 and was delighted for his teammate. 'Now he's got his stage and he's going to be an integral part of me winning this race.'

The day hadn't just been 'incredible'; it was, Dave Brailsford enthused, one of the highlights of his own career – not a bad compliment for Froome given the Sky supremo's long list of illustrious achievements in cycling. 'It couldn't have been more perfect. That stage will stay with me forever,' Brailsford said later. It was the Tour moment Brailsford had been waiting for since 2010's catastrophic debut and Wiggins's abandonment in 2011. Sky executed their pre-race plan – 'to put the hurt on the rivals and turn on the gas on the climbs' – to perfection.

Winning on the hilltop finish, outsprinting no less than Tour champion Cadel Evans, gave Froome an enormous confidence boost for the rest of the Tour. More importantly he'd silenced the sceptics who had wondered whether his performance at the 2011 Vuelta had been a fluke. After an indifferent start to the season, plagued by illness and poor form, he had even started questioning his own abilities and power. Maybe the naysayers *were* right? Well, they *weren't*. Victory in the Vosges mountains helped remove any lingering doubts from his mind. 'Winning on top of La Planche des Belles Filles was a huge reassurance to me that I am capable of duplicating, and possibly even bettering, the form I had last year,' he said.

Sean Yates, the master at reading roads, had already surveyed the Stage 8 route on behalf of the team, and from his vantage point in the Team Sky car recognised a familiar decorative plot by the roadside. 'We had a bit of a laugh when we came through,' he tells me, cackling with laughter down the phone. 'We were calling it Froomey's Flowerbed! This time Froomey squeezed the brakes at the same turn and finished seventh on the stage. I think Thibaut Pinot won it.'

Bradley Wiggins had been marshalled safely to the finish in Porrentruy by Froome and his other Sky helpers to end a tough first day in yellow. Froome was now lying sixth on the GC, just 1:32 behind his Sky teammate. And there was no sign of the loose-cannon tendencies of old. What a difference two years had made. The new, mature 27-year-old seemed, at last, to have curbed his tendency toward reckless over-enthusiasm although his daring leap away for stage victory at La Planche des Belles Filles had shown that he is, by nature, a quick-fuse attacking rider – an essential element of his winner's nature.

Froome had already learned a lot from riding at the front of the race with Wiggins and noted how smart his team leader was at conserving energy. 'Bradley has become a master at gauging his effort,' Dave Brailsford told me. 'He won't take a single pedal stroke too many, and then, when he has to make a move or put in a big effort, he knows when and how to do that. I think Chris learned an awful lot from being up there at the sharp end of the race with Bradley.'

Froome saw from watching Wiggins at close quarters that he could be competitive and win big bike races without having to ride flat out all the time. It entailed being canny, watchful, timing his efforts and reining in his impetuous instincts. 'I think he deserves a lot of personal credit for managing that impulsiveness because he's recognised it, understood it and learned where to direct his effort,' Brailsford says. 'You only have so much energy in the tank, and he's learned how to use it and not just pour it all out at once.'

At the press conference in Porrentruy Wiggins discovered the downside of leading the Tour when the full glare of the world's press turned on him. He took serious umbrage at a journalist asking him for his response to rumours circulating on Twitter alleging that he and Team Sky were doping. The Londoner let rip with an expletive-laden rant, railing against the cynics who were in his eyes no more than Internet trolls: 'fucking wankers

… who sit under a pseudonym on Twitter and write that sort of shit rather than get off their own arses in their own lives and apply themselves and work hard at something and achieve something.' He had a point. It may have been foul-mouthed but it was timely. He has spent his entire road racing career slamming dopers and dealers.

The gossip had been provoked by the team's overwhelming dominance of races such as the Dauphiné, in which four Sky riders had finished in the top ten, and had grown more feverish as they stomped all over the opposition in the opening salvos in the mountains of the Tour. Sky had managed to have three or more riders providing support for Wiggins deep into every stage, while his main rivals, Evans and Nibali, often found themselves alone and vulnerable, with no teammates to help in the crucial final kilometres of climbing.

By dint of scrupulous preparation to ensure that their riders arrived at the start line in superlative condition, Sky exerted a clinical level of control not seen in professional racing since the early 2000s heyday of Lance Armstrong's US Postal team. Since Armstrong and a number of riders on that team – including Tyler Hamilton, Floyd Landis and Roberto Heras – had subsequently either been busted or confessed to doping, it was natural for fans to be sceptical about seeing something that appeared, at least to their eyes, to be a similar invincibility.

An article in the cycling press the day before had only served to stir up the rumourmongers even more. The piece questioned the ethics of team doctor, Geert Leinders, the Belgian appointed on a part-time basis in late 2010 after Sky had pulled out of the Vuelta a España following the death of Txema González.

Former Rabobank manager Theo de Rooy alleged that systematic doping had been tolerated at the Dutch team in the mid-2000s. Leinders had been one of the doctors on that team. The story had been simmering away in the background since May 2012. Dave Brailsford had been quick to deny any wrongdoing by Leinders at Sky, although to safeguard their reputation he promised an investigation into the doctor's past.

Froome posted a comment about the press conference on Twitter that evening: 'Critics need to wake up and realise that cycling has evolved. Dedication and sacrifice = results. End of story!'

9 July 2012
Stage 9: Arc-et-Senans–Besançon, ITT, 41.5km
'It is good to know you are on track for a good time, but you have to be careful you don't overcook it. It's a fine line to gauge that effort,' said Froome after judging his exertions to perfection on the twisty riverside time-trial route. He had reconnoitred the route four weeks prior and knew all about the climb to the first time check at 16.5km at Abbans-Dessus, whose steep gradient had looked easier on the stage profile than on the ground. Indeed it wrecked the performance of numerous riders who were taken aback by its sharp incline. Sky sports director Servais Knaven, winner of Paris–Roubaix in 2001, acted as Froome's co-pilot, a nerve-shredding responsibility, firing course details and time splits into his ear through the race radio. Froome scorched round the course behind his team leader, and Sky stormed to a brilliant 1-2 finish.

Wiggins took his first ever Tour stage – the third of the race for Sky – and handed out a drubbing to his rivals to strengthen his grip on yellow. Evans lost 1:43; Nibali 2:07. The astonishing Froome ceded only 35 seconds to come second on the stage and climb from sixth to third overall on the GC. 'Time trials are by far the hardest discipline in cycling,' Froome said afterwards, looking forward to a ceasefire in the action on the first rest day.

Having proved in the Alps they were the two strongest climbers in the race, Froome and Wiggins had now laid strong claim to being the best time triallers too, particularly since reigning world TT champion Tony Martin had cut a sorry figure since sustaining a fractured wrist in a Stage 1 crash. The German soldiered on for another week to finish an admirable twelfth in Besançon before dropping out to give his injury a chance to heal in time for the Olympics.

Coming from a background in track racing, the 32-year-old Wiggins had gained a reputation on the road of always being in contention with the bona fide time-trial specialists, such as Martin and Cancellara. In the opening half of the 2012 season, on his way to winning Paris–Nice, Tour de Romandie and the Dauphiné, he had proved to be indomitable against the clock. Froome had also shown what he was capable of by beating Wiggins in Salamanca, his breakthrough performance at the previous year's Vuelta. He'd always had a natural ability for the singular discipline of time trialling. But he'd also worked extra hard with Bobby Julich and Tim Kerrison on his physical condition.

A fine balance has to be maintained in order to be both a top climber and time triallist – the two crucial skills required to be capable of challenging for the overall GC in a Grand Tour. Wiggins describes himself as a time trialler who can climb, whereas Froome is a climber who can time trial. The primary aim of Froome's training with Kerrison and Julich had concentrated on increasing his capacity to maintain a very high output for up to an hour, while maintaining a low body weight and lean body composition to enable him to compete with the best climbers in the mountains. The training was clearly paying dividends – Froome and Wiggins weren't just staying with the flyweight mountain goats, they were burning them off their wheels.

CHAPTER 15

Making up for Lost Time

12 July 2012
Stage 11: Albertville–La Toussuire–Les Sybelles, 148km
At the team meeting on the morning of the first high mountaintop finish at La Toussuire, Froome asked the team directors
for permission to attack 3km from the finish, so long as Wiggins
was free from harm, untroubled by predators, his yellow jersey
safe. The lost 1:25, which Froome felt had been stolen from him
by Stage 1's puncture, still rankled. OK, team orders decreed that
he sacrifice his own ambitions in the service of Wiggins, but he
still craved a place on the podium, and if they were to eliminate
Evans and/or Nibali on Stage 11 as meaningful threats, then
wouldn't it be feasible for Froome to be set free and secure his
place on one of the top three steps in Paris? 'It's unlikely,' the
sports directors responded. Froome apparently nodded in silence.
He had been here before. Sky's hesitancy to give him free rein at
the Vuelta, forcing him to continue working for Wiggins when
he was in a better position than his team leader to contest the
overall win, had arguably cost Froome the race.

While there *were* certain echoes of that Vuelta, this situation was
different. Wiggins already had a substantial two-minute advantage on
Froome and the rest. Sky obviously felt that unleashing Froome too
early, to gain time on Evans and Nibali, could risk those same riders
also eating into Wiggins's lead. It is a constant worry, especially in
the mountains, that an attacking *super-domestique* like Froome risked
offering Sky's rivals an armchair ride, *if* they were up to it. It was
agreed that if Froome felt good he could jump away in the last
500m and possibly improve his own position on the overall standing.

As it transpired, Evans launched a long-range kamikaze attack on the Col du Glandon with 56km remaining of the stage. This was audacious – an extremely risky tactic. There was a lot of hard riding still to do. In an obviously pre-planned move, Evans's BMC team had sent a decoy up the road in the shape of young American Tejay van Garderen, with the idea that the Australian would leap clear of Wiggins's yellow jersey group, hook up with his teammate and the pair would work together to inflict damage on Wiggins and Sky. At least that was the theory . . .

Road captain Michael Rogers lifted the pace, told Wiggins not to panic but to maintain a steady tempo on the climb. There was a long way to go – down the Croix de Fer, up another ramp to the Col du Mollard, a Category 2 climb, a super-fast, tricky descent to Saint-Jean-de-Maurienne, and then the 18km climb to the finish.

Team Sky was already familiar with the climb to La Toussuire since it was where Wiggins had claimed his first overall victory at the Dauphiné in 2011 with a strong tenth place finish on the mountain. Rogers's clear thinking was that there was no way Evans could sustain his attack even as far as the summit to the Croix de Fer, let alone open a decent gap. He was right. Sky reeled him in 2km from the top of the Croix de Fer, and from that point on the defending champion was a spent force. He dropped 90 seconds on the climb to La Toussuire and slipped to fourth overall.

(What happened between Froome and Wiggins in the final 4km of the climb to the out-of-season ski station – which was already being dubbed the 'Treachery of La Toussuire' – has already been covered in the prologue of this book.)

The immediate aftermath of the stage produced further intrigue. Froome had ridden to safety just beyond the finish line, after he'd found himself besieged by a scrum of journalists, stranded in no man's land, getting bombarded with questions about his putative attack on Wiggins. A few hundred metres away, in the press centre, the Sky leader was adding ambiguity to the confusion. He said that at the vital moment when Froome had accelerated away he could hear only incoherent snatches of what Sean Yates was saying through his radio earpiece over the racket being made by the crowd. Seconds later Wiggins claimed he had 'taken [his] earpiece out'. Television images contradicted his assertion, showing a small black disc firmly lodged in his ear before and after Froome's spurt.

The Froome–Wiggins *imbroglio* drew striking parallels with the 1985 Tour when Bernard Hinault started the race as the uncontested leader of the La Vie Claire team, going for his fifth win, with the young American pretender Greg LeMond as his designated second-in-command. Hinault took the yellow jersey but faded in the final week after a crash. LeMond got stronger and sensed he might be able to win the race himself. On the key seventeenth stage to Luz Ardiden in the Pyrenees LeMond joined another escape with other GC contenders and left Hinault behind. He was, however, ordered not to collaborate; rather to police the break, in much the same way Froome had been reined in at La Toussuire. LeMond remains convinced to this day that if he'd been allowed to ride for himself he would have won the 1985 Tour.

The Sky plot thickened when Sean Yates admitted he was 'pissed off' that Froome had taken it upon himself to deviate from The Plan, which was to win the Tour for Wiggins. Within seconds of Froome's 'unauthorised' move, Yates issued an order through his radio earpiece for him to relent, at which point Froome sat up and Wiggins was able to latch back safely on to his wheel. Like Wiggins, Yates also experienced temporary loss of hearing: 'I don't know if he [Froome] had a conversation with Bradley over the radio, because I didn't hear anything. It wasn't my instruction to attack.'

Sky seemed unable to settle on a single agreeable version of events. Team director Servais Knaven reported assuredly that 'Chris had just wanted to take a turn on the front and went too fast'. This was patent nonsense. Had Froome told them this? Whatever, the TV pictures told their own story – his violent acceleration had been real, not merely part of his stint towing Wiggins up the hill.

A more titillating reaction, which had slavering journalists rubbing their hands together with glee, came shortly after the stage concluded when Cath Wiggins, Bradley's wife, posted a note on Twitter praising two of her husband's Sky teammates, Michael Rogers and Richie Porte, for their 'genuine, selfless effort and true professionalism', conspicuously omitting Froome. Taking this as a barely disguised slight on her man, Michelle Cound waded in with the prickly riposte: 'Typical!' Froome's girlfriend also wrote that she was 'beyond disappointed', presumably that Froome had not been allowed to continue his attack to the finish. In an update she said: 'If you want loyalty, get a Froome dog – a quality I value although being taken advantage of by others.'

The spat received more attention when the Scottish rider David Millar, Froome and Wiggins's British compatriot, and the latter's former teammate at Garmin, fanned the flames on Twitter with mischievous merriment: 'Oh SNAP! Sky have a WAG war on Twitter. This shit just got real.'

A few hours later Wiggins himself tried to take the heat off the squabble with a message on his Twitter account in which he singled out Froome: 'Great day today for Team Sky, boys rode incredible and Chris Froome super strong, big day behind us.'

Within an hour of the finish, Froome had already fallen back into line, speaking with the blank monotone of Laurence Harvey in *The Manchurian Candidate*. In the film, he and other members of his patrol are captured during the Korean War and brainwashed by their captors into a state of robotic obedience to instruction. 'I'll follow orders at all costs,' Froome said. 'I'm part of a team and I have to do what the team asks me to do. Our plan is to look after Bradley.' When pressed on why he believed Wiggins's chance of overall victory was better than his own he responded: 'He's just as strong as me, I think, and stronger than me in the time trial.'

Sky, so adept at batting off the media, immaculate in their ability to 'control the controllables', had suddenly – and publicly – lost control. Rumours circulated that Froome and Wiggins weren't speaking. That Wiggins had been in tears after the stage and spoke of quitting the race, going home, cheesed off with Froome's actions and the ensuing rumpus. Initially Wiggins said he felt as if he'd been 'flicked' (cycling slang meaning to double-cross or trick) by his teammate. He then changed his mind and offered a conciliatory disclaimer. Froome, he suggested, had just got a bit giddy in the heat of the moment and gone AWOL, off piste.

Either way, the truth was that Froome *had* been derelict in his duties as a *super-domestique* to Wiggins, rebelling against the strategic hierarchy in the team, dictated by GC order, to put aside his own aspirations and help Wiggins defend his yellow jersey. Froome might well have asked retrospectively about pecking orders and the tradition of defending the leader's jersey at all costs in relation to his own sacrifice while wearing the *roja* jersey at the 2011 Vuelta.

More than anything else, Wiggins hated uncertainty. He wasn't used to it. He'd been raised on a regimen of meticulous planning and obsessive preparation with access to the best facilities and coaches, not to mention the unconditional support of teammates. Since his teens he'd been nurtured by the British Cycling system and in the closeted world of track racing where the effort is short and gains and losses predictable to centimetres. And now who was this cheeky interloper, this outsider? Who was Chris Froome to steam in and upset Wiggins's precisely wrought apple cart? The Kenyan-born Brit was not from Wiggins's world of marginal gains, collated test results and blind obedience to team superiors. Aside from a few key guiding hands along the way – Kinjah, Nilsen, Robertson – Froome had spent the last ten years making his own way in cycling, ploughing a lone furrow, from riding mountain bikes in Kenya to rubbing shoulders with the elite of the professional peloton. He'd become conditioned to his own way of doing things and simply wasn't accustomed to following orders.

David Millar perhaps summed up the contrast between Froome and Wiggins best when he said: 'Brad's your archetypal class-A athlete who does everything in an incredibly detailed way; he's mechanical, very engaged and professional. Whereas Froome is a bit looser. He's a maverick; he comes from a different background. He's very much a self-made man. Brad is manufactured. Don't get me wrong, Brad has done it himself, but he's also the product of a system.'

It was more likely that Froome had simply felt frisky and full of beans in that final 4km of racing, sensed an opportunity and was unable to contain his enthusiasm or determination to win back the time he'd lost to the puncture, rather than acting as a Machiavellian schemer.

Maybe he briefly thought about that morning's team instructions and then said to himself, 'Well, let's see . . .' and made a unilateral decision to go. It was never an actual assault on his leader's pole position. He was too loyal for that. It was an honest attempt – albeit a contentious one – to ride himself on to a podium finish at the Tour de France.

It didn't dawn on Froome until afterwards that his attack had opened a massive can of worms: 'On the road my thinking was that I'd got Brad back to [Vincenzo] Nibali, our biggest challenger. Cadel [Evans] had been dropped. Nibali and I were very close on the GC, so I thought Brad was safe with Nibali.

'Nibali had been attacking and he was in the red [cycling slang for out of juice], so I thought he wasn't going anywhere. I thought then would be the perfect time to get back a bit of the time I'd lost to the puncture. Brad was safe, so it wasn't a threat, me going up the road. But obviously . . . I started going, and it was an attack, and I knew I was going clear, then I heard on the radio, team orders to say, "No, no, don't take any risks. Stay with Bradley. Just take him to the line and look after him."

'Obviously, initially I was a bit torn,' he admitted. 'I thought I was doing the right thing by attacking. But the team is the most important thing, and obviously the yellow jersey is more important than worrying about securing second place.'

The next morning Dave Brailsford fielded more questions on the mounting speculation overnight of an internal leadership battle between Wiggins and Froome. More composed than he'd been with journalists the previous evening, Brailsford played down any hint of unrest or friction within the Team Sky camp. 'We're very happy to have two riders of the quality of Bradley and Chris here. Everyone thinks it's a problem, but having the first and second rider on the GC at the Tour de France isn't a problem.'

As Sean Yates recalls, having to fend off the clamouring press and 'clarify the mission to the team' (polite-speak for a behind-the-scenes bollocking for Froome?) was a nuisance Sky could have done without. 'It didn't make our lives any easier. That's why I wasn't happy with Froomey, because we had an agreement and he didn't stick to it.'

19 July 2012
Stage 17: Bagnères-de-Luchon–Peyragudes, 143.5km
After the dust had settled on the 2012 race, Wiggins confessed that from La Toussuire onwards, throughout the rest of the Tour and to the finish in Paris, he didn't know what to expect from Froome in the heat of the battle. It made Wiggins wary of Froome, put him on edge. What if he went careering off script again? Wiggins had to wait only a week to find out.

In the interim Froome had provoked more controversy. After dropping Wiggins in the Alps he appeared to drop him in the press too, telling *L'Equipe* (in a long interview conducted in Italian) that his efforts for the Sky leader represented 'a very, very great sacrifice'. Under the 15 July headline '*Wiggins me le rendra*' (Wiggins will repay me) Froome said: 'I could win this Tour but not with Sky. I cannot lie to you, it's difficult, but it's my job.' When he was asked what he would do if Wiggins showed frailty in the upcoming Pyrenees, he replied, 'If I thought we were going to lose the Tour, I'd follow the best, which could be Nibali or Evans, in order to preserve our chances, to make sure of a Sky presence.'

Supposedly resigned to second place, sitting 2:05 back on Wiggins, now it was unclear where his ambitions lay for the race. Was he somehow hoping that Wiggins would get dropped? The interview showed how misleading Froome's genial, laidback persona could be. 'He's very polite, very well mannered. If you didn't know him better you might think, Is he too nice?' Dave Brailsford tells me. 'But as all winners have, he's got a killer instinct.'

A steely resolve lay behind Froome's amiable demeanour. Was he a wolf in sheep's clothing? Perhaps what observers failed to understand about Froome was that he lacked the cynicism – *their* cynicism – or the guile to comprehend how his honest effort to gain time on Evans and secure second place might be interpreted as cunning, rogue behaviour.

Froome also told *L'Equipe* that he expected preferential treatment the following year – *Wiggins me le rendra* – if the 2013 Tour route suited his strengths. 'In that case I would expect Sky to be honest and put my teammates at my disposal, with the same loyalty that I'm showing now. Bradley is an honest guy. I know that he'll help me.' Again there were shades of Hinault and LeMond. After LeMond helped his French team captain win his fifth Tour title in 1985 the formal agreement was that the Frenchman would assist the American to win his first in 1986. LeMond duly accomplished his goal but only after being pushed to the limit by Hinault who said he was only trying to soften up the opposition, fortify LeMond and make the race more entertaining. Twenty-seven years later LeMond is still convinced Hinault tried to win the race for himself while Hinault maintains he was capable of winning it but instead graciously, as promised, *allowed* LeMond to take the victory. Were Froome and Wiggins set to replicate their predecessors' internecine war?

Ever the accomplished diplomat, Brailsford responded to the media brouhaha following the *L'Equipe* article with: 'I think his comments were fair. I think they were measured. It just goes to show that he's a really intelligent guy. He's here. He's part of the team. We recognise he's got his own ambitions and would like to fulfil those.'

In the aftermath the French media took to calling Froome 'Robin' in a humorous dig at his being the less heralded sidekick to Wiggins's 'Batman'.

On 15 July Froome and Sky survived a bizarre incident, which marred Stage 14. A phantom saboteur scattered carpet tacks on the final, exceedingly steep climb of the Mur de Péguère, causing around 30 riders to puncture, including defending champion Cadel Evans. Unwritten Tour custom decrees that the yellow-jersey wearer in the Tour de France should not attack a close rival if they've suffered a crash or a flat tyre. On the easy descent off the Mur, Wiggins sat up and called a general truce to allow his rival to rejoin the race without any time lost. This chivalrous gesture earned him the nickname 'Le Gentleman' in the French newspapers. Miraculously, not one single Sky rider sustained a flat in the mayhem. 'I realised at that point,' Brailsford said later, 'that the gods were smiling on us.'

On the Tour's second rest day in Pau on 17 July, Brailsford made a salient point about the Froome–Wiggins dynamic. 'I've said to Chris that he is in the best possible seat in the house to learn what it takes to win this race and what it takes to be the leader of the race. Day after day, he can learn what stress the yellow jersey has to cope with and learn how to be a leader of the team. It is not just about being on the bike; it is everything else that goes with it. Bradley has learned that, and it is a massive part of being able to deliver.'

Wiggins spent an hour or more at the end of each stage visiting the podium, dealing with television interviews, fielding questions from the world's media. All this time Froome was on the bus or back at the hotel, away from the clamour and hullabaloo.

'There's no spotlight on Chris,' Brailsford continued. 'It's like being the second-in-command of a business, and the guy who's in charge says, "I'm off tomorrow. Here's the keys, good luck." You think, hold on a minute. It's very different being the leader to being number two.'

★

Two days later Team Sky endured a brutal opening day in the Pyrenees for Stage 16, in blistering heat, surmounting four huge mountain passes – Aubisque, Tourmalet, Aspin and Peyresourde – concluding with a twisting descent into the spa town of

Bagnères-de-Luchon. Froome, Wiggins and company resisted a flamboyant attack by Nibali on the swift run down the other side of the Peyresourde – one of the fastest descents in the Pyrenees – to maintain the status quo on the overall standings, a 1-2-3 of Wiggins, Froome and Nibali. Evans, suffering from a stomach upset, no longer posed any threat either to Wiggins's yellow jersey or to Froome's podium ambitions. He lost nearly five minutes by the end of the stage and slipped to seventh overall.

The next day, Stage 17, Froome teased the conspiracy theorists again, giving Wiggins further grief and causing a general head scratching among his Sky bosses and unbridled glee in the press and spectators alike when he stretched the invisible elastic between himself and Wiggins to breaking point up to the summit finish at Peyragudes.

As the riders crossed the Col de Menté, the Col des Ares, the Côte de Burs and the giant Port de Balès, the field was gradually whittled down until only eight riders were left in the select group, the strongmen elite of the Tour, a diverse bunch containing Wiggins in the yellow jersey, Froome, Tejay van Garderen, Jurgen Van Den Broeck, Vincenzo Nibali, Thibaut Pinot, Pierre Rolland and Chris Horner. The 32-year-old Spaniard Alejandro Valverde, who had returned at the start of the season from an eighteen-month doping suspension, was already up the road on what looked to be a stage-winning solo escape, having broken free on the monster climb of the Balès, the last *hors catégorie* peak of the Tour. Thinking himself the star of the show, Valverde was blithely unaware that he was merely a bit part in a thrilling narrative unfolding behind him.

Nibali weakened on the climb up the mist-shrouded Col de Peyresourde, the stepladder to the ski resort above it, and also on the last ascent of the day – and of the entire Tour – to Peyragudes. Then Valverde seemed to fade, his long-range attack taking its toll, and his lead fell from 2:35 to 1:16 with 6km to go.

The predatory Froome sniffed another chance of a stage win. Whoops, here we go again. On the mini-descent of the Peyresourde, before the final 4km haul to the finish, Froome was chatting with Wiggins. Was he asking his leader for permission to tear off after Valverde? Wiggins motioned to Froome with his right hand, said something. Froome looked down, shook his head slightly, puffed out his cheeks and smiled.

With just over 3km remaining Wiggins steamed to the front, Froome tucked in behind, and gave it his all. Was he setting Froome up to be catapulted off the front of the race in pursuit of Valverde? Froome came past his leader and took over. Nibali slipped off the back. Van Garderen cracked.

The lead group completely imploded under the relentless pace set by the two strongest riders in the Tour. Froome continued to accelerate. A gap opened, and he glanced back at Wiggins whose face was contorted in agony. Or maybe ecstasy? (He later said he had let his mind wander as it hit him that he was about to all but clinch Tour victory: 'All the way up the last climb I almost had tears in my eyes. It was a really nice feeling.')

The two Sky men could be seen talking and listening to their radio earpieces, and the outcome of their discussion was hard to interpret. With 2.5km to go, Valverde's lead dropped to 48 seconds. He was eminently catchable and Froome knew it. He unfolded himself, erect, to his full height on the saddle and looked back at Wiggins again. Then he let his right hand dangle to one side, like a boxer dropping his gloves as a taunt to a rival – 'Come on, fight,' he seemed to be pleading to Wiggins. He flicked his hand – a small come-hither gesture – to usher Wiggins to his wheel, like a dog to its owner's heel. No response.

Wiggins said later that he'd told Froome: 'I'm not coming, I'm staying here, I'm riding this. We don't need to attack.' But Froome wouldn't take no for an answer and flicked his hand again, impatiently, as if to hurry up a child.

Wiggins confessed later he was confused by Froome's gestures. He was a bit gaga. His mind was scrambled with a collage of thoughts and images of all the things he'd done to get to this point and all the people who'd helped him get to the cusp of winning the Tour de France. The realisation that he was about to achieve his childhood dream invaded his mind with stupefying force. He was enjoying the spaced-out feeling of reaching the top of the final mountain of the race safe in the knowledge that all his rivals had been, one by one, eliminated from the game. 'Froomey was egging me on. He wanted more and more, but the fight had gone from me at that point,' he said. 'I knew it was pretty much over. We rode away from the rest of the field and I lost concentration.'

Wiggins might not have had to do anything, but Froome still wanted his help to catch the faltering Spaniard. Or at least be given the nod to set off on his own, acutely aware after La Toussuire of not deserting the yellow jersey without approval. Under the 2km banner and the gap was down to 41 seconds, then 30. Again Froome had to slow and wait for Wiggins.

The gathered throng of journalists, watching the action unfold on TV in the press room in Luchon groaned in unison. 'DAMN IT GOOOOOOO' Froome's girlfriend Michelle tweeted this time. Froome continued to look back at Wiggins all the way to the line. Valverde won in the end by a mere nineteen seconds. Froome could have caught him. He almost did so, even while having a three-way conversation with Wiggins and the team car.

Sean Yates once again expressed his displeasure at Froome's amateur dramatics on the final col. 'I told them to stay together. Froome didn't listen. This was *maladroit*; he lacked tact. He's new to this level. He has a lot to learn.'

Minutes after the finish Froome couldn't hide his dejection in an interview with ITV's Matt Rendell, barely making eye contact with his inquisitor. 'I think that was an ideal stage for us. Obviously it would've been really nice to get the stage win,' he said, with a watery smile. 'But putting time into our main opposition was just what we needed going into the final time trial.'

On being asked what he had been saying to Wiggins, he replied quietly, head down, 'Just that we've got rid of Nibali and that it was about to flatten out, just stay on my wheel, encouraging him.'

Rendell asked him if Wiggins had encouraged him to go off and take the stage. 'No. The plan was just to stay together,' Froome said, downcast, 'and we did that . . . so . . . [shrugs] . . . that's all . . . that's all good . . .'

Wiggins said afterwards to journalists that, but for his own loss of concentration, Froome might well have caught Valverde but added as if to offer consolation: 'Chris has the talent, and in the years to come he'll have all the pressure of the press and so on.

'Mentally he's very strong, and I'm sure that he'll win the Tour one day. He will have his day, and I'll be there to support him every inch of the way when he does, at the Tour.' A generous sentiment but would Le Gentleman be true to those words?

The next day, on the front page of *L'Equipe*, there was a photograph of Froome and Wiggins climbing towards the summit of Peyragudes together, having vanquished Nibali and all their other rivals, with a headline that summed up Sky's supremacy: '*La Promenade des Anglais*'.

21 July 2012
Stage 19: Bonneval–Chartres, ITT, 53.5km
Another long time trial, another 1–2 finish for Team Sky. Froome, second, at 1:16 as Wiggins destroyed the opposition with an emphatic performance befitting a Tour de France champion elect. Wiggins blew away the field, perhaps fired up not only by the prospect of putting the golden seal on his – and Great Britain's – first ever Grand Tour victory, but also the added satisfaction of putting his second-in-command in his place.

It was, unquestionably, a stunning achievement by Froome to finish runner-up at the biggest bike race in the world. Bar the pesky puncture on the second day it had been a fabulous three weeks for him. Form-wise, he hadn't wilted once. However, in the final reckoning, the man from Kilburn had proved himself to be a worthy winner over his Kenyan-born partner, reluctant or otherwise.

Talking to *Procycling* magazine in Chartres after the time trial Froome attempted to clarify that his hand gesture had been simply instinctive, with no scheming intent: 'I knew that Nibali had been dropped – it was just like, "Come on [Bradley], get on my wheel. Let's make the most of this." It wasn't a, "Come on, hurry up, you big oaf", or whatever. It wasn't like that at all.'

22 July 2012

Stage 20: Rambouillet–Paris (Champs-Élysées), 120km

Wearing the rainbow jersey of world champion, the brash, effusive *roi du sprint* (king of the sprint) Mark Cavendish, normally the centre of attention, found himself to be a bit-part player at the 2012 Tour in a game that, for once, wasn't about him. Nevertheless he propelled himself to his 23rd Tour stage win, his third of the race – poor by his standards, but then Sky had put all their eggs in Wiggins's basket and neglected the Manxman's needs – and fourth victory in a row on the grand boulevard of the Champs-Élysées. It was a typically swaggering display by Cav – a brilliantly sustained burst of power and panache taking him past the pushy new rival for his sprint crown, the young Slovak Peter Sagan.

Froome was overjoyed to reach Paris in second place, and his emotions were stirred by the reception that awaited him and the other 152 riders who had survived to the French capital. 'Getting onto the Champs-Élysées and hearing the eruption from the crowd as we came through the first tunnel sent chills right through me. It hasn't sunk in yet what we have achieved here. Standing next to Bradley on the podium has only inspired me. It was quite an emotional day. I'm 27 and I hope to win the Tour one day. If you had said to me a month before the Tour that I would be second, I wouldn't have believed you. I'm very happy.'

On the alleged enmity between him and Wiggins, Froome said it had all been blown out of proportion by the media. 'There really is no friction between us. We've worked together for years and we've done really well together as everyone has seen,' he told *Cycle Sport*. 'I think people are trying to sensationalise the race and bring a gossip side to it that doesn't actually exist.'

How did he feel about taking on the responsibility of team leadership, with all the pressures it entails, and trying for the top step of the podium in Paris next time? Was he ready for that?

'Yes,' he said, smiling. 'There's only one way to find out.'

CHAPTER 16

A Puente Too Far

In late July 2012 Olympics fever hit Great Britain. In fact the hype had been building for a long time, since 2005, when London pipped long-time favourite Paris to win the right to host the world's biggest sporting event. Over seventeen days of breathless excitement a sports-mad nation giddily arose to acclaim a host of new sporting heroes.

Film director Danny Boyle thrilled a worldwide audience of billions with a spectacular opening ceremony that went from a vision of pastoral Britain through the Industrial Revolution to quintessential British pop culture. The Queen appeared in a skit with James Bond. British athletics' poster girl Jessica Ennis smiled down from giant advertising billboards all over the country. Seventy thousand volunteers helped catalyse a mood of collective goodwill and became the Games' most potent cheerleaders. Suddenly the British capital felt like an altogether more pleasant place to be. Londoners even talked to one another on the Tube.

When the action began, the highlights flowed thick and fast. Chris Froome was about to make a name for himself too, albeit without quite the same level of hoopla that surrounded the likes of Ennis, Mo Farah, Sir Chris Hoy and Usain Bolt's triumphs.

He had been selected to ride for Great Britain in the men's road race on 28 July followed by the time trial four days later. In the first race Froome would form part of a five-man team with the purpose of winning the gold medal for his Sky teammate, Mark Cavendish, fresh from their joint success on the Champs-Élysées ten days earlier.

For Froome the 2012 London Olympics represented the end of

a long journey dating back to 2006 when the fresh-faced 21-year-old Kenyan was approached by British Cycling's Doug Dailey in the team pits at the Commonwealth Games in Melbourne. Possibly weary of the assumptions that he was some kind of 'plastic Brit' he was keen to remind anyone who asked that he had carried a British passport since birth. 'They think I swapped a Kenyan passport for a British one later on, but that wasn't the case. I had always had a British passport,' he said.

The tough road race route necessitated climbing the same hill nine times. Box Hill – a summit in the North Downs of Surrey – isn't the steepest or longest of ascents, but when you climb it nine times it becomes the equivalent of riding a major Alpine pass in the Tour de France. But Froome and the rest of the Great Britain dream team – Bradley Wiggins, David Millar and Ian Stannard – were there in sole support of Cavendish, the overwhelming favourite for the gold medal. He'd won the try-out race on the course the year before. After Wiggins's and Froome's historic performance at the Tour, Britain had gone cycling mad. The nation expected Cavendish to continue the country's glorious winning streak by racing to gold on The Mall.

On a dizzy high after their Tour de France exploits, the Great Britain team had similar expectations.

Unfortunately there was to be no repeat of Great Britain's phenomenal collective effort in Copenhagen the year before, which had resulted in him becoming only the second British rider ever to win the World Championships road race. Not to say the British quintet didn't give it their best shot. For 200km Froome and his colleagues rode with all the drive and discipline that had brought Cavendish his rainbow jersey but they were undone in the final 50km by a cleverly timed attack from a large group that included the eventual gold medal winner, Alexandre Vinokourov. The 38-year-old Kazakh rider was an unpopular Olympic champion.[22]

Cavendish finished 29th, 40 seconds down, while Froome

22 Vinokourov served a ban for blood doping after a positive test at the 2007 Tour de France but has never admitted his guilt, expressed regret or condemned the use of doping techniques in his sport.

came home 108th, almost nine minutes further back, completely spent having helped drive the pace of the chasing peloton for the majority of the race in cahoots with Wiggins, Stannard and Millar. It was a gallant effort and the four-man team of *deluxe domestiques* was so shattered by their mighty exertions they could barely speak for half an hour after the finish. Cavendish's gold medal dreams had been dashed in the end by a combination of a strength-sapping course, canny opponents and, arguably, a dash of pre-race cockiness.

Having helped Cavendish win his world title in September 2011, worked tirelessly for Wiggins at the Tour and flogged himself into the ground again for Cavendish in the Olympic road race it seemed a fitting personal reward that Froome then went on to take a deserved bronze medal in the time trial. As was widely expected, Wiggins won gold. Germany's reigning world time-trial champion, Tony Martin, took silver.

Froome put in a fabulous performance, unseating his Sky team-mate, the Australian Michael Rogers, three-time world time-trial champion, at the 30km split on the 44km circuit which took in some of London's most iconic landmarks. The partisan home crowds gasped as Martin came flying past to knock Froome off the top spot, before going wild as Wiggins hurtled down The Mall to his fourth career Olympic gold.

David Millar was suitably impressed by his fellow Team GB man's performance. 'For a climber like Froome to be so good at time trialling is exceptional. He's like [Alberto] Contador in that respect,' he told *Cycle Sport* magazine. 'He's untidy,' the Scotsman said with a laugh. 'On a time-trial bike Froome looks like he's on a motorbike that's going too fast for him. But he and Contador are the biggest threats to Brad in future Tours.'

Doug Dailey, the man who had stuck his neck out to back Froome's nationality switch, took great satisfaction that his discovery had reaped the rewards after missing out on Beijing. 'I get a personal thrill watching guys that I've been close to doing well, and one of them is Froomey,' he says. 'All I wanted for him was that he would have the opportunity, and if he had continued riding under a Kenyan licence then he would never have reached his full potential.'

For the second time in a fortnight Froome stood on one of the biggest podiums in cycling – at the Tour, now the Olympics amid the palatial grandeur of Hampton Court. Only Martin had spoiled another Wiggins–Froome 1-2. But Froome cared not a jot. He was 'chuffed to bits' with what he said was a surprise Olympic bronze medal and later said it was his favourite memory of 2012.

His emotions had been stirred by the rapturous support of the British public. They were, of course, his home crowd now. Via Kenya and South Africa Froome had taken the long road back to the land of his heritage. 'The roads were just lined with people, not just cheering but screaming our names. It leaves me with goose bumps thinking about it,' he said. 'Every time you wanted to ease off and take a few breaths or take a few easy pedals, you'd have another couple of hundred people screaming your name.'

On Twitter, on that woozy, late summer evening of 1 August, Froome posted a link to a photo of himself with a huge cheesy grin, proudly holding up his Olympic bronze medal, and the tagline: 'This photo says it all. Thank you for all the phenomenal support!!'

Wiggins vowed to let his hair down, after keeping the champagne on ice after his Tour triumph in France, with 'a few vodka tonics', before watching his old track cycling teammates in action at the London Velopark. Froome could only afford one day off to 'soak up the Olympic spirit' before returning to his Monaco base to prepare for professional cycling's third biggest stage race, the Vuelta a España, to be held later that month.

★

Happy to be back training on the roads around the Côte d'Azur for the first time in six weeks after his Tour and Olympic exploits, Froome took a wrong turning and found himself lost up a goat trail, finally making it home as dusk fell. It was like a scene from his teen years with David Kinjah; a confrontation with some local wildlife thrown in for good measure, this time thankfully of a more benign variety than that found in the Ngong Hills. 'I almost collided with four donkeys on the way down. Luckily I found a gap and squeezed through or I'd probably still be out there.' You can take the boy out of Kenya . . .

Despite his early-season setbacks – enforced periods of recuperation and a lack of racing days – caused by the return of the bilharzia bug it had been an exceptional 2012 season, with his form building gradually from fourth place overall at the Dauphiné in June, throughout the Tour – where, puncture aside, he didn't have a single bad day on his way to a milestone second place – and on to the Olympics, the selfless slog of the road race and recovering brilliantly to win time-trial bronze.

The 27-year-old's chances of bagging his first Grand Tour title in Spain rested on his answering two key questions. The first was: did he have the legs to go the extra mile, or rather, the extra 3,360km, from Pamplona to Madrid? He had never tackled two Grand Tours back to back and admitted that 'it wasn't easy to retain my focus after the Tour, and the schedule has made it harder because I've not had time to tailor my training specifically for the Vuelta, so I'm not going into it the same way I did the Tour'. The timing of the Olympics had prevented Froome and Sky, normally obsessive in their race preparations, from carrying out detailed recces of the race route, particularly the key mountain stages, where the race would be won or lost.

In the three-week trek around Spain, Froome would be up against arguably the world's best climbers – with the exception of the missing Vincenzo Nibali and Frank and Andy Schleck – in a race route designed for *grimpeurs*, that included eight mountain stages, ten summit finishes and 36 mountain passes. After Sky's utter dominance of the Tour, the Vuelta promised to be a far more competitive affair.

Twice in the past year Froome had been obliged to sacrifice his own ambitions for Bradley Wiggins – at the 2011 Vuelta and 2012 Tour – and twice he had finished runner-up. Now, with Wiggins absent, for the first time Froome was handed the opportunity by Team Sky to be their undisputed leader at a Grand Tour.

The second big question concerned how he would handle the pressure of leadership. Was he too nice to dictate to others what he required from them in the heat of the battle? 'It's a fantastic opportunity for him to learn, to take the mantle,' said Dave Brailsford. 'The key thing is, how much did the Tour take out of him?'

It is worth stressing that, amid the incessant media attention about Froome sacrificing personal ambitions for the greater good of Team Sky's Plan A – Wiggins's personal glory – and his so-called 'treachery', cycling is a team sport, a feudal pursuit, the traditions of which go back over a century. And Froome knew that. In fact he was happy to play his part in Wiggins's victory. Sure, he was gutted at not being allowed to go after some more stage wins. He's a highly tuned, top-class athlete, who felt alive to the possibilities of what his body could achieve and the Froome-dog was straining at the leash to be set free. But it was his job as a professional to ride for Wiggins. And he was being handsomely paid to do that job. Robert Millar, the Scottish cyclist who had been the highest ever British finisher at the Tour de France before Wiggins and Froome, when he placed fourth overall in 1984, put it aptly: 'Froome signed up for that role. No one made him accept that, and though he and some of his fans may be miffed at having to rein in his talent, the bigger plan had been to put Wiggins in with the chance of winning the Tour de France.'

The role of *domestique* had evolved somewhat from the old days when a rider would sometimes stop at a stream to fill his team leader's water bottle – a kind of 'Jeeves on wheels' as some wags saw it – and then dream of spending his cut of the team's paltry prize money on a modest abode in the French countryside. The job description hasn't changed that much but the rewards have, especially at a big-bucks operation like Team Sky where a talented *domestique* can be promoted to *super-domestique* and eventually team leader. Similar to the fast-track career path Froome was now on. He'd worked hard to get into the position he was in – team leader of the number one ranked cycling team in the world at the third biggest race on the calendar.

'I don't know if it's just the Vuelta or if it's because this is the position I've wanted to be in for so long; I don't actually feel like it's a huge weight on my shoulders,' said Froome. 'I've been quite relaxed.'

Froome's Monaco neighbour and closest friend in the peloton, Richie Porte, offered a different take on his state of mind. 'Chris hasn't really ridden as a leader in any other race and he goes into the Vuelta with the whole team behind him; there was a little bit of stress. I know for a fact that he had a bit of guilt in the back of his mind that guys were sacrificing their chances for him, but I guess that's Froomey. He always thinks of other people.'

★

The fierce opposition at the 67th edition of Spain's premier stage race presented themselves in the shape of local favourites Alberto Contador, Alejandro Valverde, Joaquim Rodríguez and Froome's 2011 conqueror, Juan José Cobo. But for *domestique* duties and time bonuses, Froome might well have won the 2011 Vuelta. He covered the 3,300km in the lowest aggregate time, but the wily Cobo nicked enough time-bonus seconds over the three weeks to pip Froome by a scant thirteen seconds. Froome was out for revenge.

Contador was returning to Grand Tour action for the first time that season after completing a backdated six-month ban on 5 August. Having won the 2010 Tour de France and 2011 Giro d'Italia he was stripped of those titles when a sample given during the 2010 Tour tested positive for Clenbuterol. (He blamed the tiny trace found of the banned substance on contaminated meat he'd eaten on the second rest day during that year's race.)

Froome had every right to be wary of Contador ahead of their first major showdown. The 29-year-old Spaniard is perhaps the most complete stage racer of his generation – one of only five men in history to have won all three Grand Tours – the Tour de France in 2007 and 2009, the Giro d'Italia and Vuelta double in 2008. He rode with style and panache, and displayed a terrifying ability to dance away from other riders on the most brutally steep climbs. But El Pistolero, who hailed from the small town of Pinto, near Madrid, also expressed his admiration for the British rider, articulating the belief that Froome 'showed last year he could have won the Vuelta . . . and proved that he was the strongest at the Tour de France with a spectacular performance'.

Fully aware that the trio of Spaniards, headed by Contador, would gang up on Froome in the mountains, Sky furnished their first-time leader with a team packed with climbing talent, notably the Colombian pairing of Rigoberto Urán, who had come second in the Olympic road race and seventh at the 2012 Giro d'Italia, and Sergio Henao, who finished ninth in the Giro. The Australian climber Richie Porte, seventh in the 2010 Giro, and a key man in Wiggins's Tour triumph, completed a strong trio of mountain *domestiques*.

Froome would need all the support he could get. Contesting the general classification in consecutive Grand Tours was an arduous task. Staying switched on mentally and physically in the space of a few months to compete with the best in the world over three weeks and thousands of kilometres of highly charged action was no mean feat.

Froome's Sky finished seventh in Stage 1's TTT curtain-raiser in Pamplona. Instead of running ahead of a dozen snorting, galumphing bulls, the unhinged highlight of the Navarre city's annual San Fermín festival, the riders raced against the clock on a 16.6km circuit, whose tricky second half had the teams careering through the same narrow, snaking streets as the famous bull run and ending in the Plaza de Toros bullring. Just three seconds separated Froome and Contador. The top seven teams had been split by only five seconds before Cobo and Valverde's Movistar squad wiped out the rest of the field to take victory by an impressive ten seconds.

As the race headed west into the Basque Country, the Spanish favourites flexed their climbing muscles straightaway, and the Arrate summit on Stage 3 provided the first glimpse of who was on form. Free from any shackles, the difference in Froome's modus operandi, as Sky's designated number one, became instantly clear and he displayed Wiggins-esque patience to continually reel in the skittish Contador when he surged again and again – six times in total – on the final climb. Only Froome, Valverde and Rodríguez could follow the Spaniard, with Froome taking the longest of the three shadows to do so, still managing to sneak past Contador on the line to finish third and pick up a time bonus.

'The old Chris maybe would have started jumping after the riders and then blown up. Now he rode with his head and he rode them back. He wouldn't have done that two years ago,' said Sky sports director Marcus Ljungqvist.

The next day red-jersey holder Valverde was left fuming after he was caught up in a crash with 30km to go to the finish of Stage 4. Froome's Team Sky train, looking to split the peloton in the stiff crosswinds that buffeted the race on the run-in to the day's final climb, paid no heed to the red-jersey holder's plight. As the peloton split into four echelons and Valverde got caught up in the carnage, Sky failed to call a truce to racing, thereby snubbing a collective nose to the unwritten rules of cycle race etiquette – never to attack the race leader in the event of a crash, puncture or toilet stop. 'They didn't have the balls to stop, they chose an unsporting way,' Valverde said, stung by Sky's perceived lack of respect, after he'd lost his race lead to fellow countryman Rodríguez.

For the first week Froome matched his trio of rivals pedal-stroke by pedal-stroke until the eighth stage, on 25 August, a 174.7km slog across rugged terrain from Lleida up into the Andorran Pyrenees and a brutal final climb to the summit of the Collada de la Gallina, where he was unable to respond to a piercing attack from Contador in the final kilometre. New to the 2012 Vuelta, the Gallina's slopes zig-zag 7.2km to a leg-shredding average gradient of 9% in the last 4km. Sky's super-climbing duo of Urán and Henao obliterated the main bunch on the lower slopes, leaving small groups scattered down the road.

When the Colombian pacemakers tailed off, out of juice, Froome was left to set the tempo alone almost all the way up the unforgiving ascent, with Rodríguez, Contador and Valverde tied to his wheel, like tin cans trailing off the back of a wedding car, to conserve energy. At one point, in the final 3km, Froome slowed down to a near stop and motioned to Contador to take over but he shook his head. The Spaniards then upped the pace, Contador darted away, Froome couldn't respond and Valverde won the sprint to the line ahead of Rodríguez and Contador, while Froome came in fourth. He'd lost ground, 15 seconds, but remained second overall, 33 seconds down on Rodríguez. He was still in the hunt for the overall title but for the first time he really knew what he was up against. Asked afterwards if it was Chris Froome versus Spain, he laughed and said, 'I hope not!'

In Barcelona Rodríguez caught Froome, Contador and Valverde napping when he attacked on the hill at Montjuic, in the shadow of the Olympic stadium that hosted the 1992 Games, 4km from the finish of the ninth stage, netting a crucial eight-second bonus for finishing second. In two days Froome had gone from ten seconds off the lead to 53 adrift. It would need a special performance in the upcoming time trial from Cambados to Pontevedra.

With Spain's August holiday season in full swing, Vuelta route directors Abraham Olano and Paco Giner, responsible for mapping the time-trial course, had been forced to steer clear of main traffic routes along the Galician coast and stick to minor roads. Subsequently the hillier course on Stage 11 played into the hands of pure climbers like Rodríguez, and he pulled out the time-trial ride of his life to cling on to his overall lead by one second from Contador. Froome was relegated to third in the stage and on the GC. The Briton wilted on the upper slopes of the Category 3 climb of the Alto Monte Castrove as a turbo-charged Contador soared to the top and flew down the spine-chillingly narrow descent like a toboggan on the Cresta Run, sucking 22 seconds from Froome by the finish to take second place behind Swedish thunderbolt Fredrik Kessiakoff.

It was a day of good news and bad news for Froome. On one hand he'd closed the gap on Rodríguez by 37 seconds – who'd limited his losses brilliantly – but on the other he'd lost his second spot to Contador who expressed great satisfaction at having beaten Froome. The gap was a mere fifteen seconds, but the psychological advantage of going ahead of his British rival was important to the Spaniard. An upbeat Froome insisted, 'There's everything to play for – with that little time between the top three, it's not over by any means.'

Glowering in the near distance was a triple bill of altitude summit finishes – on Stages 14 to 16 – in the high mountains of Asturias, on whose terrifying slopes it would not be so much a case of who seized the upper hand as of who cracked first. 'The Vuelta has only just begun,' Contador said with ominous intent. 'And we're moving into my terrain.'

Before they'd even hit Contador country, Froome had shed more time on Stage 12's cruel climb to Mirador de Ézaro thanks to a virtuoso climbing display by Rodríguez.

After 190km racing along the Galician coast, in cahoots with his compatriot Contador, Rodríguez attacked Froome on the lower slopes of the Mirador de Ézaro ascent that, at 29% in places, are even steeper than the dreaded Angliru. Nicknamed 'El Purito' (The Little Cigar), Rodríguez is a master at scrambling up the short, sharp ascent. He was the reigning Flèche Wallonne champion, conqueror of its famed Mur de Huy, and he had marked the stage beforehand with a cross in his route book. Froome simply didn't have the legs to keep apace and lost 23 seconds by the summit.

Rodríguez now led Contador in the GC by thirteen seconds, but the race leader's gap to Froome in third had stretched out from sixteen to 51 seconds.

Froome was on the ropes now with the triple terror of the Asturian Mountains up next – three stages that would decide the outcome of the race. On 1 September, in a thrilling duel on the last and toughest of Stage 14's five categorised climbs – a steep, 9.5km, Category 1 haul up to Puerto de Ancares, Contador – who had clearly targeted this as the day he would attempt to overhaul race leader Rodríguez – shot off the front with a full-throttle burst 2km from the finish. A tired-looking Froome seemed down and out but rallied superbly to launch his own counter-attack and left the red jersey trailing along with Valverde. But Rodríguez somehow summoned hidden reserves of energy to storm past Froome in the final kilometre and take Contador on the last bend, the latter's face etched in panic and pain, for his third stage win of the race.

Froome was now on the brink of slipping out of the top three overall after losing another 38 seconds to Rodríguez on the line. Meanwhile, the Sky man's tenacity earned him admiration from within the peloton. 'He's the toughest rider I know,' said Dutch climber Robert Gesink, lying 5th overall by Stage 12.

On Stage 14 Froome yo-yoed up and down the mountain – he was there, then he was gone, then he fought back, only to fade again. Each time he slipped off the back of the elite group, partisan Spanish radio commentators confidently predicted he was finished, only for Froome to appear once more and prove them wrong, his long back arched, elbows akimbo, nodding his head with that distinctive little swivel to the right – reminiscent of the marathon runner Paula Radcliffe. It was a testimony to his true grit, that facility to go deep into the dark depths of suffering and re-emerge. 'Maybe that's the word for the Vuelta: suffering,' said Ljungqvist. 'Chris can suffer. He's a great bike rider, but if you don't have that ability to suffer, you'll never finish at the top.'

His endurance wasn't in doubt, but there was no question that the 27-year-old was struggling to find the spark that lit up his legs at the Tour and Olympics. Rodríguez's irresistible form seemed far from waning, and, increasingly fatigued, Froome's chances of becoming Britain's second Grand Tour winner of the year now appeared slim. The battle for the red jersey was now between Rodríguez and Contador.

With three mountainous stages still to come before the second rest day on 4 September, Froome was clinging on to a podium place by his fingernails. Valverde, fourth, had joined Froome on the same time, 1:41, behind the race leader, and was hovering with intent. Not that he was about give up the fight.

It had been a long eight weeks since his impressive stage

victory in the Tour at La Planche des Belles Filles, and it was an enormous ask for him to hold his form for another eight days to the finish in Madrid. In the Tour Froome was often at his most dangerous when he appeared vulnerable. As the 2012 Vuelta approached its tantalising *dénouement* his vulnerability was real.

The climb to the summit of Lagos de Covadonga, the first *hors catégorie* peak of the race, is not long but it is devilishly steep and features two hideous ramps at La Huesara (The Boneyard) and the Mirador de la Reina (literally the Queen's Lookout). And what a 'lookout' it is. With its two lakes beneath the summit, the Enol and the Ercina, there is a spectacular view over the Picos de Europa mountain range. Ironic that in an area of such unspoiled beauty the climb's tarmac should have inflicted such pain and suffering on participants in the Vuelta since its first inclusion in 1983. Five-time Tour winner Miguel Indurain ended his glittering career at the foot of the climb in 1996, stepping off his bike, having had enough of the Vuelta and cycling.

Similar thoughts probably crossed Chris Froome's mind as he approached the final 13.5km climb to Lagos de Covadonga on Stage 15. Contador attacked again and again in attempt to shake Rodríguez, which he couldn't manage, the race leader hanging onto his 22-second lead by the finish. Froome was first to buckle and the weary Brit came home in a big group 35 seconds behind the leading Spanish pair and was helpless to prevent Valverde leapfrogging him into third place.

Worse was to come on a disastrous sixteenth stage, which took in four categorised climbs, including a brutal summit finish, 19km to the Valgrande-Pajares ski station. The final stretch up to the finish at Cuitu Negru had prolonged ramps in excess of 23%. Froome lost a further two-and-a-half minutes on Rodríguez, who once again fought out an exhilarating joust with Contador, thwarting his repeated attacks with audacious counter-bursts to gain more bonus time on the line and racing to third place on the stage. Now 28 seconds better off than Contador, El Purito had one hand on the winner's trophy with five stages left to Madrid.

Visibly in pain on the lower slopes Froome inched home

up the tarmacked ski slope 5:11 behind stage winner Dario Cataldo; all hopes of repeating his 2011 feat of a podium place were now over. Valverde had an insurmountable lead of 2:48 over the punch-drunk Brit. 'It's really hard mentally to know you're not the best,' Froome admitted frankly afterwards, 'knowing the inevitable was coming but trying to block it out and cope with it as best as possible.'

After his heroic exertions at the Tour and Olympics the ailing Froome was near to collapse, and, as the final huge mountain stage to Bola del Mundo loomed on the penultimate day, it was looking more like a case of damage limitation. Now he wasn't thinking about gaining time, he was concentrating all his remaining energies on avoiding a horrible freefall down the overall standings. Steady does it, pick up the pace by a few watts, he gave up trying to follow Contador's sudden bursts of acceleration and in the final week dug deep, perhaps deeper than he had ever done before in his cycling career.

Following the second rest day, Rodríguez went into a surprise meltdown on Stage 17, on 5 September, to lose his overall lead by a massive 2:28 to stage winner Contador, who went on to secure the overall title in Madrid. Another daring attack in the final 3km of the gruelling climb from El Pistolero saw Rodríguez's prospects of winning a first-ever major stage race disappear into the Cantabrian mountain air at the summit of Fuente Dé. Froome lost nearly five minutes but retained his fourth place.

Three days later, on the steep road up to the summit of Bola del Mundo and the soaring TV masts that stand guard over the Navacerrada network of ski resorts and the Madrid sierra, Froome was once again confronted by the dispiriting sight of Contador, Rodríguez and Valverde coasting away from him. As Denis Menchov rode to stage victory, Froome went into the red and lost another 4:48, but his fourth place was secure. That last climb had been, however, 'a kick in the head,' he said. Several riders were in need of assistance to prevent them falling from their saddles when they crossed the line at the mountaintop finish.

The old adage that you learn more in defeat than in victory

surely applied to Froome's 2012 Vuelta. He didn't win the race. He didn't finish on the podium. But it said a lot about his remarkable progress and revised ambition that a fourth-place finish at a Grand Tour could be seen as an anticlimax. Despite this, he felt that he hadn't delivered the goods or lived up to pre-race expectations. He thought that he'd let down his teammates. 'It's mind-blowing to think that I was only moderately happy with my fourth place, because a year and a half ago if you'd have told me I'd be in that type of position, I'd be ecstatic,' he said.

Still, he'd proved that mentally and physically he could handle two Grand Tours *and* an Olympic Games, and he'd learned, from watching Wiggins, how to ride economically and lead a team. No other rider had such strong successive Grand Tour results in 2012. The boy from Kenya had come a long way in a short space of time.

But he had trained for the long, steady climbs of the Tour – always his preference – not the Vuelta, where the gradients required explosive, punchy riders in the mould of Contador and Rodríguez. His fatigue was unsurprising given the two months that had preceded the race. 'I've reached the end of the line,' Froome said. 'As an athlete if you just go from competition to competition you're bound to run out of reserves at some point.'

Team Sky also hadn't recce'd the Vuelta route in anything like the microscopic detail they had done for the Tour. Dave Brailsford had chucked all their resources at winning the Tour for Wiggins, his main objective since long before the team's formation. The Vuelta was a comparative afterthought with a team leader who was knackered. Perhaps trying to win two Grand Tours back to back in the modern era *is* impossible? It begged the question: could Froome have won the Vuelta if he'd targeted it as his one and only priority of the season?

Froome's coach Bobby Julich gave his answer in *VeloNews*: 'What he has shown here at the Vuelta is grit and determination. What he showed on the Tour de France was amazing numbers [in terms of power output]. Put those two together and, if he'd had this as his objective, I'd have to say yes.' Julich said he was prouder of how Froome had raced in Spain than anything he achieved at the Tour or the previous year's Vuelta. 'He's learned how hard this sport can be, and this will give him more of a boost in many ways than if he were winning.'

His young charge viewed the race as a voyage of discovery, a journey to the extreme boundaries of where his pain and form thresholds lay. 'I've never done two Grand Tours back to back,' he said. 'After this I've probably learned that I can't do that. Maybe I need to target one Tour for stages or use as a build-up to the second one, but I don't think going for the overall in two successive Grand Tours is something that can be done.

'What I've learned most about myself is that my biggest characteristic is that I can take the best out of everything,' he concluded. 'I've not been the best here – and that's a horrible feeling – but I'm not giving up and going home to sulk.'

He also had the invaluable experience, the privilege, of riding against Contador for the first time and seeing up close how the Spanish climber was able to unleash staccato spurts of acceleration on the most evil ascents, over and over again – to feel the explosive waves of energy vibrating off the back wheel of his bike. It was fieldwork that Froome would never have been able to do by watching the race on TV. It would help him to formulate a plan to cope better next time the pair met, at a future event that he only referred to as 'the race'.

'The obvious thing that stands out is how I'm going to play the race differently, knowing that Contador has that advantage of the explosive attack. I think tactically I'm going to have to come up with some kind of plan, a scenario for the team to be able to deal with that.'

It could safely be assumed that 'the race' is the Tour de France. It was the perfect winter homework project for Dave Brailsford and Team Sky: 'How do you go about beating Alberto Contador at the 2013 Tour? Discuss.'

And who would lead the team against the dashing Spaniard? Froome said Wiggins would repay him for his loyalty in 2012 and help him towards his own aims of winning the Tour. But could the reigning champion be expected to lower himself to being a super-deluxe 'Jeeves on wheels' for Froome in July 2013?

Talking of which, what about Froome's leadership skills at the Vuelta? Can nice guys really be winners too? Could someone as unassuming and laidback as Froome possibly play the alpha male role? Teammate Porte had nothing but praise for his friend. He said Froome led the team 'like Brad Wiggins' on Stage 8 to Andorra, and he couldn't recall seeing him stressed or irate during the entire three weeks. As roommates and training buddies they had shot the breeze about any subject in the world except cycling, but then, Porte said, Froome could flick the 'on' switch to train and race like a man possessed. It was clear that Froome had been stung at having to play second fiddle to the Spaniards, but Porte warned: 'Alberto and those guys should fear Chris Froome for the future. Before last year's Vuelta, if someone had said Chris Froome was going to be the next big GC rider of this generation, you'd have thought he was mad. But if he can improve even a small percentage on this year, that's a pretty scary bike rider.'

CHAPTER 17

2013 . . . Lucky for Some?

Ten years ago Chris Froome was pulled over by an irate traffic policeman for riding his bike down a busy Johannesburg highway, taking a cheeky shortcut home from boarding school to spend the weekend with his father. Despite the fresh-faced youth's, no doubt polite protestations, the patrolman failed to see the funny side.

On 11 January 2013, almost exactly a decade on, Froome found himself involved in an incident that served as an amusing, and enlightening, bookend to the original encounter. He was back in South Africa for the European winter months, revelling in the wonderful scenery and weather, and doing interval training along the R27 highway, on the Western Cape coast near Saldanha Bay, when he was chased down by a SAPS (South African Police Service) vehicle and ushered to the roadside. This time there was no angry ticking off. It transpired that the constable, a cycling fan, just wanted to shake Froome's hand.

After his second place finish at the 2011 Vuelta, Froome would have been able to walk around in public unnoticed, just another face in the crowd. It was a different story after the Tour de France and the Olympics. In the space of one glorious summer, he had become quite famous.

'It is a bit strange now,' he told *Cycle Sport*. 'I go for a coffee and I realise a lot of people seem to be looking at me, saying little hushed words. It almost makes you a little self-conscious. It was quite a shock in the UK, walking around London after the Olympics, people asking me for photos and autographs.'

He might have exploded into the consciousness of cycling fans at the Tour and Olympics, but it was an overnight success ten years in the making. It had been an erratic and arduous journey. Everything around him had been altered in the last year by his incredible success, but it hadn't changed him. 'I'd like to think that I'm pretty grounded. I'm not feeding off all this attention,' Froome said. 'I actually think I'm a bit the opposite – I tend to shy away from it and prefer a quieter life.'

★

On 22 October 2012, two days before the official presentation in Paris of the 2013 Tour de France route, Lance Armstrong was stripped of the seven Tour titles he'd won between 1999 and 2005.[23]

Team Sky released a statement saying they wanted to 'reaffirm' their commitment to a clean sport following the damaging effect of the Armstrong case on cycling's reputation, sullied for too long by doping scandals. Sky's zero-tolerance approach to drugs resulted in them asking all staff to sign a statement pledging no previous involvement in doping. Dave Brailsford informed his squad of the policy on the first day of their annual end-of-season camp in mid-October. Sky had said that anyone who refused to sign would be sacked.

Froome said his interview was very straightforward. He was asked if he had 'done anything' or was 'likely to be linked to anything'. When he answered 'no' he was told to sign the statement. 'I wish it was that simple for everybody on the team,' Froome said. '[But] we have staff and riders who rode in that time [the Lance Armstrong era].' He called on Armstrong to confess to doping to 'help the sport move forward and close the door on that era of cycling'.[24]

23 On 22 October 2012 the Union Cycliste Internationale (UCI), cycling's governing body, announced that it had accepted the findings of the United States Anti-Doping Agency's (USADA) investigation into systematic doping and stripped Armstrong of the seven Tour de France titles he won in successive years from 1999 to 2005. Armstrong was also stripped of all race results since 1 August 1998 and received a life ban from USADA for what the organisation called 'the most sophisticated, professionalised and successful doping programme that sport has ever seen'.

24 Over two consecutive nights, 17–18 January 2013, Lance Armstrong finally ended years of denials by admitting he used performance-enhancing drugs during all seven of his Tour de France wins, in the most incongruous of settings, or perhaps the most apposite, given his propensity for showmanship – the *Oprah Winfrey Show*.

'The sport needs new figures to look up to, clean winners who aren't going to get their titles stripped. Personally it gives me a lot of motivation, it gives me a goal, something to aim for and hopefully inspire people.'

Sky's refusal to employ riders, coaches or backroom staff with a prior history of doping claimed its first victim on 25 October. Bobby Julich, Froome's coach and mentor for the past two years, publicly confessed to using EPO from August 1996, when he was riding with Armstrong's Motorola squad, until July 1998. It was announced that he would be leaving his job at Sky. 'That was quite a shock,' Froome told the *Guardian*. 'It's sad to have lost Bobby. But you look at all the negativity around doping and the chaos it's causing weekly. You don't want any ties to it.'

Brailsford told the BBC it was 'highly likely' more staff would go, and on 28 October came the news that Sky's senior sports director Sean Yates was retiring from cycling due to ill health and to focus on his family. Sky said Yates's departure was not forced by an admission of any kind.

Another Sky sports director Steven de Jongh was the third staff member to vacate his position after confessing to taking a banned substance earlier in his career. Michael Barry, Froome's Sky teammate, had announced his retirement in September. The Canadian, a key witness in USADA's Armstrong investigation, also confessed in October 2012 to doping during his time with Armstrong at the US Postal Service team he joined in 2002. Suddenly they were dropping like flies.

Brailsford strongly refuted the suggestion that these measures were draconian. Froome said he wasn't 100% behind the new policy and lamented that good people would be lost from the sport because they'd be 'painted with the same brush. But it is where we need to go with the team.'

Still, Froome was upset to lose Julich. The American had been instrumental in guiding him to his epiphany at the 2011 Vuelta. However, Sean Yates says that Froome won't miss Julich's influence. 'With Bobby's help Chris has moved on to another level and so he doesn't need him like he did then. Froomey's pretty damned determined. He knows exactly what he wants. He knows the tools he has to use to get even better, and Tim Kerrison is one of those tools.'

With Julich gone, Froome was now working full-time with Kerrison, Sky's head of performance support, the man often referred to as the team's 'secret weapon' by Brailsford. Not such a secret any more. Kerrison's cover had been blown after he overhauled Wiggins's training programme and masterminded his Tour and Olympic wins. Froome would now hope to be the beneficiary of his Midas touch.

★

As the sport digested the Armstrong doping scandal the route of the 100th edition of the Tour de France was unveiled in Paris. The defining theme of the 2013 race was mountains, and specifically two iconic climbs: Mont Ventoux and L'Alpe d'Huez. It would be the first time the Tour peloton would tackle these two mountains as summit finishes on road stages in the same Tour. And to add further spice to an already heady mix, Alpe d'Huez's concertina of hairpins would have to be climbed twice. This was to be on the pivotal Stage 18, on 18 July, a finishing circuit from hell after 168km of racing from Gap.

A tough opening three days, on the Tour's first visit to the rugged island of Corsica, with two stages akin to a hilly Classic, are to be followed by a pair of potentially race-defining mountain stages in the Pyrenees. And as if scaling Ventoux and Alpe d'Huez wasn't quite enough climbing for the final week, still to come was a hilly final time trial from Embrun to Chorges then argu-ably the hardest of the three Alpine stages, to Le Grand Bornand, and an intense penultimate stage to Semnoz, above Annecy, in the northern Alps.' The centenary Tour looked set to be one of the most keenly fought and most exciting in years.

With the total length of the time trials reduced to 65km from 100km in 2012 it was a *parcours* that played to Froome's strengths as a climber more than time-trial expert Wiggins. In Paris for the unveiling, Froome said he was certain that he could contend for overall honours on a route with four summit finishes. 'It's very well suited to me, more than last year which was predominantly decided in the time trials. This coming Tour will be decided in the mountains, no doubt about that. It's going to be very tough, but I think I can win the Tour. The legs have to do all the talking when they hit those mountains.'

He knew he wasn't capable of matching the ferocious bursts of acceleration by Alberto Contador, whom he declared 'the hot favourite for the Tour', so his work with Kerrison over the winter of 2012, then at the training camps in Mallorca in January and Tenerife in May, would focus on his ability as a climber to maintain a steady tempo that could reel in the Spaniard.

After it was clear that the centenary Tour would be decided in the mountains, it made perfect sense for Sky to reverse the leadership roles from 2012 and have Froome as Plan A with Wiggins providing back-up. If only it were that simple. Over the coming months and into 2013 there were to be more twists to the saga.

Wiggins said it was 'more than likely' that he would sacrifice defending his Tour title to support Froome in the 2013 race. He would instead concentrate his efforts on trying to be the first British rider to win the Giro d'Italia in May.

★

On 8 November 2012 Wiggins released a book, *My Time*, a personal account of his 2012 Tour victory. In the book he described Froome as lacking knowledge of the sport and being guilty of tactical naïvety. Wiggins said he felt that he was as much under attack from Froome as from any of his opponents on other teams.

Any perception of disloyalty still rankled with Froome: 'I was annoyed that people played on that. I know there were moments of miscommunication which could have been portrayed as me going against Brad, but I always did my job.'

Then Wiggins reneged on his intention not to defend his Tour title and concentrate solely on Italy's national tour when he told BBC Radio in mid–December that 'my goal is to win the Tour next year. Whether that is realised or not, I don't know really.' He said the problem of 'how to service both mouths' was a problem for Dave Brailsford to figure out.

Meanwhile Froome reiterated to *The Times* that he had been assured by Brailsford that he would be sole Sky leader at the 2013 Tour. 'The team are saying they are going to back me for the Tour. That's directly from Dave,' Froome said. 'He [Brailsford] said: "You're our man for the Tour. Focus on it."'

The ongoing debate of who would lead Sky's Tour team had been turned on its head again. Wiggins's unorthodox suggestion of having two leaders raised the tantalising prospect of the Londoner going head to head with his Sky teammate Froome for cycling's ultimate crown. Perhaps the Hinault–LeMond comparisons weren't so far off the mark after all?

★

At the team's Mallorcan training camp, where, among other stiff training tests, Froome and his Sky cohorts tackled the 26 hairpins of the formidable Sa Calobra climb on the northwest of the Spanish island, Froome and Wiggins appeared together for joint media appearances, and the stark difference in character and personality – not to mention status – could be gleaned from their slightly uncomfortable double act. Wiggins oozed confidence and was bullish about his prospects, fully befitting a man who cleaned up in 2012 with a Tour and Olympic double. Deferential and diplomatic sitting next to Wiggins, Froome radiated a quiet self-belief when interviewed on his own. He calmly stressed to Donald McRae of the *Guardian* that he was '100% certain' to be confirmed Team Sky's leader at the 2013 Tour ahead of Wiggins.

'We've got a perfectly good working relationship . . . we do what's needed of us,' Froome said. 'I wouldn't say I spend time with him off the bike. We've always felt an element of competition, especially over the last twelve months. But we're both professional about it. We both get along and we do our job.'

Wiggins answered the same question with: 'I haven't seen him since the Olympics.' But then they had different objectives for the season, which dictated a different racing and training schedule, and Froome had been in South Africa over the winter.

Not to say that the Froome–Wiggins rivalry wasn't real, but, channelled through Team Sky's tightly run ship, it merely provided an impetus for both men in an anything-you-can-do-I-can-do-better way. 'The reason I got back on my bike in early November was that I knew there are guys ready to jump into the position I've had for the last couple of years as team leader,' Wiggins said. 'We all push each other because we know that if you take your eye off the ball for one minute someone else is more than willing to jump into the position and get all the support.' Definite parallels with Hinault and LeMond, then. In many ways Team Sky is Wiggins's team – Brailsford built the team around him – in the same way that La Vie Claire was Bernard Hinault's team. His American teammate LeMond was, like Froome at Sky, very much the outsider.

Such rivalries as those between Froome and Wiggins are part of the age-old inner world, the closed circuitry of professional cycling. It's an individual sport run on a team basis. But, confusingly, it's not a team sport at all, because the riders are individuals torn between their personal competitive instincts and their professional obligation to conform to team orders. Froome, and many before him, had compromised his own desires for victory in order to become a team player. But, as is the case with Wiggins, it is not in his nature not to try and win. Possessing a champion's winning mentality, loyalty to another champion, even a reigning champion, only stretches so far. As Froome sniffed weakness in Wiggins last year so Wiggins will be ready to pounce if Froome has a bad day in the mountains.

★

As the 2013 season got under way, the cycling world didn't have to wait long to see Froome and Wiggins competing in the same stage race for the first time since the 2012 Tour.

Froome and Team Sky would get an early opportunity at the Tour of Oman, starting on 11 February, to test how their winter training had gone and what marks Brailsford and Kerrison would get for their off-season school project: How best to tame Alberto Contador in 2013?

The pecking order for Oman saw Froome as Sky's number one – by happy coincidence the way it was expected to pan out for the Tour – with Wiggins there in a support role for the first time.

The six-day stage race meandered through the vast gravel desert plains and the Hajar mountains of the oil-rich Arab state. It was too early in the season for the Grand Tour contenders to go full bore. Many riders were still in the initial throes of their training programmes, far from peak condition. But on certain days over the undulating Oman course – especially Stage 4's ascent of Jabal al Akhdar (Green Mountain) – there was a chance for climbers to test their legs and those of their rivals. The race was a little like the prologue of the Tour de France, an opportunity for the peloton to size each other up, score a few psychological points.

Come Valentine's Day and the Green Mountain stage, Froome had ridden himself into thirteenth place overall, 36 seconds behind race leader, Cannondale's young Slovak sprint sensation, Peter Sagan. It was the first real mountain showdown of the new season and the perfect place for Froome to lay down a marker for his Tour rivals. He hadn't been able to match Contador's kick for the line in the previous day's stage finish at Wadi Dayqah Dam, won by Sagan, his second stage win in a row. The 152.5km fourth stage was largely flat, winding around the Wadi Bani Khalid from Al Saltiyah in Samail to the summit finish at Green Mountain.

In baking conditions on the final 5.7km climb, with the last 2km at a joltingly steep 13.5% gradient, Froome and Joaquim Rodríguez out-manoeuvred and out-gunned big rivals Contador, Cadel Evans and defending champion Vincenzo Nibali in the final kilometre to take a 1-2 on the line putting the British rider in the race leader's red jersey by 24 seconds over Evans. Wiggins, although providing sterling support work for Froome, had already dropped out of overall contention on day one, perhaps wilting from the intense desert heat.

The next day Froome clinched overall victory with a brilliant Stage 5 win at the Ministry of Housing in Boshar, west along the Gulf of Oman from the capital city, Muscat. After a trio of tough climbs he led out the sprint into a headwind and had the speed and power to hold off Contador, with Rodríguez third. He closed out the first ever professional stage race win of his cycling career on the final day, protected by Team Sky on the high-speed circuits along the Corniche, a beautiful 3km stretch of beach road leading into Muscat. Beaming at the finish, Froome reserved special praise for talented Tasmanian climber Richie Porte, who was rapidly turning into his trusty lieutenant.

As Sky race coach Rod Ellingworth had astutely pointed out at the team training camp in Mallorca: 'Chris's big challenge for this year is to stay consistent – that's how he will get the belief of the guys in the team on the road.'

He'd never ridden consistently from week to week, race to race, throughout his five-year professional career. Significantly, however, 2013 marked the first time in three years that he was healthy, able to start a season free from the debilitating effects of the bilharzia bug. Not that he could relax completely. Following a routine check in mid-January Froome found that he required another dose of medication to keep him in the clear for at least another six months.

★

In the first week of March Froome travelled south from his Monaco base back to his former domicile of Italy for Tirreno–Adriatico, the 'Race of the Two Seas', so-called for its snaking path between the Tyrrhenian coast to the west and the Adriatic coast in the east.

On 9 March Froome made the decisive move of the race on Stage 4 after a startling display of collective power from his Sky team on the final 15km ascent to Prati di Tivo. The British outfit laid down a ferocious tempo – driven by Dario Cataldo, Sergio Henao and Rigoberto Urán – on the snow-banked climb to the ski resort, high in the Apennines, ripping the peloton to shreds and allowing Froome to put in a fearsome dig 1km from the finish, to leave the likes of Contador and Nibali for dead. It was a stylish win for Froome and left him perfectly placed at four seconds behind race leader Michał Kwiatkowski going into the final three stages.

When the race rolled alongside the Pescara river into the city of Chieti on the Adriatic coast on Stage 5, Froome had done enough to usurp Kwiatkowski with a twenty-second buffer. Nibali lost more time and cursed 'the infernal rhythm of Froome's team'. Consecutive victory in stage races seemed to be on the cards for Froome. But no one would have accounted for the manner in which the GC was turned topsy-turvy on the sixth stage. The brutal, rain-soaked leg, which saw the peloton ride a 209km looping route in and around Porto Sant'Elpidio and tackle a 27% incline up the Muro di Sant'Elpidio three times, forced over 50 riders – including Mark Cavendish and Andy Schleck – to retire early. Many of the riders turned up over-geared, and were forced to dismount in front of the crowds to scrabble up the slippery, rain-drenched slopes, pushing their bikes on foot or getting a helpful shove from a spectator. Froome was one of the riders who found his 36x28 gearing was not low enough to spin easily but he dug deep and stayed out of the broom wagon. The general shambles caused a considerable shake-up of the overall standings with Froome the main loser.

By the finish Nibali had stolen nearly a minute to relieve him of his blue jersey by 34 seconds – an advantage which Froome couldn't make enough impression on in the closing time trial in San Benedotto del Tronto the next day. The punitive nature of Stage 6 prompted the race director, Michele Acquarone, to admit on Twitter that 'if you lose half your peloton, you just have to be honest and learn from your mistakes. If the riders are not happy, fans are not happy and I'm not happy too.'

Vincenzo Nibali was happy. And the Italian used his second

successive overall win at Tirreno–Adriatico to take a swipe at Sky's tactics, accusing them of 'racing by numbers'. He said they were over-reliant on their SRM power meters to control their efforts on important climbs. Nibali suggested that Froome spent more time staring at the plastic SRM box on his handlebars than looking at where his opponents might be on the road. Ban them, he said on a Twitter post, to make for more exciting racing. 'Sky has a way of interpreting the race that's scientific,' Nibali said. 'However, in a stage like that [Stage 6], where you couldn't make a fast rhythm, you need strong legs and courage.' He talked of using his own racing nous to make his race-winning move rather than listening to the sports director in the team car behind.

'I think we're developing our own tactics at the moment, and a lot of people are criticising us saying it's boring,' Froome said. 'But I think it's quite exciting because other teams have to plan their own tactics against ours.'

Brailsford hit back at Nibali, saying the Italian and anyone else accusing Sky of riding to numbers should do their homework first. The Sky boss said the team had ridden with compact chain sets on the stages in question and didn't even have SRMs on their bikes. It's about riding to a plan, Brailsford said: 'That's racing as far as I can see.'

*

Sky's early-season dominance had tongues wagging about more than just a perceived obsession with SRM technology. An increasing number of sceptical observers were questioning how a single team could be so successful. Sadly, given European cycling's tarnished history, such dominance has been too often synonymous with doping.

After winning the fourth stage of the Tirreno–Adriatico, Froome rejected the suggestion that the British team had anything to hide. 'There's no secret,' he explained. 'It's just continuing to work the way we worked in the last few years: training, measuring the training and going back and doing it again. It's about getting the basics right. Cycling isn't always predictable, but the more control you have over things the easier it becomes.'

Numbers. Marginal gains. Controlling the controllables.

At the race in Italy Dave Brailsford again took issue over what he described as 'innuendo' regarding Team Sky's indomitable start to the 2013 season. Questions had been raised about why they had hired Dr Geert Leinders, the former doctor to the Rabobank team, to work with them in 2011 and 2012. While Brailsford accepted that hiring Leinders had been a mistake, he condemned insinuations of any wrongdoing at Sky. 'Hiring one doctor for 40 days, does that mean we're doping now, are we? How does that work? There are plenty of journalists who like to think we're at it. But when you read some of the things that are written on the Internet, the accusations and the innuendo, they're incorrect.'

Having just experienced a tough race on Italian soil, Froome was asked if he had any tips to offer Bradley Wiggins in his bid for the Giro d'Italia title in May. He replied: 'There is only one word to win the Giro, I think it's *grinta* [aggression, fierceness]. That's it.'

Nibali's barbs bounced harmlessly off Froome. More importantly he was rising to Ellingworth's training camp challenge: to show consistency and earn the trust of the team. And he'd taken the scalp of Contador for the second time in the fledgling season, giving him, he said, an important 'mental advantage'.

Asked who between Contador and Wiggins would be his main rival at the Tour, Froome replied: 'Brad is my teammate, he's not a rival. I was not against Brad last year . . . Contador is my biggest rival.'

★

Froome followed up victory in Oman and second place in Italy – and celebrated his engagement to his girlfriend Michelle the week before – with a stunning solo ride in Corsica to claim the two-day Critérium International over the weekend of 23–24 March.

On Stage 3 Froome launched a daring, unplanned attack with 5.5km remaining on the ascent of a fog-shrouded Col de l'Ospedale – overlooking Porto-Vecchio where the 2013 Tour was set to kick off on 29 June. Richie Porte, the overnight race leader after a terrific time-trial victory on day one, didn't have the legs to follow, and Froome reached the summit finish 30 seconds ahead of the Tasmanian to leapfrog him in the final overall standings.

With Porte in the yellow jersey, Froome's acceleration had echoes of his attack on Wiggins on the La Toussuire stage at the 2012 Tour, but any questions about more Machiavellian skulduggery were quashed as the two embraced after the finish. Froome called the weekend a 'worthwhile exercise for the team' – an understatement, which, added to Sky's swaggering start to the season – Porte was fresh from his own triumph as the first Australian to win Paris–Nice – would have sent shivers down the spines of his Tour adversaries.

The year before, Wiggins, like Porte, had been in yellow at the summit of Col d'Èze for a trailblazing win at Paris–Nice that set in motion a flawless run of victories, which culminated in a triumphant Tour campaign. In that spring of 2012 the French media accused Team Sky of exerting a vice-like grip on the peloton and of racing like 'a steamroller'. This year's model – with Froome and Porte seemingly on a similar red-hot streak to Wiggins' – was even more dominant.

On 21 April Froome returned to Belgium for the first time in a long while to take part in the last race of the spring Classics season, Liège–Bastogne–Liège. He finished 36th, his best ever showing in four appearances at *La Doyenne*, 1:14 behind Irishman Dan Martin who outsprinted Joaquim Rodríguez in a thrilling finish.

★

In recent years the Tour de Romandie had become a particularly revealing stage race in the build-up to the first two Grand Tours of the season. Cadel Evans and Bradley Wiggins emerged victorious in Switzerland at the end of April in the previous two editions. Both went on to win the Tour two months later.

Froome got off to a flying start on 23 April in the 7km prologue time trial from Le Châble to Bruson, edging out Garmin-Sharp's young American Andrew Talansky by six seconds to take the stage win and the race leader's yellow jersey. In a commanding week-long performance Froome retained the jersey from start to finish.

Dismal weather conditions saw the *parcours* altered on the queen stage, 4, a tough 188.5km ride over mountainous terrain from Marly. The original steep final ascent of the Col de la Croix was removed from the route and replaced with the shallower climb of Les Mosses before an 8km-long plateau to the finish in Les Diablerets. Froome made certain of overall victory when he broke free with Katusha's Simon Spilak 500m from the top of Les Mosses and the pair worked together to stretch their lead to over a minute over a fractured, fatigued peloton. Spilak easily dispatched Froome in the two-man sprint to take the stage win.

Froome sealed final overall victory the next day with an assured ride in Geneva, by placing third in the final time trial, behind a dominant world time-trial champion Tony Martin. It was a great win for Froome; his third stage race triumph of the season. He was on an eerily similar road to the one Wiggins had so success-fully ridden on his way to Tour victory in 2012.

'It is definitely a good omen, but the Tour is still two months away, and I need to do a lot of hard training before then,' Froome said.

★

While Bradley Wiggins began his bid for glory at the Giro d'Italia – the 96th edition of the Corsa Rosa started in Naples on 4 May – Sky's final pre-Tour training camp in Tenerife beckoned for Froome again. In the Teide National Park, on a road from nowhere that climbs inexorably through a hostile wilderness to 2,100m above sea level, Tim Kerrison would put Froome through his final paces.

Every turn of a pedal Froome takes would be recorded, analysed and then benchmarked against Kerrison's training models. The rider who can generate the most power for the longest duration while weighing the least usually wins. From a mass of data, Kerrison had to calculate what it would take for Chris Froome to win the Tour de France.

Physical and mental conditioning complete, Froome would travel to France to compete in one final race – the Critérium du Dauphiné, from 2 to 9 June – three weeks before the Tour's *Grand Départ* in Corsica. The 33-year-old Wiggins was the current holder of the Dauphiné, and had also taken overall victory in 2011. If Froome could take Wiggins's Dauphiné crown – he finished fourth behind his team leader in 2012 – it would signal his clear intention to wrest the biggest prize of all from Wiggins's shoulders, the *maillot jaune* of the Tour de France.

On 6 May 2013 Dave Brailsford finally put an end to frenzied media speculation, hissy fits on Twitter, claims and counter-claims between Froome and Wiggins about who would lead Sky's challenge at the 2012 Tour when he said: 'Given Chris's step-up in performances this year, our plan, as it has been since January, is to have him lead the Tour de France team.'

★

The young lion lopes towards Chris Froome and clambers all over him. Froome laughs and wrestles playfully with the animal, pawing off its advances with gentle jabs. The lion nuzzles its chin into his face. They are at ease, completely relaxed, like a couple of old friends, just fooling around. In the caged enclosure of a South African safari park Froome is in his element, at one with nature.

In December 2012 a France TV crew filmed Froome in his natural African habitat for a short documentary piece titled *Chris Froome, L'Africain*. They follow him on one of his favourite training runs to the Suikerbosrand Nature Reserve, 50km south of Johannesburg. He is riding with his friend Alex Pavlov. The pair have known each other since their junior days together at the Hi-Q SuperCycling Academy. As they cycle by, zebras graze in the near distance, long-tailed baboons scuttle across the road behind them and a cluster of antelope glides with supple grace across the savannah.

Training ride over, Froome drives his car through the main gates of the reserve's safari past a wandering giraffe and stops next to a pride of lions lolling in the sun by the roadside. A lioness laps water from a pond as her three cubs play-fight beside her. The life of a professional cyclist, he explains to the camera, is spent eating, sleeping, training, cycling, all year round. He needs to come home to Africa during the winter off-season, to train and be around his friends and family. It adds some normality to an abnormal existence. 'It's really nice for me to come to a place like this and just watch the animals, to see that there's a different life out there . . .'

He gazes out of the car window at the family of lions, snaps some pictures on his iPhone. 'I feel like I could sit here all day and watch their behaviour,' Froome says. 'It's very calming and peaceful for me.' As he speaks, the weight of the cycling world, and all the pressure and expectations that accompany it, almost visibly lift from his shoulders. He smiles, sighs, and an expression of complete contentedness settles on his youthful face. 'Africa has always felt like home to me,' he says quietly. 'I was born here. It's just a way of life.'

Throughout his professional career Froome has spoken openly about his dream of establishing a cycling foundation in Africa. 'In the next few years I hope to create an academy and organise mountain-bike safari holidays in Kenya,' he said. He wants to use his new-found fame as an African-born professional cyclist to inspire children to take up the sport, especially if they're from similarly unconventional, non-traditional cycling countries. His desire to create a place to nurture young talent in Africa has always seemed as important to him as any personal ambitions as a rider. He keeps in touch with his old friend and mentor, David Kinjah, and has said he would like to return to Kenya when his career is over and help him with his Safari Simbaz project.

'David Kinjah is doing something really great,' Froome says. 'He's taking orphans off the street and training them. It's a process of guiding the children on to the right path, and it's great to see something like that happening. They are really talented youngsters out there.'

But Froome's future plans for Kenyan cycling will have to wait. Health and motivation permitting, he has at least another six or seven years left at the top. 'It's been an epic journey to get here,' he says. 'It's by no means been plain sailing. I've had to fight every step of the way.'

From the Kenyan bush via the Highveld of South Africa to the podium of the Tour de France, Froome's extraordinary story is unlike any other in the history of a sport steeped in tales of outlandish derring-do and astonishing endeavour. And it's by no means over yet. 'There have been a few ordeals along the way . . . but if you have a dream, you'll find a way to make it happen,' Froome says.

In the wake of his 2012 Tour de France triumph, Bradley Wiggins was fond of saying that a kid from Kilburn wasn't meant to achieve such feats. So what about a kid from Kenya?

CHAPTER 18
The Heights of Greatness

'It is a rough road that leads to the heights of greatness.' Seneca

On 31 May 2013 Chris Froome was relieved of what he described as a 'pain in the neck', when Bradley Wiggins was ruled out of defending his Tour de France title through injury. An inflammation in Wiggins's left knee left him with insufficient time to train properly for the 100th edition of the event. The 33-year-old triple Olympic gold medallist had pulled out of the Giro d'Italia two weeks before with a chest infection after a calamitous twelve days of racing.

It was a blessed relief for Froome to be freed from constant media pressure as to who would lead Team Sky into the Tour. The debate had been quietened, if not finally put to rest, by Sir Dave Brailsford's pronouncement in May that Froome was their designated number one. Wiggins, the charismatic mod geezer with a penchant for self-deprecating back-chat – would have been good for the Tour, good for the media hype, given the incessant coverage devoted to Sky's top pair, but not necessarily good for Froome.

While Froome said he had sympathy with the injured Wiggins he made it clear that the champion would only have ridden as his *super domestique*. The decidedly more mountainous *parcours* of the 2013 race suited Froome's natural climbing abilities far better. 'I wouldn't necessarily think that he would have been defending his title, as such; the course is so different this year,' Froome said.. But Froome conceded that the team would miss Wiggins's strength against the clock in the team time trial and 'he could have been with us in the mountains to play that support role for me. That's definitely unfortunate.'

Not that Wiggins would have relished such a diminution in his status. Playing the support act was not Wiggo's style, and the issue of who was really leading Team Sky would have dogged the pair throughout the Tour, raising the prospect of internal conflict within the team. 'I know a lot of people would have still aimed that leadership question at me,' Froome said. 'I wouldn't say it was stressful but it was a bit of a pain in the neck to have to keep repeating myself.'

A magnanimous Wiggins told the *Guardian* in June that there had been a natural selection in 2013. He conceded that Froome was Team Sky's *de facto* leader and he'd struggle to oust him from the number one slot. 'Chris has really stepped up, he's delivered now and he looks like he's going to be there for a few years to win a few Tours,' Wiggins said. 'I can live with that.'

Froome's early season run of success testified to Wiggins's claim of sporting Darwinism at Sky. He had taken impressive stage race victories in the Tour of Oman, Critérium International and the Tour de Romandie, and also finished second overall to eventual Giro champion Vincenzo Nibali in the Tirreno–Adriatico in March.

At the prestigious Critérium du Dauphiné (2–9 June), traditionally the final dress rehearsal before the Tour de France, Froome and Team Sky recorded their third consecutive win in a key pre-Tour event, repeating 2012's 1-2 for Wiggins and Michael Rogers, with Froome and Richie Porte topping the GC. The British and Tasmanian climbing partners were dominant throughout, and Froome stamped his authority on the race in Stage 5, the first true mountaintop finish, to the *hors catégorie* Valmorel. He reeled in a late attack by Alberto Contador before sprinting past the Spaniard with a perfectly executed acceleration to take the stage win and yellow jersey, which he kept until the race finish.

Froome's pursuit of perfection as the Tour approached was relentless. Instead of a long lie in bed he left the next morning to reconnoitre the Alpine climbs that would figure in the Tour in July. He rode the route of Stage 17's hilly time trial from Embrun to Chorges. Recces complete he travelled to Châtel in the French Alps for a pre-Tour training camp.

As the days counted down to the Tour start in Corsica on 29 June, Froome was in the best physical condition of his life. He was consistently hitting numbers on his power meter that he'd once felt were 'exceptionally good' but were now quite comfortable. Tim Kerrison, Sky's head of performance, said that in Châtel the team intentionally replicated some of the training from 2012 and found that Froome was 'a good couple of per cent better than he was last year'.

Although yet to win a Grand Tour – finishing second both in France in 2012 and in the 2011 Vuelta a España – Froome had set his sights on winning a series of Tours de France, confident he could become the man to beat in stage races for years to come. 'I've got my goals and personally where I want my career to go is to target the Tour,' he said. 'Not just this year but for the next seven or eight years, and each time to line up at the Tour ready to try and contend for yellow. I am driven by that goal.'

★

The Tour was making its first ever visit to the craggy Mediterranean island of Corsica. Hilly stages on the opening two days and an early team time trial prompted Sky to surround the race favourite with a strong team of all-rounders who could do the business on the flat but also when the road tilted skywards.

The experienced Spaniard David Lopez, the Belarusians Vasil Kiryienka and Kanstantsin Siutsou and Norway's Edvald Boasson Hagen, a double stage winner in the 2011 race, joined three riders who'd come through the Great Britain academy – Geraint Thomas, Peter Kennaugh and Ian Stannard. The selection of Thomas, the versatile Welshman, was expected, but the Isle of Man rider Kennaugh, who provided exceptional support to Froome in the mountains of the Dauphiné, and Stannard, a former British road champion, each making his Tour debut were more of a surprise. Thomas, set for his fourth Tour appearance, and Kennaugh won team pursuit gold and broke the world record at the London Olympics in 2012.

Only Froome and his close friend Richie Porte, winner of the Paris–Nice stage-race in March, fitted into the category of pure climbers.

★

The 213km opening leg, from the swish resort of Porto-Vecchio, dubbed the Corsican Saint-Tropez, north to the bustling old port of Bastia, on undulating roads skirting the less rugged east coast of the island, was meant to serve as a gentle introduction to the race for the peloton. Instead it left the 198 riders in a state of disarray, many battered and bruised from a dramatic crash close to the finish that scuppered the hopes of pre-stage favourites Mark Cavendish, Peter Sagan and André Greipel.

Froome got off to a dreadful start. Rolling along in the neutral zone – the initial, non-competitive 8km of the stage before the race proper began – he punctured on the outskirts of Porto-Vecchio and got a new rear wheel. Then he was forced to stop for a second time when he struck a concrete barrier and had to change bikes. Just five kilometres into the 3,404km of the three-week race and Froome was already in trouble. Anxious moments for Froome, but he kept his cool and was paced back to the peloton by Sky teammates in the nick of time for the official race start as five riders immediately leaped off the front to form the break of the day.

Cavendish's Omega Pharma-Quickstep team led the chase, eager to set up their star sprinter. A 24th stage victory for the Manx Missile would also add the *maillot jaune* to the leader's jerseys of both Giro and Vuelta.

Sky and Froome, with little or no sprint finish ambitions beyond all-rounder Boasson Hagen, were able to sit back for most of the stage. But after a stint of keeping Froome sheltered from the wind and with just over 10km to go, the former British champion Ian Stannard was brought crashing to the ground and badly roughed up when two Garmin Sharp riders – Ryder Hesjedal and Rohan Dennis – got snagged on some advertising hoardings lining the road and the Sky workhorse had nowhere to go but follow them onto the tarmac.

Meanwhile, bizarrely, the Australian Orica-GreenEdge team bus had somehow got wedged under the gantry at the finish line. The driver, Garikoitz Atxa, on his first day on the job, had arrived late into Bastia and was instructed to drive through. But the scaffolding which housed the digital race timer had been lowered after the other 21 team buses had safely passed under. and the roof of the Orica bus, too high to clear the gap, got stuck.

With the finish line blocked and the peloton 8km away, thundering towards a mass sprint climax, the president of the race jury decided to move the finish to 3km out. Team directors frantically relayed the information to their riders via radio. Gendarmes swarmed around the scene; the fire brigade was called. Hydraulic equipment was brought in but to no avail. Atxa sat at the wheel of the bus with his head buried in his hands, the team from Down Under's cheery kangaroo mascot beside him. Jokes were already flying around that he'd be the first coach driver to win a stage of the Tour.

Finally, in a desperate attempt to extricate the vehicle, the tyres were deflated, and Atxa was able to reverse the bus off the course, clearing the passage. With the main bunch bearing down on the rearranged finish at the 3km marker, ASO hastily moved the finish back to its original location. The indecision caused chaos.

Almost immediately, 5km from Bastia, as the latest newsflash filtered through to the peloton, a wave of riders went down in a horrific crash that took out a host of big names, injuring around twenty riders and eliminating most of the potential sprint trains. As Greipel surged forward through the pack, another rider's pedal caught on his *derailleur*, ripping it off. The German sprinter escaped with just a broken bicycle as carnage reigned in his wake. Froome got stuck behind the tangled mess of bikes and bodies but emerged unscathed. Green-jersey favourite Sagan hit the deck, Froome's chief GC rival Alberto Contador, grazed his left side and world time trial champion Tony Martin sustained a bruised lung and severe road rash 258 that left his back looking like it had been mauled by a wild animal. Even worse for Sky, their road captain Geraint Thomas was catapulted over his handlebars and fell heavily on his left side. Secondary medical checks the next day revealed a small fracture to the left side of his pelvis. Due to the shambolic *denouement* the stage was neutralised and the peloton was given the same time as the eventual stage winner and first yellow jersey of the race: Argos-Shimano's 25-year-old German Marcel Kittel.

Miraculously all 198 riders started next day and Jan Bakelants won a pulsating Stage 2, a rolling 156km run from Bastia down the backbone of Corsica to Ajaccio, birthplace of Napoléon Bonaparte.

On the short, sharp climb of the Côte du Salario, 12km from the finish, Froome thrillingly showed himself for the first time in the race when he glided off the front just before the summit, laying down an early marker that he was in frisky form. Froome said later that the main reason he broke free of the bunch was to negotiate the tricky descent on his own terms but confessed that keeping the other GC contenders on their toes was also part of the plan.

The French sports paper *L'Équipe* wrote that whereas Wiggins's 2012 Team Sky had a 'predictable style and an absence of panache and attacking spirit; their goal was simply to win in the most effective way,' the unexpected early spurt from Froome in Corsica suggested that 2013 would be different.

★

The Tour's giddy lap of the stunning rural wilds of Corsica came to its conclusion on the 145.5km ride up the sinuous west coast from Ajaccio to Calvi on Stage 3. Orica again stole the headlines and a redemption of sorts. Simon Gerrans pipped Sagan in a dash to the finish line after an expert lead-out from designated team sprinter, Daryl Impey.

Geraint Thomas, who needed help just to swing his leg over his bike that morning and said the final two days in Corsica were 'probably the most I have ever suffered on a bike', made a valiant thrust to the front of the peloton at the 100km mark, drew up alongside Froome and Porte, just to let them know he was still in the race and yelled at his teammates: 'Yeah! C'mon!' before drifting back down the bunch again.

'That made us all smile,' Froome said. 'He's Welsh, he's got fighting spirit. He's in pain but he's up for it and that really lifts us.'

Thomas – who had ignored pleas from his mother to quit the race – would need all the courage he could muster when the race crossed the Mediterranean Sea back to mainland France and Nice, the setting for the team time trial on 2 July.

Happy just to get round Corsica in one piece – 'this is a beautiful island, but I'm glad to be leaving it behind us,' Froome said – Team Sky proceeded to execute the most efficient evacuation of Corsica since Lord Horatio Nelson's withdrawal of the Royal Navy in 1796, by way of a private jet

★

On the morning of Stage 4's team time trial, Richie Porte posted a playful photo on his Twitter account of himself and roommate Froome larking around in the hotel room in their time-trial skin suits, thumbs aloft cheesy grins. A few hours later the pair got down to serious business on the short, flat 25km out-and-back seafront course centring on Nice's famous palm-lined Promenade des Anglais. Sky rode a smooth, disciplined race from start to finish, with Froome taking long stints on the front. It was expected that the badly crocked Thomas would quickly lose contact with the back of the Sky train, thereby hindering their ambitions for a high finish. On the day he performed heroicallyand stayed in rotation until the *flamme rouge*. Under the circumstances, it was an incredible ride. Sky finished third, two seconds behind world champions Omega Pharma-Quickstep who had the stage victory agonisingly snatched from their grasp by 0.76 seconds following a scintillating display by Orica GreenEdge. The Australian team's second win in a row put Stage 3 winner Gerrans into the *maillot jaune*. Froome soared to seventh overall at three seconds, the highest placed of the GC contenders.

It was a perfect result for Froome. Team Sky kept any time losses to an absolute minimum while avoiding the stress of having to defend the yellow jersey too early in the race. 'Motivating and humbling to see how G pulled through today,' Froome tweeted that evening in reference to Thomas's gritty ride.

The next day the race headed 219km west through Provence, from Cagnes-sur-Mer to Marseilles, a stage town in the first ever Tour in 1903. With 1km to go, Mark Cavendish surged clear of Sky's Boasson Hagen and Peter Sagan of Cannondale in the bunch sprint for his first win of the centenary race. The victory took his career tally of Tour stage wins to 24, one shy of Andre Leducq, and behind Bernard Hinault (28) and Eddy Merckx (34). A large pile-up in the final 200m split the peloton as Gerrans retained the leader's yellow jersey. Froome avoided the crash, but Belgium's Jurgen Van Den Broeck, fourth in the 2012 race, injured his knee and was forced to retire.

★

For the first time since the stage to Alpe d'Huez in 2008, one team-mate passed the yellow jersey to another with Gerrans unselfishly leading out Daryl Impey in the final kilometre into Montpellier for the South African to finish thirteenth behind stage winner André Greipel, enough for the 28-year-old from Johannesburg to become the first rider from his country to lead the Tour de France. Rather than feeling pangs of envy that Impey, his old buddy from their Team Barloworld days together, had stolen a march on him Froome tweeted: 'Incredible day for African cycling, a Saffa in yellow! Congrats @darylimpey & kudos to @simongerrans for setting it up.'

Seven stages into the race, Peter Sagan broke his run of second places to win the 205.5km run from Montpellier to Albi. Impey held onto his leader's jersey, and Froome and Porte were perfectly positioned in seventh and eighth place on the GC, at eight seconds.

In post-stage encounters with the world's media Froome was consistently self-effacing and polite, treating the Tour as if it was any other race. When Sky sent the room-sharing list round ahead of the start in Corsica, Froome was the only rider in the team given a single room; a privilege afforded the team leader. But Froome refused the offer. He wanted to share with his mate Richie Porte, as he almost always does at stage races. The concept of special treatment was anathema to him. Is he as cool as he appears? a journalist asked. 'Totally,' confirmed Porte. 'He is no different here to any other race.'

★

Now the Tour was set for the first proper shake-up of the main contenders in the rugged, verdant heights of the Pyrenees: two days that would go a long way to proving whether or not the inscrutable Froome merited the tag of race favourite.

Team Sky's plan for the first foray into the high mountains was that Froome would attack on a steep 700m section, four kilometres from the summit of Ax-3-Domaines, the Category 1 climb to the ski station at the summit finish, made famous by Carlos Sastre's dummy-sucking win in 2003. Close enough to the end not to take Froome beyond his threshold but enough to hopefully gain significant time from his rivals.

Brailsford said Froome was 'like a year's worth of coiled spring, just waiting and waiting to burst until he couldn't keep it in any longer', but he and Tim Kerrison, Froome's personal coach, preached caution: to be patient, gradually wear down their opponents and then strike to take the biggest chunk of time as possible.

On a searingly hot day the peloton set off from Castres on a rolling excursion through the Tarn and Ariége *departements* before hitting a slowly ramping, twisting 15km drag up the *hors categorié* Col de Pailhéres, at 2,001m the highest point of the race.

Sky, Movistar and Belkin led the pacesetting to the foot of

the Pailhères. Forty kilometres from the finish, Robert Gesink of Belkin attacked, pursued by Europcar's ace chancer, Thomas Voeckler. Ahead of them was Christophe Riblon, sole survivor of a four-man breakaway.

Colombia's pint-sized *grimpeur* Nairo Quintana then took flight and sailed past Voeckler and Gesink. The 23-year-old Quintana, on his maiden Tour, was born at an altitude of 3,000m, and grew up in a settlement near the town of Cómbita in the Andes. Every day, on a $30 mountain bike, he would ride 16km up the side of a mountain to school. It had clearly stood him in good stead, as he scaled the Pailhères with nonchalant ease and was first over the top to claim the Souvenir Henri Desgrange.

But the Movistar rider lost time on the tricky descent down to Ax-les-Thermes, taking the wrong line too often on the sharp hairpins, while Sky's Kiryienka, then Kennaugh, led the chase, in tandem with Froome and Porte. Kennaugh brilliantly commandeered the Sky train down the mountain before wasting himself in one last effort for Froome's cause on the early slopes of the final 7.8km haul to Ax-3-Domaines. Quintana had already caught and dropped Riblon to deny the Frenchman a repeat of his stage win here in 2010.

Porte then assumed the mountain *domestique* duties and the Tasmanian's savage pace whittled the leading group down to an elite handful of five chasing Quintana: Froome, Porte, Contador, Alejandro Valverde and Roman Kreuziger.

As the two Spaniards and Czech rider struggled to hold Porte's wheel Quintana came into view with just over 5km to go. Froome sensed his moment and exploded up the mountain, leaving Porte to dog Contador's fading efforts. Meanwhile, scattered further down the slopes were a shellshocked gaggle of Froome's supposed main GC rivals: Cadel Evans, Tejay van Garderen, Andy Schleck and Joaquim Rodriguez.

Froome, in imperious climbing form, unceremoniously dropped Quintana and flicked a switch to time-trial mode for the final 4.5km incline to the finish to take an emphatic stage win and his first ever *maillot jaune* – the sixth British rider and second

African-born to do so. The roar from within the Team Sky bus when the gangly Brit dropped the 'F-bomb' on the Colombian was deafening. Even after his almighty effort, Porte still had enough left in the tank to take second on the line, at 51 seconds, and second on GC. Sky and Froome had massacred the opposition . . . again.

Sir Dave Brailsford said the team plan had been executed with the perfection of 'a nine-dart finish'.

'This is incredible!' Froome said. 'We have worked for months to be in this position. I wasn't holding anything back. Every second counts.'

After such a dominant performance it was inevitable that Froome would be forced to field questions about doping. When asked by an American journalist, who said Sky's exploits reminded him of how Lance Armstrong's US Postal used to destroy the peloton, to confirm that what he had achieved was totally natural, Froome replied with Zen-like calm: 'One hundred per cent.' He said he was on a 'personal mission to show the sport has changed' and insisted he was clean of drugs.

'I know the results I get are not going to be stripped ten years down the line. Rest assured that is not going to happen. I think if people got more of a look into [my training] they would see that that work equals these results, and it's not something that's so wow, so unbelievable. It does add up if you look and see what actually goes into this.'

★

The big question after Stage 8 of the 2013 race was: how could Froome and Team Sky be beaten? The British team was invincible during Bradley Wiggins's procession to Paris, and had carried on that swaggering form in the 2013 season, winning every stage race where they had taken their A-team.

But for the first time in the two years since Sky rose to domi-nance, chinks appeared in the seemingly impregnable carapace.

'Our aim is to cause chaos,' Garmin-Sharp's Irish all-rounder,

Dan Martin, had vowed on the eve of the Grand Départ. And Jonathan Vaughters's American team was as good as their word, a day after many had feared Sky had already killed the Tour as a contest.

On a Pyrenean rollercoaster from Saint Girons to Bagnères-de-Bigorre Team Sky's long, stressful day in the saddle got off to a bad start when Ryder Hesjedal knocked Kennaugh into a ditch at the side of the road, just 17km from Saint-Girons, on the lower slopes of the Col de Portet-d'Aspet. As the Canadian attempted to thread his bike through a narrow gap on the left side of the road he caught the Sky rider's handlebars, and he tumbled down a steep slope and disappeared into the bushes. Kennaugh emerged from the greenery and clambered back up the hillside, his helmet askew, a bloody wound on his left arm. He remounted and set off in what would be a futile day-long struggle to rejoin the front of the race.

By the top of the Portet-d'Aspet, Froome's three trusty lieutenants from the previous day's heroics – Porte, Kennaugh, Vasil Kiryienka – had been blown away, in part due to a series of blistering accelerations by Garmin's David Millar, Dan Martin, Jack Bauer and Tom Danielson and then a series of devastating surges from Movistar. Kiryienka's collapse was such that he finished outside the time limit and was eliminated from the race.

Worse was to come on the second climb, the Category 1 Col de Menté, when Porte was dropped. Froome's wingman tried to catch the leading group, failed, sat up and eventually finished eighteen minutes back, surrendering his second place and any hopes Sky had of repeating their 1-2 GC finish of 2012. Porte, who had been somewhat dismissive of Quintana's early raid on Stage 8, was made to eat his words.

Now Froome's rivals had him exactly where they wanted him: alone, isolated, vulnerable to attack in a 30-strong group controlled by Movistar. He was forced to ride without protection for over 100km of the loopy 168.5km route, fending off numerous assaults on the way.

Movistar made more than half a dozen attempts to drop him. With 35km to go Quintana, a classic Colombian *escarabajo* – flying beetle – who climbs for fun, unleashed the first of four short attacks on the final climb up the Category 1 Hourquette d'Ancizan, drawing a cool reaction from Froome who shut down the danger each time. 'Not easy, definitely not easy to follow the Colombian,' he said later.

It was a courageous performance from Froome worthy of comparison with the likes of Bernard Hinault, one of the great patrons of the past. If he could ride out the stage alone, losing no time to his chief rivals and retain the yellow jersey, then the stage could arguably be considered even more important in the final reckoning than his victory the day before. 'I did start thinking about a few things. It would have been easy to just sit in the bunch and not follow the attacks of guys like Quintana,' Froome said. 'But I thought, I've worked bloody hard to get here, I'm not going to let this race ride away from me just because I'm on my own.'

Ultimately Valverde's Movistar team squandered a golden opportunity to inflict serious damage on Froome. The Spanish team appeared to be more intent on distancing Porte although Froome admitted afterwards that he had suffered 'one of the hardest days I've ever had on a bike'.

A slowing in the peloton after Quintana's first attack just over 4km from the summit of the final climb provided the springboard for Daniel Martin and Jakob Fuglsang who jumped clear and held off the chasing pack before collaborating smoothly on the 30km drop to Bagnères-de-Bigorre to fight out the stage honours. Martin, nephew of 1987 Tour champion Stephen Roche, triumphed over the Dane after a final kilometre game of cat and mouse to become the fifth Irishman to win a stage of the Tour, 50 years after Shay Elliott took a pioneering victory in Roubaix in 1963. Froome and the main overall contenders came home together 20 seconds down on Martin.

Team Sky had expended so much energy putting Froome in yellow atop the Ax-3-Domaines that it was normal, he said, for them to have an off day. 'They are human and they can't keep doing that every day. Some days you can be there and some days you can't. That's bike racing.' If they were only human, what was Froome?

★

At Sky's rest-day press conference in La Baule on the Atlantic coast, after a long transfer north from the Pyrenees to Nantes, Froome established a routine where he would place the microphone on the table between each question to allow himself time to think before speaking and developed a physical tic of nodding in affirmation at the end of every response.

'Given the history of cycling, people are going to ask questions because there are great performances which have been linked to doping in the past and now we're bearing the brunt of those questions,' Froome said. 'But the sport has moved on, and I know what I'm doing is right. Outside of that, I don't know what else I can do.'

Brailsford was asked if he felt he could do more to show his team's veracity beyond looking journalists in the eye and asking them to believe he was telling the truth. He said he was reluctant to release Froome's power data to be probed by what he termed 'pseudo-scientists'.

Reformed doper David Millar jumped to the defence of Sky and Froome when he said: 'I believe they are clean and they deserve respect and admiration for it. They feel they're doing it all right and perhaps rightfully so they're just defensive about that. They think they're being lumbered with another generation's mistakes. It's one thing satisfying the sceptics, but at the same time they don't want the other teams to know what they have to do to beat them. Their trade secrets are their training.'

★

On 9 July Froome negotiated his way through a dramatic conclusion to Stage 10 as the sprint teams duked it out in Saint Malo. With an anticipated switch from a headwind to strong crosswinds in the final 20km, the overall contenders moved up to the front of the race to stay safe from any possible splits in the peloton, creating a nervous atmosphere in the main field as it wound through twisty roads towards the coast of Brittany.

Froome was brilliantly marshalled by Ian Stannard and Edvald Boasson Hagen as the 197km trek from Saint-Gildas-Des-Bois reached its dramatic climax, and he crossed the line safely alongside his teammates following a fractured finale between the opposing lead-out trains.Marcel Kittel narrowly pipped fellow German Andre Greipel to victory, but Kittel's team-mate Tom Veelers was sent tumbling in the last 100m after peeling off into Mark Cavendish's sprint line and then being bumped on the shoulder as the Manx Missile produced his final kick.

Fortunately, Veelers' crash didn't have any repercussions for the rest of the peloton, and there was no change in the general classification which saw Froome maintain his 1:25 advantage over Alejandro Valverde.

★

The race organisers had plotted a truly stunning finish for the first individual time trial of the centenary Tour de France, a 33km, flat, fast course from Avranches to the towering citadel of Mont-Saint-Michel.

Chris Boardman, nicknamed Mr Prologue, who wore the *maillot jaune* after the opening prologue of the 1994, 1997 and 1998 Tours, once said that the knack of the time trial is to continually ask yourself the question: 'Can I go on?' – and never be sure of your answer. Froome increasingly relished the singular challenge against the clock, buoyed by the knowledge that he had made technical advances during practice sessions in a wind tunnel at Southampton University in May. He bolted across the salt marshes to obliterate his opponents for overall victory and threatened to pinch a remarkable stage win from the German chrono specialist Tony Martin, the reigning world champion in the discipline.

As Froome rode towards the ramparts of Mont-Saint-Michel,

rising out of the shimmering sea like Camelot, he faded a little in the high winds on the exposed final stretch along the causeway to the finish, but only in comparison with the peerless Martin, pushing an awesome 58x11 gear, who posted the third fastest average speed for a Tour time trial of a similar length. Martin confessed later that he went through agony watching Froome beat his times at both intermediate checks and 'nearly started to cry' as the Briton came close to stealing victory. He missed by just twelve seconds.

Froome described his 36:41 ride through the fields of Normandy as 'a blur of noise and colour'. But his performance in placing second on the stage brought unarguable clarity to the overall rankings. The closest finisher to the race leader was Bauke Mollema, 1:48 back. Valverde clung on to second place but was now 3:25 behind. Only Mollema, Contador and Kreuziger remained within four minutes. Indeed, no Tour leader since 2001 had enjoyed such an advantage after eleven stages.

★

On the morning of Stage 12 Brailsford revealed that Froome was close to renewing his Team Sky contract. 'It's no secret that we want him to stay. It's not signed, but we're in agreement.' Sources estimated Froome could earn around £3.44m (€4m) a year.

That was the good news. The bad news was that Edvald Boasson Hagen got caught up in a high-speed crash 2km from the finish on the outskirts of Tours, a pile-up comprised mainly of Lotto riders. He had sustained a fracture of his right shoulder and was flown home the next day. This reduced Froome's support riders to six. Moreover, Geraint Thomas was still hampered by a fractured pelvis. 'It was a hard day,' Froome said. 'Every time I cross the finish line, I breathe a little sigh of relief.'

In an electrifying sprint finish Cavendish was beaten by Kittel, who came out from behind him to overtake and win his third stage with what German cycling website Radsport-News vividly described as his 'Tigersprung' acceleration.

Stage 13, a 173km run from Tours to Saint-Amand-Montrond, was expected to be a quiet day for the peloton, the overall contenders saving their legs for Mont Ventoux and the sprint teams focused on controlling the race so their speed merchants could battle it out for the stage win.

An early six-man break looked set to be off the front for much of the day but instead the race took a dramatic twist just before the 100km mark. The hot, sweeping crosswinds of central France, as the route followed the River Cher, suddenly generated waves in the cornfields and created echelons in the peloton.

Disaster had already befallen Valverde, Froome's closest rival lying second overall on GC, when he punctured after 84km. Rather than take a Movistar teammate's bike and quickly rejoin the bunch, the Spaniard opted to take a rear wheel, wasting precious time fitting it, a costly decision. Omega Pharma-Quickstep drove the pace at the front of the lead group in an attempt to distance Kittel who was also stranded with Valverde in a group of stragglers. Belkin, with Mollema and Laurens Ten Dam in the hunt for a podium place, helped OPQS at the front on the long, straight exposed roads through rural France, making it impossible for Valverde's Movistar team to bridge the gap.

With around 50km to go, the wild gusts across the flat plains caused the 90-strong yellow jersey peloton to splinter. As the wind buffeted the leaders, Saxo-Tinkoff – ironically former Sky man Michael Rogers engineering the move – made an audacious leap off the front in an attempt to gain time on Froome. It worked. Sky missed out on joining a fourteen-man breakaway which included a dangerous sextet of Saxo-Tinkoff riders, including Contador and Kreuziger. Omega's Cavendish was last man to jump onto the back of the mini-express train as it rapidly disappeared into the distance, leaving Froome and co. adrift.

Saxo's magnificent six rode in team time-trial mode to the finish. Cavendish, led out immaculately by Sylvain Chavanel, beat Sagan in a sprint finish to win his 25th Tour stage.

Valverde, second overall at the start of the stage, reached the finish a massive 9:54 behind Cavendish. Contador and Mollema pulled back more than a minute on Froome to inflict a psychological blow to Sky as Ventoux and the Alps loomed. Froome's lead had fallen to 2:28 ahead of Mollema. Contador was now third overall at 2:45. A flat stage had done as much damage as a mountaintop finish.

★

On Bastille Day – 14 July, Stage 15, at 242.5km, the longest stage of the Tour – as the peloton crested a rise somewhere in the Drôme region they caught sight of the strange, solitary cone of Mont Ventoux, the Bald Mountain, rearing up 1,912m in the south, its intimidating white summit a limestone moonscape of bare rocks – courtesy of a deforestation programme carried out by Napoleon to furnish his navy.

It was the first huge test for Froome and the peloton as the race entered arguably the toughest final week in Tour history. The last eight stages consisted of 244.3km of climbing, over 35 category climbs, including six *hors categorié*, reaching a combined height of 35,441 metres – the equivalent of scaling Mount Everest four times.

Quintana was first to state his daring intentions when he danced clear of the yellow-jersey group of Froome, through the oak woods, with over 14km of climbing still to go up the unremittingly steep road to the observatory. Quickly settling into a comfortably seated style reminiscent of illustrious Colombian forebears such as Luis Herrera, twice winner of the King of the Mountains title at the Tour, Quintana sat expressionless, barely opening his mouth to breathe, as he swiftly opened up a 50-second lead on Froome's group. He caught and dropped earlier escapee Mikel Nieve and looked likely to continue irresistibly to the summit and a stage win.

'I think I attacked too early,' Quintana reflected later. His nose had started to bleed at the start of the 20.8km climb, an early ill portent for an ascent that the philosopher Roland Barthes called 'a god of Evil, to which sacrifices must be made. It never forgives weakness and extracts an unfair tribute of suffering.'

Porte took up the reins from Kennaugh – completely spent, he slowed to a virtual standstill – and slashed Quintana's advantage, simultaneously shattering their elite group containing Contador, Rogers, Kreuziger, Mollema and Rodriguez to pieces, with only Contador able to stay with the Sky tandem of Froome and Porte.

Then, with just over 7km remaining, Porte whispered a few words to Froome and his leader was gone. 'Alberto [Contador] was the only guy left, and as Richie came to the end of his turn I thought: Now is the time,' said Froome.

The yellow jersey produced a sudden, violent acceleration, spinning his pedals at an intense rate, and blew a startled Contador off his back wheel. Froome then revved round the bend and up a vicious incline like a motorbike in a velodrome. He bridged the gap alone – briefly knocked off his stride at the 6km mark when a boisterous spectator waved a flare under his nose – and was soon on Quintana's wheel.

Another spurt from Froome saw him briefly take a 14-second lead over Quintana, but the poker-faced Colombian soon drew level again as the relentless climb continued out of the forest at Chalet Reynard and onto the lunar landscape of Ventoux's upper reaches. Froome leaned across to Quintana to talk about the terms of their collaboration.

'He told me to work with him because Contador was losing time. He said that if we were still together when we got to the finish then he would let me win,,' Quintana said.

A noble proposition from the yellow jersey, but, as they passed the Tom Simpson memorial, just over 1km from the summit, Froome made sure Quintana wouldn't be with him at the finish. He delivered a coruscating burst of speed to pull away from his erstwhile accomplice. He paused briefly then launched another blazing attack, pedals spinning at a stupefying speed – he'd stayed in a lower gear so as not to risk derailing his chain. Buffeted by a driving tail wind, remaining seated for the aerodynamic advantage, he took off into the fortuitous slipstream of a television camera motorbike, which helped propel the decisive moment. It was thrilling.

Simpson, the 1965 world champion, collapsed and died on Ventoux during the 1967 Tour, with a cocktail of alcohol and amphetamines found in his system. Froome, typically modest, and not one for delivering weighty messages, said the timing of his attack as they rode past Simpson's memorial was merely coincidental.

Froome forced his bike up and around the final bend to take a famous victory in the shadow of the observatory. He'd gained an astonishing 29 seconds on Quintana by the finish line in a staggering display of superiority that extended his overall lead to 4:14 on Mollema and his advantage on Contador to 4:25. On Bastille Day, in the 100th Tour, on cycling's most revered mountain, dazzling in hisyellow jersey, Froome had comprehensively destroyed his rivals.

He'd dug so deep into his physical capacities to triumph in, what he called, the 'mental warfare' on the mountain, that he had to be given oxygen at the finish. 'It was a full gas effort to the finish and I felt quite faint and short of breath,' Froome said. Coincidentally, in 1970 the great Belgian Eddy Merckx, the last yellow jersey to win here, rode himself to the brink of collapse while winning Stage 14 to the summit of Mont Ventoux and received oxygen.

'His [Froome's] physical make-up is amazing,' Brailsford purred at the finish. In Brailsford's opinion, Froome is an outlier, a freakishly talented physiological specimen aided by the most advanced scientific training regimen in cycling. The Sky supremo stunned pundits and sent shudders through Froome's rivals when he suggested his number one rider could have climbed Ventoux even faster.

The race has only scaled the mountain fifteen times with ten summit finishes and those victories are highly prized. 'I didn't know about Merckx winning here,' Froome said, still, endearingly, no scholar of the race's history. 'This is such an incredibly historic climb and it's such an emotional win for me to know the names of those who have won here before. It's the biggest win of my career.'

On 15 July, the second rest day, in Orange, the whispers of innuendo that swirled around Froome after his impressive stage win in the Pyrenees turned into an almighty din in the wake of his extravagant show of strength on the Ventoux.

L'Équipe's front-page headline read: 'Froome naturellement', Froome of course.

At the restaurant of the Park Inn hotel in Orange, less than 24 hours after climbing to victory on the summit of Mont Ventoux, in a brief but intense press conference, Froome found himself once again being compared to cycling's most infamous drugs fraud. 'Lance [Armstrong] cheated,' Froome said unblinkingly. 'I'm not cheating. End of story.'

Sadly for Froome he had inherited a poisoned chalice, his success burdened with the legacy of Armstrong and Generation EPO. Armstrong and others' sinister heritage is that any cycling performance viewed as being even remotely out of the ordinary – although what defines ordinary, no one is quite clear about – is open to interrogation.

Froome should have been basking in the splendour of his Bastille Day triumph. But there was barely a mention of him having produced one of the all-time great Tour rides. Two thirds of the questions directed his way alluded to doping. According to Tim Kerrison, Sky's head of performance, Froome's young mountain *domestique*, Pete Kennaugh was laughing at the end of Stage 15. As Kerrison explained: 'Peter said the way Chris rode that climb was exactly what we do in training every second day.'

It was in essence a relatively routine piece of riding for Froome, who had spent a week in May training exclusively on the 21km drag up the Bald Mountain. It involved a kind of interval training that Kerrison refers to as 'spiked efforts'. Froome has worked hard on being able to handle sudden changes of pace while already at or above his anaerobic threshold – to go from, say, 350 watts to

650 watts for a few seconds in order to launch an attack and get a gap on a rider and then come back down to 350 watts. This drop to sub-threshold helps clean out the lactate brought about by the effects of the initial burst of acceleration. All Sky's climbing training is based on these spiked efforts.

'The guys in the team who train that way look at [Froome's attack] and think, "He's rehearsed that way of riding, three or four times a week for the last two years",' Kerrison said.

In the face of more intimations of doping a frustrated Brailsford offered to turn over all Team Sky's performance data to the World Anti-Doping Agency for it to make an independent assessment of whether the squad's riders were drug-free. 'They can have everything we've got,' he said. 'They can come and live with us. They can see all of our data, every single training file that we've got. They could then tell the world whether they think this is credible or not.'

David Millar called for the cynics to 'have some bloody respect' for his Team GB colleague. 'I pity those who doubt Chris Froome or don't believe in him,' he fumed. 'It's his misfortune to be wearing the yellow jersey on the Tour in the year after Armstrong was exposed. I feel sad for Chris. It is every cyclist's dream to win or lead the Tour de France in the style he has, but he's paying the price for the history of the sport . . . I know Chris. I know the volume of training that he does. I know he's clean.'

It was clear that Froome had grown weary of the accusations. His unfailingly polite demeanour began to crumble slightly when he was asked if all the negativity about his achievements was beginning to tarnish his Tour experience.

'I just think it's quite sad that we're sitting here the day after the biggest victory of my life, quite a historic win, talking about doping,' he replied. 'My teammates and I, we've slept on volcanoes to get ready for this, we've been away from home for months, training together, just working our arses off to get here, and here I am, basically being accused of being a cheat and a liar, and that's not cool.'

★

On 14 July 2003, during the ninth stage of the Tour de France, Joseba Beloki was sitting second overall (just 40 seconds behind Lance Armstrong) and negotiating a sharp right-hand turn at high speed while descending from the Côte de la Rochette, just 4km from the stage finish at Gap. The Spaniard skidded wildly on a patch of tarmac softened by the baking sun, hit the deck hard and broke his right femur in two places. Armstrong, who was right on his tail, famously rode cyclo-cross style across a field and back on to the road.

Almost exactly ten years later Froome and Contador found themselves in an eerily similar situation, one bend below where Beloki's career as a premier bike racer was effectively ended.

All the way up and down the final climb of the Col de Manse, the Saxo-Tinkoff team attacked the yellow jersey. With 18km to go of Stage 16's 168km, Contador fired the first shot from Froome's group, and this prompted a pursuit by Porte and his team leader. Then Kreuziger went, followed by Contador again, ripping the pelotonapart. Five times the Saxo duo tested the resolve of the Sky pair with a 1-2 punch routine on the ascent.

The attacks continued on the descent to Gap and with 7.5km to go Contador lost control of his bike on a sharp turn. Froome was following immediately behind and swerved to avoid him. The yellow jersey wound up on a grassy verge and had to unclip his pedals to lift his bike back onto the road. The GC rivals both remounted – Froome shaken but unhurt while Contador was left nursing a bloody knee and an injured hand – and set off to rejoin the race, with Porte pacing Froome safely back to the elite front group.

Up the road, in the second race of the day, separate from those vying for the *maillot jaune*, Rui Costa sprung clear of a 26-rider group which was given its head an hour out of Vaison-la-Romaine and the Portuguese *rouleur* proceeded to outsmart, outclimb and outpace everyone else on a fast, sweaty day of racing to take a deserved stage win in Gap.

Afterwards Froome accused rival teams of becoming 'desperate' and taking 'uncalculated risks' on the descent, with harsh words reserved for Contador. 'I think he [Contador] was taking too many risks down there. He couldn't control his speed and was struggling to control his bike. I was trying to keep safe but he was pushing the limits.' Contador responded by saying that there was no motivation for him to sit twiddling his thumbs on Froome's wheel in the lead group. He would attack at every opportunity.

It had been a lucky escape for Froome, who said: 'One moment you can be going for the finish, the next lying in a ditch with a broken bone.'

★

The route for the seventeenth stage ITT skirted the shores of Lac de Serre-Ponçon, in the heart of the high Alps. A climbers' time trial, the tough, technical 32km course headed from Embrun up into the hills above the north side of the lake, taking in two Category 2 climbs, the Côte de Puy-Sanières and the Côte de Réallon. Froome knew the *parcours* well having recced it on 10 June, the day after he sealed overall victory at the Dauphiné.

Rated one of the most difficult time trials the Tour had ever seen, Froome had expected to limit his losses on GC rivals by racing conservatively on a course that rewarded risk-takers, so the fact that he took his third stage win of the race seemed to come almost in spite of himself. In doing so he became only the second British rider, along with Mark Cavendish, to take three stages in a single Tour.

Thunderstorms were forecast, the prospect of which would have made the slaloming descent of the Réallon even more treacherous. In the end two key factors contributed to Froome's victory: favourable weather conditions and a brilliantly executed change of bikes. After Tejay van Garderen had set an early time to beat, a mid-afternoon downpour forced the middle of the field to deal with very wet conditions. Luckily for Froome the rain eased and the slick roads dried up by the time the later starters set off.

Most riders opted to use standard road bikes for the time trial because of the lumpy, technical nature of the course. Froome opted for a cunning combination of bikes that proved to make the difference. On the morning of the stage, Froome and Porte had ridden the course in its entirety. Porte tested a road bike on the descent of the Réallon down to the finish in Chorges, with Froome on his regular time trial machine. The aerodynamic advantage the specialist time trial bike offered Froome was significant, and a plan was hatched to swap bikes just before the crest of the final summit.

Froome overturned a twenty-second deficit on Contador, who had led at both intermediate time checks, on the second climb of the day up the 6.9km Réallon. He then lost ten seconds to the Spaniard as he switched from the road bike to the time trial bike but flew down the descent into Chorges to beat Contador – who remained on his less-aerodynamic road bike with tribars – at the finish by nine seconds. Contador, captured on TV in the hot seat, shrugged his shoulders and shook his head in disbelief as Froome crossed the line.

The risky bike swap had paid off. Froome had strengthened his position at the top of the rankings on all of his rivals. Mollema had a disastrous day, coming home 2:09 adrift of Froome to slip to fourth overall. But Froome never relaxed on even so healthy a lead as the 4:34 buffer he had on second-placed Contador. 'Every night I'd go to bed thinking, OK, I've got this big advantage but at any second something's going to challenge that. I've been so fortunate. Not to have a mechanical at the wrong time, a crash, anything going wrong.'

★

In an intriguing development Sky supremo Dave Brailsford made another attempt to prove Froome and his team were racing ethically by providing the French sports newspaper *L'Équipe* with all the climbing data Froome had produced in the last two years: eighteen ascensions dating back to the 2011 Vuelta a España when he made his big breakthrough by finishing second overall. The data was examined by the newspaper's in-house physiologist Dr Fred Grappe, who has worked with the Française des Jeux team since 2000 and was the French Cycling Federation's scientific adviser for ten years. None of the data was made public in the newspaper, at Sky's request, but Grappe concluded – under a portentous 18 July headline 'Froome. Le Dossier' – that Froome's performances were 'coherent' and consistent and humanly possible without doping.

Grappe said that Froome had 'a certain reserve compared to other athletes', which he estimated to be around an extra twenty watts of power. 'This gives an indication of why he is capable of performing on the final climbs. It is this difference that can be seen between him and his main rivals on the climbs.' The Briton, Grappe added, has 'an extraordinary high aerobic potential, close to the limits of known physiological science'. He concluded: 'Intellectually speaking, it would be wide of the mark to attribute [Froome's] performances to doping.'

Sky also released data showing how many drug tests Froome had undergone during the race so far: nineteen times, thirteen blood and/or urine tests and six biological passport profiles. Throughout the season he had been tested 29 times, 23 times in competition, six times out of competition. Meaningless in terms of a definitive test of Froome and Sky's probity but evidence that they were being intensely monitored.

★

On Stage 18, the much anticipated Queen stage of the centenary Tour, the rain that had threatened the cancellation of the second ascent of Alpe d'Huez held off, France earned its first stage win of the race thanks to the unheralded Christophe Riblon, and Froome was docked twenty seconds for illegal feeding in the final kilometres after he suffered a hunger knock.

For the first time in Tour history the fabled slopes of Alpe d'Huez featured twice. After the first time up the 14km climb, the riders would carry on through the ski resort up to the Col de Sarenne and hurtle down the vertiginous, technical drop to La Ferrière before looping round and climbing the Alpe again.

There were fears that the narrow, dangerous descent of the Sarenne – already closed off to spectators for safety reasons – would be too perilous if the threat of rain materialised. Froome had even called for organisers to excise the descent from the stage if the weather turned ugly.

In the end, food, or a lack of it, not inclement weather, provided Froome with his trickiest moment of the race so far. He had looked a little shaky at the foot of the second ascent, toiling at times to stay with teammate Porte, although he had enough in his legs to dispose of Contador on the lower slopes of the second ascent. The Spaniard was unable to respond to the Sky leader's acceleration, but Quintana and Joaquim Rodríguez did get across to the yellow jersey. Porte also scampered across to this trio, and oh how Froome needed him higher on the climb. The effort of dropping Contador had taken Froome over the edge and with 5km to go he urgently signalled to his team car, raising his right arm in the air. Porte eased off from pacemaking duties to confer with his leader, then dropped back to the team car to pick up an energy gel. As Froome took on board the sugar to alleviate his 'bonking' – as British cyclists call hypoglycaemia – Quintana and Rodriguez wasted no time in surging away, both riders gaining over a minute on the Briton and two on Contador. Porte nursed Froome to the finish with the grateful yellow jersey holder patting his friend on the shoulder as they crossed the line. It was Froome's worst day of the Tour but he still gained 57 seconds (37 after his 20-second penalty) on Contador to extend his overall lead to 5:11.

On the eve of the stage, two Sky carers had filled the cooler box in the number one team car with ice in anticipation of a sweltering day ahead. They topped up the ice again in the morning but the previous evening's ice had begun to melt. On the way down the Col d'Ornon, 15km from the first ascent of Alpe d'Huez, mechanic Gary Blem, in the back seat of the car, heard water sloshing around in the cooler. Unbeknownst to him the water was leaking out and dripping into the electronics of the Jaguar.

On the descent from the Col de Sarenne, the car – driven by sports director Nicolas Portal and assigned to be at the front of the race to look after Froome – conked out. They were forced to wait at the side of the road for the second team car to catch up, switched cars and then set off in an attempt to regain their place at the head of the cavalcade. But it was hopeless. By now the leaders were climbing the Alpe for a second time and the road was jam-packed with delirious fans making it impossible to overtake. Froome, in desperate need of sustenance for the final climb, sent Kennaugh back to the team car, but it wasn't there. Seven kilometres from the summit Portal had managed to snake his way through some of the race traffic and heard Froome's frantic voice on the two-way radio: 'Nico, sugar, sugar. I need sugar.' It was the dreaded hunger wolf. But it was too late to allow Froome to refuel legally.

There is a rule against taking food from a team car in the final 20km of a race. For the finish on Alpe d'Huez, feeding was banned 6km from the finish for road safety reasons. But Froome was suffering. He was in danger of losing a heap of time to his rivals in the final stretch of the mountain. To hell with the rules. Portal still had some overtaking to do before he was close enough to Froome. Then Porte dropped back to the second team car, picked up some sugar-rich energy gels and brought them to his team leader. Froome scoffed one, panic over, and the Tasmanian ushered him to the finish line.

'It's a horrible feeling,' Froome said. 'If you've ridden a bike or done any kind of endurance sport, you know the feeling I'm talking about, when you have no energy left, no more fuel in your body.'

Froome knew that he and Porte could afford to take the twenty-second penalty. The latter, stronger on the day than his team leader, lamented: 'It's just a shame that Chris had that hunger knock, otherwise we could have done more damage.'

Porte's team leader offered a more positive spin on events: 'I'm just happy to get through this stage and come out of it with more of an advantage. If that was a bad day for me, I'll definitely accept that.'

The drama involving Froome wasn't the only action in the final kilometres, which saw an enthralling pursuit match between Christophe Riblon and the young American Tejay van Garderen, who had led for much of both ascents and looked set for victory. Riblon pegged back the BMC rider, who had slowed to a crawl, with about 2km to go and sped past as an ecstatic home crowd roared him on to a first French stage win of the 2013 Tour.

Afterwards Riblon sympathised with Froome when he said that the way he was being put on public trial was 'scandalous' and personally he would prefer to know Sky's training secrets so he could improve his own performances.

The Sunday Times reported a series of disgraceful incidents directed at Froome and Team Sky. David Walsh wrote that on the way up Alpe d'Huez unruly fans screamed at some Sky riders while mimicking the act of injecting into their arms. Two men, allegedly French, ran beside Froome, wielding syringes filled with an unknown liquid. One man got close enough to squirt Froome in the face. The yellow jersey instinctively lashed out and walloped the man. 'Some of the stuff went into my mouth, it might have been beer, but I was conscious of not wanting to swallow even a drop and just kept spitting it out,' Froome said. 'I was thinking, What if there's some product in that stuff?'

The climbs of Alpe d'Huez had unsettled Froome. On a mountain notorious for attracting masses of delirious spectators, the crowds seemed denser and rowdier than ever, a result perhaps of the novelty of a double ascent for the 100th Tour. Shrieking hordes, instilled with a gormless belief that it is wonderfully helpful to the riders to brandish cameras, banners and flags in their faces and pull away at the last possible moment, or sprint alongside them dressed only in a pair of day-glo underpants, had turned the road into a pantomime of goons.

Sky's chief doctor, Alan Farrell, said the team's cars had been booed at, pelted with eggs and sprayed with beer and water on the way up the Alpe. One car, which had slowed to almost a halt on the steep incline, was rocked back and forth by a jeering mob. 'Once there were riots in Kenya and my mum and I got stopped going through a particularly dangerous township,' Froome said. 'The protesters rocked our car, we didn't know what was going to happen – Alpe d'Huez reminded me of that day.'

★

Stage 19, a mountainous 204.5km route from Bourg d'Oisans to Le Grand Bornand, over five tough climbs, including the giant Col de la Madeleine, did not deliver the expected attacks on a relieved Froome, who only really came under pressure in the final 20km of the day on the Col de la Croix Fry. Contador's Saxo-Tinkoff team set the tempo on the way up the 11.3km climb, but the only move of note came from fifth-placed Joaquim Rodriguez of the Katusha team, who was tracked by Contador, third-placed Colombian Quintana and Froome.

Contador hurtled kamikaze-style down the 13km to the finish line in torrential rain, but Froome stayed on his Spanish rival's wheel in an otherwise drama-free stage, maintaining his 5:11 lead over Contador and with only one more Alpine stage to negotiate before the traditional procession into Paris.

Rui Costa cruised to his second stage win after breaking clear on the Croix Fry and snuffed out lone escapee Pierre Rolland's bid for glory as the sky darkened and the heavens opened.

'I definitely had a sigh of relief after getting today out of the way – this was one of the stages I was most worried about,' Froome said. 'But I don't want to get complacent at this stage. Tomorrow's stage is only 125km, but it is still one more day to get out of the way before relaxing and heading into Paris.' It was highly unlikely that Froome would lose over five minutes in a single stage of just over 75 miles. All he had to do was remain vigilant to ensure an historic victory.

★

On the morning of the penultimate stage of the 2013 Tour de France, Froome showed how preternaturally laidback he was even after three weeks of tense competition and even tenser cross-examination by the press. At Sky's hotel in Annecy he was ringleader in a prank involving his older brother Jeremy.

On the second rest day, on 15 July, Jeremy and three family friends, the Jethwa brothers, Kiran, Sam and Jaimin, turned up at the Team Sky hotel in Provence. Froome had no idea his brother and friends had travelled from Kenya, a marathon journey that for Jeremy began with a flight from the Nandi hills to Nairobi, from there to Abu Dhabi, then to Paris and a TVG to Marseilles, and, finally, a camper van to Orange.

That morning in Annecy, Froome, Porte and others dressed Jeremy up in Team Sky kit and a yellow jersey and sent him out on a fake errand to the team bus. Much to Froome's amusement, his brother was mobbed by fans. With his own imminent coronation as Tour champion just over 24 hours away, the 'real' Chris Froome would have to get used to such displays of public adulation.

Two kilometres from the finish of Stage 20, a short, sharp, mountainous 125km from Annecy to Semnoz, Froome was finally able to believe it was really going to happen and experienced a similar wobble to the one that Wiggins had felt on Stage 17 of the 2012 race, on the final climb to Peyragudes.

That moment, Froome said, was 'overwhelming' – so much so that he could hardly focus on turning the pedals. 'I thought: I've actually done this, I'm in yellow, this is the last day of GC, and nobody is going to take it away from me,' he said afterwards. 'It was hard to concentrate, to think of carrying on, of tactics, of trying to sort out the last two kilometres. It was a very emotional feeling.'

On the brutal final climb up Annecy-Semnoz, Jens Voigt's brave solo bid for glory was thwarted and Contador's GC hopes melted in the hot July sun. The final act of the race for the GC saw Froome riding away with Quintana and Rodriguez, leaving Contador behind. The jaded former champion not only conceded time again to Froome, he lost over two minutes to Quintana and Rodriguez, and, with it, his place on the podium.

Not even Froome could beat Quintana. The yellow jersey attacked with just over 1km to go but could not sustain the acceleration, distracted by the bigger picture, on the cusp of glory. Quintana caught him and glided past, and then Rodriguez too, but it was of no matter. Froome's job was done. He rolled over the line grinning widely, thumbs up. Quintana took a deserved first stage win and in the process secured two jerseys – the polka dot for King of the Mountains and the white jersey for best young rider – and second place overall. Rodriguez was rewarded for a magnificent ride with a guaranteed third place on the podium.

'This is an absolutely amazing feeling,' Froome said. 'What this represents – the journey I have taken to get here from where I started riding on a little mountain bike on the dirt roads in Kenya to the biggest race in cycling – it is difficult for me to put into words.'

★

'Oh, I'd give anything just to see her smile with me coming into Paris,' Froome said wistfully, as he thought about how proud his late mother might have been if she could have witnessed her shy boy pedal from the Palace of Versailles into Paris, christened by *L'Équipe*, as Le Roi Soleil, the Sun King.

Jane Froome died in the summer of 2008, ten days before her youngest son made his debut for Team Barloworld in the Tour de France. She was the one who had encouraged his cycling from the very beginning. She had introduced him to David Kinjah, put him on the path to a cycling career in Kenya, South Africa and ultimately Europe. As a reluctant economics student at the University of Johannesburg, when Froome told her he didn't want to make a career in business she urged him to 'Go and ride your bike. Follow your dreams.'

And he did, all the way to an astonishing victory in the 100th Tour de France, one which the cycling world hopes will help mark Froome out as a fitting new champion, a clean champion, one who will inspire a new generation and a sport ready to rid itself of the lingering shame of Lance Armstrong, who hovered over the 100th feast like the ghost of Tours past.

'In a way I'm glad that I've had to face those questions after the tarnished history over the last decade,' Froome said. 'All of that has been sort of channelled towards me now, and I feel like I've been able to deal with it reasonably well and send a strong message that the sport has changed. And it really has. The peloton aren't going to stand for it any more.'

★

As Froome pedalled round the Arc de Triomphe in the Paris gloaming , his yellow jersey jazzed up with sequins to glitter in the night lights, the red, white and blue vapour trails of *la patrouille blanche* – the French Red Arrows – dissipated in the breeze. The race climax had been put back several hours to finish as the sun dipped over the French capital. It was an appropriately spectacular finale to three weeks of terrific racing. But despite the party atmosphere of Stage 21 – Froome posed for pictures at the start line in Louis XIV's sumptuous gardens at Versailles with a cigar, and rode along for a short stretch with a glass of champagne in hand – there was still a race going on. German powerhouse Marcel Kittel sprinted to his fourth stage win to deny Mark Cavendish a fifth consecutive victory on the most famous boulevard in the world.

Such was Froome's advantage – 5:03 over second-placed Nairo Quintana – -he could even afford to sacrifice 43 seconds, slipping off the back of the pack on purpose in the final kilometre along the Champs-Élysées to share the final moments of their epic 3,440km journey with his Team Sky teammates and cross the line together holding hands. 'It brought tears to my eyes coming over the line with the guys like that,' Froome said. 'I expected it to be big, but this is something else. I'm speechless. This really was an amazing way to finish off a fitting 100th edition of the Tour de France.'

Asked to pick one factor that he felt contributed the most to Froome's victory, Dave Brailsford highlighted his star's outstanding 'mental resilience'. 'His ability to stay calm in the face of adversity, to keep his cool in the face of non-stop questioning, the same questions a million times, is phenomenal.'

In his speech atop the podium on the Champs-Élysées, Froome spoke in French to thank his hosts and then switched to English to pay tribute to his teammates' efforts. He then dedicated his victory to his late mother. 'Without her encouragement to follow my dreams, I'd probably be at home watching this event on TV. It's a great shame she never got to come see the Tour, but I'm sure she'd be extremely proud if she were here tonight.'

Froome ended his speech by responding to the suspicions surrounding his commanding victory with a pointed reference to Lance Armstrong's stripped titles. 'This is one yellow jersey that will stand the test of time,' he told the enormous crowds who had gathered for the finale and the *son et lumière* lightshow which illuminated the Arc de Triomphe. And, he added, he wants more. Having seized possession of the iconic garment Froome hinted that he would be unwilling to relinquish it any time soon. 'It is hard to talk too far in advance now, but, if you look at my career now and what my ambitions are, to come and target the Tour de France has to be the biggest goal.'

Brailsford believes Froome can improve even more. 'He has all the physical and mental attributes to be competitive in this race for quite some time. He is not at his best yet, for sure. I think he has all the ingredients of a multiple champion.'

Chris Froome's story is a fairytale worthy of a Hollywood movie and he hopes his remarkable achievements will prove to a new generation of cyclists, in particular African riders, that they can follow a similar path. 'I would like my performances to help inspire and motivate a lot of youngsters, especially young Africans who find it very hard to believe that they can get out of Africa and get on to the European scene, or make it into a pro peloton,' he announced. 'My experiences are an example that if you really want to make something happen, you will find a way. You will make an opportunity for yourself.'

Acknowledgements

Many people made this book possible, giving of their time and knowledge with generosity and goodwill. I'm grateful to the British Library, particularly Darren Townend, for providing me with access to their archives of *Procycling* (2007–2013) and *Cycle Sport* (2007–2013); to Paul Johnson and staff at ITV Sport; to Abby Burton at British Cycling and Chris Haynes at Team Sky; to Professor Paul Hagan and Michael Barrett; and to Toni Williams at St John's College, Johannesburg.

Special thanks to John-Lee Augustyn, Michael Barry, Sir Dave Brailsford, Claudio Corti, Steve Cummings, Doug Dailey, David Kinjah, Allan Laing, Andrew McLean, John Robertson, Michel Thèze, Conrad Venter and Sean Yates for their time and insight.

The following books were helpful: *My Time* by Bradley Wiggins; *Sky's the Limit* by Richard Moore; *21 Days to Glory* by Sarah Edworthy and Scott Mitchell; *Mountain High* by Daniel Friebe and Pete Goding; *Tour de France* by Graeme Fife.

Thanks to my agent Kevin Pocklington and to my editor Alison Rae and everyone at Birlinn.

I'm especially grateful to Graeme Fife for his constancy as a friend and his tirelessly creative help, encouragement and good humour.

Thanks and love to my mum Cathy, sister Carol and the Macdonald clan of Largs: Hector, Ellie, Freya and Evan.

Were it not for the unstinting love and support of Lesley Allan none of this would have been possible and this book would not exist. Thanks, Les!